The Complete Book of
Aquarian Magic

The Complete Book of Aquarian Magic

Marian Green

With a foreword by JUDIKA ILLES

A Practical Guide
to the Magical Arts

WEISER BOOKS
San Francisco, CA / Newburyport, MA

This edition first published in 2015 by Weiser Books
an imprint of Red Wheel/Weiser, LLC
With offices at:
665 Third Street, Suite 400
San Francisco, CA 94107
www.redwheelweiser.com

Copyright © 1983, 1985 by Marian Green
Introduction © 2015 by Judika Illes

ISBN: 978-1-57863-583-2

Library of Congress Cataloging-in-Publication Data available upon request

Cover design by Graham Lester
Text design by Jane Hagaman

Printed in the United States of America
MG
10 9 8 7 6 5 4 3 2 1

This book is dedicated to William, Dora, and Richard with love and gratitude. Bless you all.

Dedicated to all my friends on the Paths of Magic.

CONTENTS

Foreword   ix

PART I
MAGIC FOR THE AQUARIAN AGE

Introduction   xv

1. What Is Wrong with the World?   1

2. Questions   7

3. Meditation   13
   The Art of Stopping Time

4. Visualization   25
   Creating a Place in Infinity

5. Getting Fit for Magic   39

6. The Experience of Religion   49

7. Divination   61
   Stretching Your Senses

8. The Equipment of Ritual   73

9. The Rite Way to Work   87

10. A Week of Magical Work   101

11. The Many Paths of Magic   113

Conclusion   125

Further Reading   127

Index   129

PART II

EXPERIMENTS IN AQUARIAN MAGIC

Introduction   133

12. Opening the Doors to Your Inner Mind   137
13. Journeys to Vision   149
14. The Nature of Healing   163
15. Creating a Magical Temple   183
16. The Patterns of Ritual   195
17. Magical Experiments with Time   205
18. The Magic of Space Travel   221
19. Minds over Magic   235
20. The Arts of Talismanic Magic   249
21. Gods for the Future   263
Conclusion   279
Further Reading   281
Index   283

FOREWORD

"Following the lessons in this book will help you become a better Aquarian person, self-sufficient yet able to share skills, abilities and activities with other people to your mutual benefit."

In a nutshell, that quote establishes precisely why Marian Green's *Complete Book of Aquarian Magic* is an important and significant book.

We stand on the threshold of a new era—or perhaps even a little beyond that threshold—and those of us who seek to thrive are learning to become better Aquarian people. The *Complete Book of Aquarian Magic* is a tremendous resource. Its availability comes not a moment too soon. Reading it has inspired me to reminisce about my own magical journey and education.

When I was in the fifth grade, my classmates dubbed me "The Mystic One." It was not meant kindly. I was perceived as "weird." Some child had decided that each member of the class needed a nickname determined by something—some trait—that would immediately identify us and a small group enthusiastically took to naming the rest of us. It was done quickly and semi-spontaneously and there were children who fared far worse than I did, as you can imagine.

My passion for the occult was apparent, even then. At the time, the nickname made me self-conscious, as it was intended to do, and it taught me to be more discreet. Decades later, however, in retrospect, I consider it a badge of pride.

I was ten years old when I was in the fifth grade and I openly read every metaphysical book available to me. I consumed any book I could find on witches and witchcraft, whether fantasy or fact. I scoured school and public libraries for books on folklore, Halloween traditions, and stories featuring ghosts or spirits. (I lived in a liberal and very secular school district that hadn't banned such books or at least hadn't yet.)

At home, I had access to greater esoterica. My older sister shopped at the Weiser Book Store in New York City, which was then among the very few exclusively metaphysical book stores in the world. She brought home books on tarot, astrology, numerology, palmistry, and the nature of dreams. I read every single one, cover to cover. I memorized Zolar's *It's All in the Stars* and devoured Leo Martello's *Weird Ways of Witchcraft*. I read obsessively and I learned a lot.

However, I did not *choose* any of these books. I was a kid and had no money or the ability to shop for myself. I was dependent on the whims and preferences of relatives and librarians. I read a lot of wonderful works, but also plenty of filler, and way too much dross.

My generation of occultists, like those that preceded us, typically read whatever we could. The books found us, rather than vice versa. Of course, it is quite the opposite today. It is now common to be overwhelmed by the sheer quantity of available choices. Albeit in different ways than during my childhood, one must still sift the dross to reveal the treasure.

Marian Green's *Complete Book of Aquarian Magic* is one such treasure. I wish I had encountered this book in my earlier days. Had I done so, I suspect my enrollment in the School of Hard Knocks would have been shorter and my magical path less circuitous. Whatever *your* path, there is useful information in these pages for *you*.

Dear readers, there is a tremendous quantity of practical magical information in this carefully crafted and lucid work. Clarity is something to be prized, especially in books of magic. Too many chroniclers of the magical arts, both now and in the past, apparently think that their credentials are proven by *obfuscation*, which the dictionary defines as "making communication confusing, willfully ambiguous, and difficult to interpret."

I, on the other hand, was explicitly taught that that those who cannot explain something simply in a comprehensible manner do not understand the material either. Marian Green very clearly understands what she teaches so well and with precision, humor, and kindness.

The Complete Book of Aquarian Magic is a genuine textbook of the magical arts. If there was a true academy of the magical arts—

a real life Hogwarts—then the *Complete Book of Aquarian Magic* would be required reading.

- If you are beginning your magical path, I recommend this book wholeheartedly. It will answer many questions and help you accomplish desired goals
- If, like me, you have long pursued your magical interests, you will be pleasantly surprised at how much new and useful information is to be found in these pages

The *Complete Book of Aquarian Magic* is intended to help ease the transition from the Age of Pisces into the new Age of Aquarius and so is very much a book for our present time. The concept of the Age of Aquarius frustrates astronomers: its precise start date is contentious. For others, the concept is nothing but a clichéd vestige of the Summer of Love or the Broadway musical *Hair*. However, many mystics await the changes this new era heralds; some with apprehension, fearing the worst, but most of us, I'd like to think, hoping for the dawning of a more enlightened, tolerant time.

As Marian Green writes:

"We are changing from the astrological age of Pisces, in which people acted like schools of fish, all following the same rules and the same patterns of life, to the new age of Aquarius. Aquarius is usually shown as a man with a water pot, pouring out a stream of water. This symbolizes individuality . . ."

She further explains:

"The Age of Aquarius is the age of the individual selecting his or her own path."

Wherever your own particular individual magical path may lead, *The Complete Book of Aquarian Magic* offers needed illumination.

—*Judika Illes, author of* The Encyclopedia of 5000 Spells; Encyclopedia of Witchcraft; Pure Magic: A Complete Guide to Spellcasting; The Weiser Field Guide to Witches *and other books of magic.*

PART I

MAGIC

FOR THE

AQUARIAN AGE

INTRODUCTION

This is a book of wonders. It is full of adventures, of strange and unimaginable experiences—not those of other people, but ones that you can try for yourself. It unwraps the secret magical inner YOU that is capable of solving all your own problems, and assisting many of the people in the world around you. The only limits as to what you can achieve are set by your own feelings, and there are keys here to open the doors to a magical new universe once you have learned to use them.

Some books contain rituals and spells and expect the novice to feel safe and work competently through strange invocations, calling upon archaic gods and using words of power in languages few people understand. This book is not like that. It is a map exactly adapted for you, the seeker living at the end of the twentieth century, rather than the crumbling remains of an ancient rite which might have had some relevance in the fourteenth century. Magic is a matter of experience and reality. It is a combination of inner skills everyone can develop, given time, dedication, practice, and the application of universal laws of nature. There are a number of magical exercises that have to be tried; there are the patterns upon which a personalized ritual can be built; there are notes on symbolism, divination, and equipment to be studied and fitted into your own life pattern.

The Age of Pisces encouraged people to act like fish, all flowing with the tides and currents in a bunch, all doing the same things in the same way. Now we are on the brink of the Age of Aquarius when everyone will learn to become his or her own person, directing life and knowledge in an individual way. Each of us is different, so each can apply these techniques, master the arts as an *individual*; and although the skills, methods, and symbols are as old as the hills, they are still relevant if they are applied in the ways of the modern world. All the necessary keys are available to you in these pages. What use you make of them will depend on your commitment to magic, your patience, and your determination to learn the old arts. No one can direct your path but yourself, guided by your inner self—and the gods and goddesses if you desire to know them.

To be effective all the time at magic requires patience and perseverance, but so does the acquisition of any physical or mental skill. Nothing can make you an 'instant magician,' but if you follow the various exercises, ideas, and experiments in this book, within a very short time you will begin to notice new perceptions, hunches, and feelings of self-confidence.

This is not a book of old methods, ancient rituals, and decayed ceremonies but an instruction manual which, together with the parts and tools needed to build it up, can create for you a system that is not merely up to date, but is designed for your own future and for the twenty-first century, not the fifteenth. It may contain some surprises, some subjects that may not appear to be immediately relevant—but everything mentioned is important for the magical Aquarian Age. Consider each suggestion with an open mind, try the exercises, no matter how familiar or simple or unimportant they might seem to you now, and soon you will be able to judge the fruits of your own effort. You may well be in for some surprises, some new experiences, feelings of health, of joy, and of being able to cope with the world instead of being swept along like a twig in a stream.

Read this book carefully: It may open your eyes to another universe. Have fun!

MARIAN GREEN

WHAT IS WRONG
WITH THE WORLD?

Many people feel that there is something drastically wrong with the world and the way they have to live in it. Some people are content to suffer the miseries produced by this state of affairs, but more and more are becoming determined to *DO* something about the situation they find themselves in. This book is written for them.

Certainly, there is no simple answer, no miracle panacea that will instantly improve the whole scene, right the wrongs, and grant a heart's desire—at least not in a manner one might expect. The world can be changed, improved, and made the beautiful place of peace and plenty many of us dream of—potentially, it has all that is needed. What has to be changed is *us,* the perceivers of this world.

By changing our point of view, by developing our own inner skills, each of us can learn to help shape the world into the perfect planet everyone yearns for. I will not say this transformation is likely to be instant, nor is it easy; but anyone who has a vision of a better place, a happier state, and a more peaceful and beautiful environment has the keys.

For thousands of years there have been schools of students taught in secret arts and crafts that have been called 'magic' because they were not fully understood. These ancient skills have been preserved and live on today. They involve methods of healing, of understanding the patterns and tides of nature, and of working in harmony with these to gain the greatest help from nature herself. They help to explain man's position in the universe, and the part he has to play in its future. Most importantly, they have taught each individual to seek within and find the keys of his/her true self, and by understanding these inner strengths and weaknesses, become the best person they can. It is these particular skills that can be learned, and by altering the point of view from which we look at the world, we begin to see how distorted our former view of it was.

To get a clear view will require a lot of hard work, for in one sense you will be embarking on a voyage of discovery, climbing a new peak of personal experience, and that is no easy task. However, you will not be making this journey of exploration alone, for over the ages many thousands have trodden the hidden path, clearing the way and making the steps safer. Today there are thousands of people who realize that life has more to offer than may be obvious at first, and they too are traveling in the same direction.

This book consists of a number of exercises, both mental and physical, to help you to improve your body, making it fitter and more able to cope, and what might be called 'spiritual' or 'psychic' exercises. These are designed to awaken perceptions and senses that have been blunted by living in a modern, stressful world. Many of them may seem rather strange at first, if you have never tried consciously to alter your state of awareness, except for trying to fall asleep; but all are quite safe. You may think it odd that you are advised to try a different diet or break old habits, but the objective of all these practices is to get YOU in total control of your SELF. Often it is easier to slop along, scarcely aware of what is going on around you, acting out of habit with no more will power than a caged animal. If you wish to improve your world, that will have to change—the comfort of following the herd, acting like an automaton, will have to go. You will have to take a grip of all your activities, physical, mental, and spiritual, and you will soon discover what you have been missing all these years.

There is no reason why you cannot be extremely healthy, full of zest and energy when you wish, in control of your own life pattern and the way in which it unfolds, *if you want to*. Too many of us have forgotten what it is like to be really alive, although as children, the summer days were golden and all was right with the world. To regain this youthful freedom you will have to be prepared to sacrifice some long-held ideas, to think in new ways, to act differently, and to shoulder the burden of personal responsibility. You cannot go on passing the buck or walking away from problems that you have caused with a clear conscience, if you become more aware—life just won't let you. The rewards for living life to the full cannot be estimated, but you will begin to feel liberated from a long term of imprisonment, during which you were your own jailer.

The secrets of ancient magic can be yours, but you will discover them only through experience. The exercises will need to be done, the experiments tried, the new experiences assimilated and thoroughly understood to get consistent results. Like learning anything else, magic requires practice and patience—it is not instant, although its results can be! Work steadily and you will be in for some surprises. Whatever may happen to you will be the result of some part of your self being awakened. It is in no way harmful, or 'evil.' It may seem strange, but then so is being able to swim, or balancing on a bicycle. Look upon it as an adventure that may lead you to explore new areas, discover exciting new talents, experience interesting and rewarding sensations, and get more fun out of life.

Identity

Today, many people are suffering what is called 'an identity crisis.' They are uncertain where they fit into the changing patterns they see around them. Things used to be simple, organized and obvious; there was a clearly defined path from birth, through school, marriage, and work to old age. Everything was straightforward; the roles and expectations were clear; the choices limited. Now things are changing at an ever-increasing pace. Family life has altered from its traditional form of mother at home, father out at work all day, children (usually several) with their mother until the age of four or so and then sent off to school. Now children may only have one parent; they may be sent out to be looked after while their parent works all day; they may start school sooner, or even be taught at home.

This is only one minor way in which traditional patterns are breaking up, and the sudden shifts have caused a lot of people to feel insecure, afraid, and puzzled. They cannot see where they fit in. They are not clear which goals they should be seeking. This unsettled feeling may in turn lead to depression, phobias, and all sorts of psychosomatic health problems. Some folk cling desperately to the old situations which, when forces beyond their control break up the old, seemingly secure base, are cast into a turmoil of new experiences and situations and are beaten down by circumstances. They may turn to drugs, alcohol, or suicide, have 'nervous breakdowns' or other forms of mental disorder, not because they are actually ill, but because they cannot cope.

What this book is designed to do is to show people what aspects of their lives are under their own control; what skills they may be able to develop, given the right kind of instruction; what methods may be used to bring out all the most adaptable aspects of a person's character to help him or her through the changes. Many of these methods are very old and for a long time have been passed on by a teacher to one or a few pupils. Now some of these old techniques can be taught much more widely. They will probably never be universal, for what is clear about the people of today is that many of them are seeking individual paths through life.

How to Approach this Book

Certainly it is harder to learn by reading a book than by following the exercises or instructions of a personal teacher, but it can be done. The qualities you will most need are those of common sense and, to some extent, patience. Like learning a new language, or taking on a different activity or sport, you have to learn the rules first, get used to the equipment, and try out different parts of the process until they are familiar. The same applies to these magical exercises. If you can follow the different sections carefully, mastering each skill before going on to the next, you will find that your 'spiritual' or 'psychic' muscles develop steadily and without any trouble. If you wish to rush ahead and try things at the end of the book first, you may find yourself in the position of a boastful weightlifter who is expected to lift a world-record weight at first go! There is no advantage in rushing. The first skills are just as important (and may be the most beneficial to you as an individual) as some of the later ones.

This work is intended to be interesting, fun, and satisfying. It can be learned alone or with a companion, or in a group. You can practice indoors privately, in the garden, in a park, or even, if the mood so takes you, at an ancient sacred site, stone circle, or mound. You will need a minimum of equipment, and things you make or adapt yourself will give you greater pleasure than something simply bought for the purpose. If you have not encountered magic before, you may find some of the ideas and suggestions strange; if you are a practitioner already, you may find some of the exercises familiar. But whatever level you are at, you are in for some new experiences, which I hope you will find personally rewarding and permanently valuable.

2

QUESTIONS

'Who am I? Where am I going? What is it all for?' If these questions have been running through your head lately, you have begun the ultimate quest, which in one form is to answer questions such as these, and in another is perhaps the attainment of the Holy Grail.

In many countries, people ask these questions, and instead of turning within, where the ultimate answers must surely lie, they turn to 'experts,' 'psychoanalysts,' and 'psychologists' in the hope that other people can explain what they, the individuals, are about. Usually these experts will ask many questions and urge the wanderer in search of himself to make his own choices (which he will have to do anyway); but in doing so they will somehow make him feel more lost, more dependent on the good will of another and less sure of himself. There are probably a few people who do desperately need guidance to find themselves and to help them solve their own problems, but these are in the minority. Most people, given a fair share of personal honesty, uncritical self-examination and consideration, can go a long way in discovering their own motivations and needs. After all, only you can sense the mood of the moment, the inner need, the outward intention to express a feeling or fear. You can judge when you are hungry, determined, or sad, and it is often an inner feeling that builds up to joy, happiness, and contentment. By noting what things help to bring about these changes of mood, you can gradually map your likely reactions to any situation. In time you can find ways to change a gloomy feeling into a brighter outlook.

It might seem daunting to have to look at and map your own feelings, but you can spend a few minutes each day thinking about how you feel. You can start by going through your life, from when you were a child, and jotting down in your own secret book the things you wished for, what you wanted to do, how you got on with the people around you. There is no need for this to be in chronological order. Write notes as you recall them. You may also wish to enter today's ambitions and last night's dream.

From your own secret journal, you will begin to discover patterns of your own emerging. This is the beginning of the magical journey of inner exploration. You are mapping an uncharted country which you alone can visit totally. You can become your own expert and gradually, when you have learned to change your awareness from the immediate world to the inner one, you will be able to make long expeditions to gain new knowledge. Be absolutely honest in all that you write down. There is no need to explain or justify your feelings to yourself.

Self-Knowledge

You might ask 'How is this a magical way?', because it seems so tied up with ordinary things. Remember that written above the doors of the temple schools of mystery teachings was the phrase 'Know Thyself.' This was the purpose of much of the old mystery teaching—to train the novices to come to terms with themselves as individuals, learning what practical and magical skills they possessed, and how, like any talent, these could be improved.

The reason for concentrating on understanding yourself first of all is because *you* form the core and base upon which your magical training is founded. The more secure this foundation is, the stronger and higher you can build. If you are aware of your own feelings or reactions to a given situation, then you will be able to understand the feelings of others. You will become a crystal-clear mirror in which you may see other people reflected. By seeing yourself in your true colours, you will be able to judge others, and knowing your own faults and failings, give them a fair hearing.

The simplest way to go about gaining self-knowledge is to get a small book, one that will fit into a pocket or handbag so that you can carry it about all the time. Start with your earliest memories; begin to recall your likes and dislikes. You can have a separate page for each, and enter foods, music, situations, relationships— as

many categories of items as you can. As it is secret, n
your leg if you enter 'Dislike turnips' or 'Like cuddly

Devote another pair of pages to things you ha
achieve, such as learning to swim, riding a bicycle o
ing examinations, making friends, and so on. See
these you have done, how many you have abandon
many are still unobtained (It is never too late—Grar
hanggliding or parachute jumping, or sail singlehande
world!) Have you done more things than not? Have y
mastered things which are useful to other people, c
activities and abilities directed towards pleasing only you
your ambitions crazy, or are they reasonable, at least to y
they changed over the years, or do you still secretly yearn to
steam train or dance the lead in *Swan Lake?* Has the chang
availability or type affected your original choice of career, o
you seen new occupations or interests arise out of developme
technology, science, or other matters affecting your life?

Change

The last few decades have seen enormous, and continuing, changes
in almost every area of our day-to-day lives. But as the rate of change
has increased, so more and more people are turning towards alternative philosophies and lifestyles in the search for stability and security.

The self-sufficiency movement has led many people back to
the land, to try their hand at small-scale farming, animal hus-
bandry, and rural skills. Gurus all over the world have tried to do
something similar in the realms of the soul or spirit, teaching the
ancient arts of yoga, T'ai Chi, macrobiotic cookery, zen, and others. Religion has changed to try to meet the new needs of people
in the modern world, though in so doing has sometimes cut itself
off from the roots, which has lessened its value and impact on the
world. Many people seek alternatives and ask entry to covens or
cults, follow teachers of many colours in the hope that the inner
turmoils that affect them can be cured from without. Many are
sadly disappointed and come away disillusioned.

hough many teachers have valid messages, no one solu-
an possibly help everyone. The most important aspects of
uman character have led to our survival in hostile environ-
s—from deserts and ice caps to jungles and outer space.
han beings can adapt to new conditions, and this is why know-
to what extent each of us has been able to change and accom-
date new circumstances is so important before launching into
study of magical arts.

Magic was defined by Aleister Crowley as 'the art of causing
anges in conformity with the will of the magician.' Similarly,
ion Fortune called magic 'the art of causing changes in con-
ciousness in conformity with will.' In China, the great ancient
oracle, still widely consulted, is called the *I Ching*, which means
the Book of Changes. Change is magic, and magic is the art of
making changes.

Once you begin to see how you were as a child, in what way
you developed, and what sort of a person you have become,
you will be able to judge how subsequent changes have affected
you. If you have been frightened and made uncertain by what
seems to be happening around you, this basic understanding of
yourself may give you a solid basis on which to build. You will
learn to become calm; to cope with situations that once seemed
beyond you; to flex and bend rather than stiffly resisting until you
are forced into a different pattern. You will learn to *control* the
changes, decide upon them and carry them, out to suit your own
purposes; but you will need to understand both yourself and the
causes of change.

If you ask 'Where am I going?,' the answer can depend a lot on
where you *want* to go. If you have no clear plan for yourself, then
you can so easily be carried along by every passing current. If there
is a new religion, political party, or any other mass movement, and
you have no definite plans, then you may be swept along with it,
perhaps against your choice. You will need to list in your secret
book the directions in which you would most like to travel on the
road of life. In the fields of home, job, partnerships, friendships,
and achievement, you may already realize where you would like to

go. In each category, it is best to look closely at the next step (preferably a small one) you need to take towards your personal goal. Gradually, as you progress through the arts in this book, you may find these directions changing too. Some goals will be fulfilled, but others will shift into a new and, at present, undreamed-of form. The surprises magic can bring into your life are totally unimaginable, until you step onto the hidden path that now lies at your feet. In a year's time, if you can look back at this moment recorded in your journal, you will know what this can be like!

Summary

It would be useful, perhaps, to sum up what has been said so far in this chapter. The purpose of magic is to help each individual become the most effective, competent, and skilled person he or she is capable of being. No one can make you clever, strong, or able to work helping or healing magic except yourself. Get *yourself* right, and the picture of the world as you see it will change to a brighter, better image. You can change the world by cleaning the lenses of your self through which you view it. To help yourself, you must obey the traditional command of magical schools throughout the ages—'Know Thyself.' This can best be done by keeping a 'magical diary' or secret journal in which you record all your hopes, aspirations, ambitions, and successes. You will need to note failures and difficulties too, for it is by balancing up the good and not so good aspects of life that you will find a pattern emerging upon which you can base future plans. You will need to be absolutely honest with yourself in this, for covering up faults will not show a true picture, and in any case your journal should be secret!

When you have considered the things you wish to achieve in the ordinary world, you will be able to add to your list the things that can be assisted by magical workings. Perhaps you wish to act as a healer or counsellor to other people, or to be able to read the Tarot cards or the *I Ching* in order to see clearly what is to come. You might want to work on far-reaching projects, such as world peace, justice, or other global problems. All these things, and many more, are possible with a lifestyle in which magic is the name of a real art, as practical and effective as computer science.

The arts of magic are manifold and though most books tell you to 'believe in magic' it is better to learn to KNOW that these skills will produce results by personal experience. It is not a matter of believing that the light will come on if you turn the switch: You know it will. You may not understand how the electricity makes the filament of the light bulb come on, but you assume it will do so. Magic is the same. You may not be able to understand the stages by which what you will to come to pass actually does so, but once you have begun to get yourself balanced and tuned into the level on which magic works, you will know the equivalent action to turning on the light switch. The test of effectiveness of the various exercises in this book is simply for you to make a serious effort to try them. You can then convince yourself that magic is real, that it can widen the scope of your activities and add new dimensions to your life.

3

MEDITATION
THE ART OF STOPPING TIME

When Albert Einstein published his Theory of Relativity, he put into words something which in ordinary life is a common experience. He explained that time is relative; that a traveler in outer space would experience the passing of time at a different rate to that of his twin brother left at home. This was a revelation in a world in which it was considered that time flowed sequentially, at a regular pace, measured in standard hours and minutes wherever in the universe you might be. Our actual experience of time, however, is much closer to Einstein's relative time, if you think about it.

You are bound to have been aware how time seems to fly past when you were enjoying yourself or absorbed in some task or entertainment. You will know too how minutes have dragged by like hours when you have been waiting for something to happen. Ten minutes at a bus stop in a thunderstorm can feel like an age, yet three hours watching a good film can pass like minutes. Our experience of time is personal and relative to our own scale.

Another aspect of our life in which time does not obey clock hours is whilst we are dreaming. During the periods of sleep, which are called 'paradoxical' by modern researchers, it is possible to see by movements of the sleeper's eyes that he is following the action of some visible dream. This sort of sleep is called 'Rapid Eye Movement' (REM) sleep or paradoxical sleep, for though the sleeper might show brain wave patterns or electrical skin resistance readings close to his waking state, he would be very hard to awaken. In non-REM sleep, his dreams are not necessarily pictorial but are 'thought dreams,' and though measurements of depth would show he was more deeply asleep, he would be easier to wake up in this type of sleep. Whether they remember it or not, everyone dreams, and experimental subjects who have been awakened each time they begin to show signs of dreaming, and have thus been deprived of dream time, show symptoms of disturbance of memory and irritability.

Recent experiments have shown that there is another kind of dream, in which the sleeper is aware of being asleep and, without waking up, can communicate by eye movement that he has reached a stage called 'lucid dreaming.' Experimenters have conveyed information to the sleeper that has then been incorporated into the dream and recalled on awaking.

To meditate effectively is to reach an almost similar state. You will learn to alter the state of your consciousness, so that your immediate environment, worries, sensations, etc., do not concern you. You are totally aware and totally in control of the level at which you perceive things. This is a very old art, and every culture has its own method of helping meditators shift the level of their attention. Some rely on techniques that distract the attention by the rhythmic chanting of a prayer, hymn, or 'mantra,' or by adopting specific kinds of physical posture, such as those used in yoga. These work because they occupy the attention of the mental or physical processes so that the inner levels of what might be called 'spirit' or inner self can begin to manifest themselves.

The Inner Self

Everyone has an inner self which may or may not make itself obvious. It is this factor that can take over in a crisis, so that people in accidents or dangerous situations suddenly find incredible strength or powers of endurance. It can also offer a quiet voice of guidance, helping with the very ordinary choices which life causes us to take all the time. We are sometimes 'urged' to act in a certain way, which we subsequently find out has got us out of danger or brought about some fortuitous meeting. If you think about it, something of this sort may have happened to you. In the techniques of meditation outlined here, it is this inner voice, offering information, guidance, or actual practical help, which proves so valuable in the everyday world. Your inner self has access to a great deal of information, part of which is derived from your own memories during every moment of your lifetime. It may also be able to recall material from your past lives. It is a source of wisdom available to everyone, and it is in this context that the following exercises are directed.

The thing most beginners in the art of meditation find hardest is learning to concentrate and relax at the same time. Many of them strive hard, clench their teeth, tense their muscles, and try to force the meditative state upon themselves. It is like trying to make yourself fall asleep! What is required is almost the opposite—a state of mind in which you couldn't care less if anything happens, a relaxed body and an idling mind. It is surprisingly difficult to get into this state of 'turned-off-ness' without tensing up, worrying that nothing is happening, or thinking of some reason to give up trying and go shopping. It is easy in the beginning to be distracted by little itches or sudden thoughts because it is the inner self taking notice that you are trying to get in on the act. It is saying to itself 'Hey, who's digging in MY files. Who's walking through MY regions of this person? I don't like it and will stop it by making them twitch, or tingle, or think about buying something. . . .' It is an excellent sign!

Because meditation is a way of stopping time, or at least your own awareness of it, it is necessary to find ways in which you can keep in touch with the normal world, once you get the knack. To begin with, it is best to get rid of as many distractions as you can; for instance, other people walking in just as you settle down, or the telephone ringing at a critical moment. Obviously, you cannot in all fairness order the rest of your family or household to be silent for an hour while you do your meditation; nor is it reasonable to hog the most comfortable chair in the warmest room at a time when others might expect to share that space. Be reasonable; choose a time of day when the house is quiet, when other people are not likely to use the room you have chosen, and when other distractions can be kept to a minimum. Do not make a song and dance about your new interest: Quietly select the least difficult time and place with regard to those about you. As your expertise grows, then you can talk more freely and perhaps share your methods with others.

One way of controlling the time of your meditations is to use a record of quiet, peaceful-sounding music as a background. This is useful in two ways: First, it covers up some of the noise which might distract you; secondly, it runs for a set amount of time, so that when it finishes it will help you to come back to the ordinary time scale as gently as possible. Select any tape or record which seems to you to be peaceful and calming. It doesn't have to be heavy classical if you like modern music, just as long as it has a lulling or stilling effect on you.

Basic Meditational Technique

Although many of the eastern methods of meditation suggest you should adopt a lotus position, squatting crosslegged on the floor is not a generally comfortable posture for most Western people. Ideally, you should sit upright on a fairly hard chair with a high back. An old fashioned dining chair, sometimes known as a 'carver,' with arms is very good. It will need to be the right height so that your feet rest comfortably on the floor (use a thick book or stool, if not), and support your back upright with your spine straight. If you need to sit on a cushion or place one in the small of your back to make it really comfortable, then do so. Later on, you will be able to meditate sitting on a rock in a thunderstorm without being distracted by noise or discomfort, but it is best to make it as easy as possible to begin with.

If you have seen the pictures of the Egyptian pharaohs, sitting with their backs straight and their feet firmly on the ground with their hands resting along their thighs, you will know how you ought to sit for meditation, and pretty well any other sort of static magical work. Most people suffer from tension in the neck and shoulders and often this is a contributory factor in such things as migraine or other 'tension' headaches, upper backache, or stiff 'frozen' shoulders. Usually these symptoms are caused less by the physical position than by a mental attitude of rigidity, which leads to stiffening of muscles and joints. If these sorts of things afflict you, the posture and practice of meditation may well help to get rid of some of them.

Some people like to meditate just before they go to sleep and feel that lying down in bed is a suitable posture; but too often, these folk get a good night's sleep but no advantages from their meditations. Others suggest lying on a hard floor, kneeling, or slumping in a soft armchair; but in each case an extra strain is put on muscles, or discomfort or cramp forces the novice to give up the session before any useful shift of consciousness has taken place. Certainly when you have learned the technique, you will be able to meditate on trains, sitting, standing, or lying pretty well anywhere; but to begin with, do make it as easy as possible for yourself.

The upright position is best because there is less strain on your chest and lungs, allowing you to breathe easily. You will be in a balanced, poised posture, all your internal organs can rest in their proper places, and the nerves in your spine, particularly those in the neck, will not be compressed through being bent. For this reason it is important to learn to relax whilst keeping your head up. This ensures a clear airway and allows many muscles to relax. Breathing is used to help shift the level of consciousness at the start of a meditation, but you need to continue throughout the session. Your brain needs blood to ensure it is functioning as well as possible.

Once you have found a quiet time and place, perhaps prepared a tape or record of pleasing music, discovered a chair which meets as many of the criteria previously mentioned, and have asked not to be disturbed for a while—what next? You will need a notebook and pen, or a spare cassette or tape, so that you can immediately note any impressions, feelings, images, and so on that come to you during the session.

Because the first part of magical training is concerned with learning who you are, a simple subject on which to begin meditation is your own ordinary name. Choose your first name as a setting-off point. On the matter of breathing, all of us breathe at slightly different rates, which can vary depending on what we are doing. You will notice that your own rate will vary during the meditation and other exercises. It is possible to follow a precisely timed sequence—for instance, four seconds breathing in and four seconds breathing out.

However, this may be too fast for some people, too slow for others. If you need a natural rate to count at, use your own pulse, felt either with your fingers at the opposite wrist, or, if you concentrate, you may be able to feel it in your neck. You can even count heartbeats. Whichever you choose, begin by using a natural rate suited to your own body.

Sit upright, comfortable and still, with your hands relaxed and your neck balanced upright. Close your eyes and slowly say to yourself: 'My name is . . .' or 'I am called . . .,' making each word fall on a pulse beat and breathing in for one set of words, and then out for the next. You may wish to hold your breath in and/or out for a couple of beats also. The pace is up to you. Just concentrate on getting a steady rhythm for the first few moments.

Allow your name to become the focus of your attention. You may hear people speaking your name, or see it written. You may sense others who share that name, or receive abstract impressions based on the meaning of the name. All sorts of things may flash through your awareness when you begin. DON'T try to hold on to these fleeting glimpses, or you will find you have lost the thread. They will return stronger and clearer. When the music stops, or your time of about five to ten clock minutes elapses, stand up gently, stamp your foot firmly on the ground, and jot down in writing or on tape immediate impressions, no matter how vague. If you think nothing has happened, say so. Meditation may not produce immediate results, especially for beginners; but as you progress, you will find that impressions, pictures, feelings, and so on come both during the session and later, even in dreams.

You may well recall other items to add to your secret journal as a result even of the very first session working on your name. Jot down, too, how you felt—relaxed, cold, tense, wary, intrigued, and so on. Note any change in pulse rate, quicker or slower; any noises, feelings, or other distractions which made it harder to concentrate, or even any fascinating revelations that your first session may have produced.

You might think these instructions are very basic, and that you have done this kind of thing before, but there are many people to whom this can be a new and rather strange experience and who do need to be gently guided until they get the knack of meditation. Even if you are skilled, you might not have tried all the experiments mentioned here, so give them a go, just for the sake of completion.

Relaxation

Some people find it rather difficult just to sit down and switch off thoughts and tensions that have been part of their ordinary life, so some simple exercises can often help to relax the body at least. So long as you have enough room to stand up and swing your arms a little, you can do this in quite a confined space. The best results can be achieved by dancing to a record of your choice in order to loosen up your muscles and carry your thoughts away from worries or ordinary matters. Alternatively, try a few stretches and bends, especially movements which raise your shoulders, like reaching up. Twist and bend at the waist, sway from side to side, always trying gently to go as far as you can with each movement. Very slow and controlled movements are better than fast swings, which could cause pain in joints or muscles if you are not used to this kind of exercise.

If dancing doesn't appeal to you, or if you have a health problem or are handicapped in some other way, you can still relax yourself before settling down to meditation. If you sit in your meditation chair you can clench and relax each set of muscles, starting with your feet. Ideally, you should remove your shoes and anything tight or uncomfortable. Screw up all the muscles you can feel in your feet, and then let them relax and become limp; do the same for those in your ankles, counting three as you hold each set tensed up. Go on to your lower legs and knees, then to your thighs, clenching them hard together for a count of three. Next the abdomen, solar plexus region, and the muscles of your chest as you hold a breath for 1, 2, 3 counts. Push your elbows hard against your sides and tighten the muscles in your shoulders, each time letting every part fall loosely to a relaxed pose. Clench your fists and all the muscles in your forearms, hold for three, then let them fall limply onto your lap in a comfortable position. Next stretch your neck, raising your chin, then allow the muscles and tendons to relax. Screw up your face, shut your eyes tightly, clamp your lips hard together (don't clench your teeth or you might crack a tooth!); feel everything pull for a count of three, then relax. Take three slow, deep breaths, breathing in gently as far as you can, and counting to see how high you can go, but without strain. Hold it for a moment, then breathe right out. This should be done without effort or strain. (If you smoke a lot or suffer from bronchitis, etc., you will not be able to take very deep breaths yet, but as you learn to relax, things may improve.)

You should now feel quite calm, relaxed, and at ease, and any problems which had been chasing round your head should have evaporated while you have been concentrating on getting your muscles to relax. Close your eyes and just 'feel' around your body for any areas that still feel tense and repeat the clenching and relaxing of any part until all is comfortable. Now, allow your name to drift into your mind. See if any images, feelings, or sounds sail by. Perhaps you will see what seems to be a film with a steady flow of scenes passing by, or still pictures, or just impressions—sounds or sensations that are vague and hard to grasp. Don't worry; allow your set time limit to run out, then get up, stretch, and have a hot drink or a snack. Meditation is a 'knack.' For most people there is a period in which nothing seems to happen and then, quite suddenly, pictures appear, or ideas begin to flow. Like learning to ride a bicycle, for a while you cannot get the hang of it, but then a little practice makes balancing easier. Meditation is the same: First you cannot do it, then you can, with no in between state.

Try to have a session each day, ideally at the same time, so that you are as awake and relaxed as you can be. Be patient and jot down ANYTHING that occurs to you during each session, even if it seems insignificant.

In the old schools of magic, the students had to meditate regularly three times every day. At sunrise they would begin by saluting the rising sun, whose light symbolized the spread of knowledge throughout the world. At noon, when the sun was at its zenith, they would briefly meditate on the work that they were performing, and at sunset they would consider what they had achieved during the day. They would sum up their feelings, getting rid of any disappointments and failings, so that nothing would trouble their sleep. This discipline was laid upon them from outside by the rules of the school. Some people still feel they need to be organized and made to do things at particular times; others are more flexible and are able to meditate effectively anywhere and at any time, though they should still perform a session at least once a day.

We are changing from the astrological age of Pisces, in which people acted like schools of fish, all following the same rules and the same patterns of life, to the new age of Aquarius. Aquarius is usually shown as a man with a water pot, pouring out a stream of water. This symbolizes individuality—people being their own masters and taking more personal interest in the way they plan their lives. The water pot symbolises those experiences gained by an individual that can be shared with others. Following the lessons in this book will help you become a better Aquarian person, self-sufficient yet able to share skills, abilities, and activities with other people to your mutual benefit.

For this reason, rather than say you *MUST* meditate at dawn or at eight o'clock at night, it is best for you to find an ideal time to suit your pattern of daily activities, and which will not disrupt the activities of others in your home. Often early in the morning *IS* a good time, perhaps before the others get up and the house is quiet, or late in the evening when everyone else is occupied, watching television or in bed. Choose a time when you are not sleepy or concerned about something else. You may need up to an hour of peace in which to stretch and relax first, followed by meditation for ten or fifteen minutes, and finally a period of further relaxation and recording your experiences.

You might find that exploring the concept of your name is unsettling and that you become lost in a maze of symbols and words. There is no reason to feel upset or contemplate giving up, for you are opening a channel to a part of your inner self that has long been overlooked. Obviously it may take a little time to free the line of communication. Everyone has good and bad experiences during their life: unhappinesses, actions you later came to regret, hasty words that upset someone close, can all leave a kind of scar or residue. This is sometimes referred to as the 'psychic dustbin.' It is a part of your personal memory where the 'bad vibes' or bruises left by the knocks life has dealt you seem to remain. Part of the training in magic is to have a dig around in this pot of past experiences and stop them getting worse and overflowing into ordinary consciousness. This is done, not by supressing them and trying to cram more bad feelings in, but by trying to look at each experience in the light of your current knowledge and see if it is really as bad as you thought at the time.

This is not a job to tackle all at once, but again by gently delving, a little at a time, you will find you can cope with things that seemed unbearable at the time. It is important to tackle these past memories because, for one thing, they will have taught you valuable lessons which you may not have realised, and the less junk there is in your 'psychic dustbin,' the less chance there is of it causing you trouble later on. Quite often today's fears or phobias, dislikes, or mental disturbances can be traced back to things that may have happened years ago and have lain bubbling away in your subconscious mind and now pop up to cause trouble. Although some people seek expert help from psychiatrists to delve into this material, it is often better to 'do it yourself,' because you will not be embarrassed by thinking over former follies or heartaches. Try it. You can either begin when you were a baby, thinking of the earliest events you can recall and coming slowly up to date, again jotting in your secret book, or start with yesterday and work back. Take a section at a time and honestly note everything which might be relevant. If you wish to be a successful magician, it is important to understand what makes you tick!

One way for getting at the things you have 'forgotten' is to use a list of random words, meditating on each and seeing what comes to light. Open a book at random and point to a word with your eyes shut and then see what images and feelings it stirs up. Be patient. If you have lived for twenty or more years, you will have thousands of experiences tucked away in your memory and you cannot hope to winkle them out in a few sessions. There is no hurry: The magical school term is as long as you need to master every stage. Only you can know when you have finished each exercise to your own satisfaction.

If you can share some of these lessons with friends or relatives, you will find your companions may have different experiences to yours. There is no right or wrong way to experience things, nor is it bad to take longer to learn something new. Obviously, like playing a musical instrument, some people have a natural talent and will find it easier than others. The arts of magic are the same— some people learn to meditate, read Tarot cards, develop healing skills, and work ritual much easier than others, but in every case, patience and perseverance will pay off. You can never try for too long; though, because meditation requires a relaxed body and alert mind, it is possible to try too hard! The mind is a butterfly, not a log, and needs dealing with accordingly—although it can behave like a log sometimes!

Using your own name as a focus, allow images, feelings, and impressions to come to you. Although you will be very relaxed and become able to sink deeply into the meditative state, you will still be aware of your surroundings, able to cope with any emergency or other matter if the need arises. Remember, you are in charge and can control the speed of the process and the material which you explore. You are starting with yourself, for only by understanding your own life and motives can you reasonably hope to begin to understand what makes others tick. By exploring and turning out the contents of your memory's 'psychic dustbin,' you will be able to cope with some of your fears and past unhappinesses. Magic will lead to a fuller, happier, and more beneficial life for you and those around you.

Practise regularly, noting all your discoveries, for when you come to look back, you will be amazed what has come to light, even in blank periods; for dreams, ideas, and sudden inspiration can all enlarge or clarify the picture, even if meditation does not seem successful initially. Be patient, for you are a novice in an art that is thousands of years old. No one can be expected to become an expert in a few days, but surprisingly, many people get the knack quite quickly and start to uncover a vast source of information and guidance.

Though to begin with even ten minutes may seem a long time to try to wring information out of your inner self, as your technique improves, time will begin to flow by without any awareness on your part. Real experts can sit motionless in meditation for many hours; but avoid forcing long session on yourself until you feel you can cope. You should always feel completely alert, aware, and 'back here' after a session. Should you feel sleepy or confused, you will need to be firm with yourself: Take some deep breaths, stamp your feet, and move around vigorously. Often a hot drink or piece of fruit will get the system going. You may also feel cold if you are sitting still for a long time in a cool room, but you will soon recognize these things as ordinary happenings, and you can wrap up or sit more comfortably to get rid of any disturbances.

Often you will hear your heartbeat, the gurglings of your digestive tract, feel your pulse beating and be annoyed by itches, tingles, or odd feelings. These are quite natural and most of the time they happen without your noticing. They are a good sign in that you have begun to turn your attention away from the outer world and are sensing the complicated inner world, perhaps for the first time. Your breathing will tend to slow down and so will your pulse; you ought to feel relaxed but full of energy once you get into the swing of meditation. Even things like tension headaches, neck strain, and odd aches and pains can be alleviated by regular sessions. Once you have come to grips with the 'inner you,' you can tackle your general health and try the suggestions, later on, designed to help you become a fitter and stronger person.

4

VISUALIZATION
CREATING A PLACE IN INFINITY

Meditation is an altered state of consciousness in which you cease to be concerned with the time and place in which you are sitting and enter a world of information affecting various senses. It is an inward-looking, waiting, and perceiving state in which impressions and feelings can make themselves felt. It is an essentially passive activity, for apart from continuing to maintain a relaxed and attentive state, you are not directing the material that comes to you. Creative visualization, on the other hand, is a method of directing what you see and of creating, from fragments already in your memory, a new place or condition. It is the most important key to practical magical work and allows you to direct your will effectively, through the images you create. To do it effectively is not easy.

You will learn to direct your 'mind's eye' to any place or imaginary situation with accuracy and clear vision. To begin with, you should concentrate on things or places you can actually visit, so that you can check the images you perceive against the real thing and be certain you are not deluding yourself. Magic is an art of reality just as is cookery. You cannot throw together any old picture and expect it to be true to life, just as you cannot throw together any combination of foodstuffs and expect a perfect fruitcake. There is a right way to do both.

To begin with, you will need to repeat the same sort of relaxation exercises that you did before meditating. If you do not receive useful information from that, there is little point in trying visualization just yet. Once you are still and relaxed, you should imagine that part of you can see through your closed eyelids. Try to picture or sense (not everyone gets actual pictures) some object in the room with you: a vase, a book, the cover of a magazine or the pattern on the curtains— it doesn't much matter what. See it in colour, sense its texture, focus on a detail—is it real, is it solid, does it stay there for you to examine?

Usually not, to begin with. Objects become vague, colours and patterns shift, detail blurs. Open your eyes and look at it. How does the actual thing differ from your impression of it? Examine it, and then try again.

It is very important to be able to see an actual object clearly and in a real and lasting way, because during your magical work you will be presented with all sorts of images, symbols, illustrations, objects, and pictures which you will need to remember in order to interpret them. It is no use saying to yourself, 'I think I saw a red triangle, or it could have been an orange dagger, or perhaps a thing like the top of an iron fence gone rusty. . . .' You will need to see, quickly and accurately, whatever may come your way, and it is no use pretending; you will have to learn at least to get clear impressions, every time.

The human eye can act with extreme definition and can detect thousands of variations of colour and texture, distance and depth. The brain then interprets the data the eye picks up, and from its store of memories identifies and names what is being seen. Even if you see something for the first time, your eye and brain will tell you it is a flower, a machine, a soft, slimy substance. Think of the way children learn to name and recognize things. Within a few years of life, they know the names of colours, objects, foods, and so on. Recent studies have shown that they can even recognize numbers of dots and do sums and subtractions before they are able to recognise the numbers written as figures.

Most people use about 8 per cent of their brain. If you try very hard you might get it up to 10 per cent. This unused capacity may be full of memories, or is just waiting to be exploited through the use of 'psychic' senses. You can improve your ordinary vision and concentration by taking notice of things about you. Look at shapes, colours, and the natural world about you. Try to match designs of things seen as patterns on wallpaper with real flowers, etc. Imagine the colours of things and see if they are just as you imagined them. Ask yourself about the shapes of leaves, the way a tree branches— did you know they are all different? What about flowers, fruits, vegetables—what details do they share?

Shut your eyes and see a Rolls Royce car. What details come to mind? What about a wild rose? A tabby cat? A giraffe? Your memory is bound to be crammed with information on all sorts of animals, plants, and objects, especially since most people have been exposed to films, television, illustrated books, and so on for many years. Perhaps you have never touched a panda, but you know what it is like. When you learn to use visualization creatively, you may be able to make one to play with, to feel, and to talk to!

Inner Vision

Magic has always relied upon symbols and upon the use of items of equipment which may seem archaic or clumsy at the end of the twentieth century, but these are very powerful in the world of inner reality. In really elaborate rituals, there are long lists of instruments, regalia, banners, altars, signs, and symbols and to use all of them could mean a considerable outlay of cash. Many of these items can be seen in the mind's eye, or represented by some more ordinary objects, which, for the duration of the ceremony, appear to be the magical equivalent.

Just as a name can call to mind a whole series of impressions, so any symbol traditionally associated with ritual magic will evoke, on some inner level, a great collection of similar associations. It is these associations that make it such an effective and powerful symbol, and why, after hundreds of years, it is still used by modern magicians. There certainly is a case for gathering at least some of the symbolic objects as your personal tools, so that you can get the feel of practical work. It is much easier to remember the feel of an act if you have actually done it. If you have wielded a sword, or received a cup in a communion, felt the weight and grip of a magical wand and carved the design on a platter, it is much easier to imagine these items.

Magic is a matter of experience. Some things you can effectively imagine, but if you have personal experience of them it will be much easier. The equipment can be purchased from specialist shops, or you can do the whole thing by pretending the stick in your grip is a sword; but if you can find the determination to gather the basic equipment, making some items, altering others, you will have the most powerful tools available to you. You will need to try all sorts of practical things as you gain the skills of modern magic, just as the novices learned in the old schools. You will have to learn from a book instead of a teacher, but you can increase your own abilities by actually trying things, as best you can.

Back to the subject of visualization. You should try to fit in a training session each time you meditate. Look at an object, close your eyes and try to 'see' it, in colour and three dimensions, then see if you can alter details. Can you change the colour, the size, the shape, or texture? If you can, it is imagination not a true vision. The thing is real so it has a fixed form—try to learn that.

Another test of your ability to really 'see' is to imagine what is on top of things in your house. Look through closed cupboard doors, inside drawers, anywhere that you have not examined recently. Once you have a clear impression, go and look! Were you right?

The reason that clear inner vision is so important is that if you begin to work on seeing into the future, you will need to recognize any details that may confirm your vision. If you see a date on a calendar, for example, you will want to know what it actually is, especially if you are being warned of danger to yourself, or someone close. Car numbers, details of places, clothing, the state of flowers or trees can all help to indicate the season, place, and the people involved. The more observant you become in ordinary everyday matters, the better you will be at magical seeing. In both cases it can matter. Imagine you are the only witness to a crime and can recall clear, accurate details of what happened—you could prove a valuable witness and perhaps prevent a second crime.

Experiments with hypnotic subjects have shown that when relaxed in a hypnotic state, considerable details of forgotten events can be called to mind. The same can be true of anyone who has deliberately altered his own state of consciousness in the relaxed pose of meditation, for by remaining in control, he can carefully examine anything he sees. In both hypnosis and in meditation, the state is actually controlled by the individual whose state of consciousness is being altered. No one can compel a change of state; it has to be voluntary. The more you are in control, the more information can be discovered. The data is there; it is the recall system which needs to be tuned up!

The Magical Personality

Visualise yourself as you imagine other people see you. Are you generally cheerful or gloomy, smiling or glum? Do you have many friends or none; lots of acquaintances, or are you always surrounded by familiar strangers? What do you think others feel about you? Do you feel lonely, alienated, or are you constantly surrounded by loving friends and people you often hug and kiss? One of the other applications of creative visualization is used to create what is known as a 'magical personality.'

If you are disappointed with the way you are seen by others, or have become aware of parts of your character that could be improved in some way, now is your chance. Traditionally, the magical image a person creates is one of an adept, surrounded by novices and holding a position of power and domination within the magical lodge. In real-life modern magic, this image is the magician who has become totally himself/herself. Each of us has many talents and skills that have been overlooked, and aspects of ourselves that have been repressed by the world in which we live. By acknowledging that we can all be more effective human beings, and by striving in various ways to improve ourselves, we can make our world a better place for us, and more important, make it a better place for those around us.

Some of the old rituals talk of the 'perfect self,' the 'true person,' the 'higher' or 'inner self.' We do have an 'inner self,' and if this aspect can be encouraged to show itself and work through our lives, we can grow to match the magical image of our personality. Perhaps you wish to change your shape, be thinner or more curvy, stronger or more appealing to other people. To a certain extent these changes can be made, for once you determine to alter the body, it will help you to change the way you live. You can 'think' yourself fitter, quell minor and some major ills, become the magical image you see before you. All it takes is time and the will to make it happen.

Perfection is not a boring, self-righteous state in which you criticize everyone about you, but a widening of all your horizons. If you can see more of the picture, you can see where different factors fit into it; you can detect patterns which the narrower, unclear view cut out. By raising your state of awareness, you can sense the needs, abilities, and troubles of others, and if you have gained knowledge, skill, or understanding, you can help them. As you help others, you help yourself, for through their improvement the whole world is made a fraction better, even for you. You also gain experience. Probably you will not achieve 100 per cent perfection all at once, but think how much fun, interest, and new experience you will gain in the process. Life is infinitely more strange, thrilling, and fascinating than you can possibly imagine, and the only things stopping you seeing it are the spectacles you have chosen to wear, or which circumstances have forced upon you. (It is not your physical vision, which may also need correction, but your inner view of reality that may be at fault!)

Through experiencing the images creative visualization can show you, and by learning to see things as they are, you are moving into a greater, virtually infinite world of visions. By recognising what you see as real now, you can create a new future for that scene in which things can be changed for the better. If you have a broken leg, for example, you can see yourself out of plaster, running and jumping with no pain and full strength; you can then work towards that result. See yourself getting stronger, the bones knitting straight and firmly, as quickly as possible. It can happen!

You may need something and by creating an image of it, draw it to you. You will begin to find information you require suddenly turning up, books even throw themselves off shelves and fall open at the relevant page on occasions! You will find your meditations show you the location of bargains, or where some out-of- the-way object you want may be found. Lost items may show their hiding places and turn up even after you have searched thoroughly.

By using meditation and visualization together, you can uncover all sorts of valuable information. Visualize the thing or situation you require and then meditate upon it. A clear picture or strong indication may well come to you if you are patient. Often the solutions to difficult problems can be found, and those difficult interpersonal relationships be untangled by submitting them to the inner wisdom and clear sight of your meditative self. Don't be selfish, either. It does pay in magic to use your new-found skills for the benefit of other people. Don't meddle, though. Many of the experiences life throws at us are for a purpose that may not be clear at the time, but later on will be seen to have taught us a valuable lesson. If other people are having troubles, help as a friend, but do not expect to be able to wave a wand and make their difficulties vanish in a puff of smoke. It does not work like that. Give advice if you are asked for it, or support them through the tough time in a way you would like to be supported in similar circumstances, but let them gain whatever experiences are there for themselves. Meditate to see what might happen, and if that produces helpful information pass it on, but do not make a song and dance about inner inspiration. Most people do not understand, and you might lose a friend in consequence. Magic is meant to be a secret, so be discreet.

Try to have a session of meditation and visualization each day so that these two key techniques become second nature. Without them, the other arts of magic and of self-awareness are impossible.

Pathworking

If you have a friend to share your work with, or else a tape or cassette recorder, you can try another application of visualization and meditation which is used by most magical groups. This is usually called 'pathworking,' named after an exercise concerning the Tree of Life, the central glyph used by students of the Qabalah, a Hebrew mystical system. What happens is that a journey is described by one person and everyone tries to 'see' the scenes or images as clearly as they can. Sometimes people take it in turn to continue the story, or take up the narrative as the mood takes them. Others add details or tell of their own impressions as the visualization is continued. This is a very natural way to encourage magical vision because it is one we have known since childhood. Almost everyone has had stories read to them and have imagined the characters, scenes, and events as they were read. A vivid imagination, directed by magical training, is the most effective tool we have for changing the world, and it is something which has often lain dormant since childhood. The world of fairies is still there, but our adult eyes tend to look through it. We can regain the dimmed sight if we so wish, and with it see infinity, explore the far side of the moon, visit the lands of lost legend and the power that lies there.

Ideally, you should have a companion to read the words to you, pausing here and there to allow the pictures to grow real and solid. If you are alone, it is possible to read the narrative onto a tape and listen to it as you are meditating. Go slowly until you remember the child's skill of sensing the details, seeing any characters who turn up, and feeling the atmosphere. If several of you share this experience, take it in turn to read. There is a skill in that, too, which can be learned with practice. It is also good training for reading and performing rituals with others, as it helps you get over stage fright or embarrassment. Allow yourself plenty of time for relaxing first, for going through the script, and for pausing where there is a place to receive new impressions or information. You may need a while to jot down ideas afterwards too, so do not try to fit in a rushed session between other appointments. It can be fun and is a very good way of getting used to sharing magical experiences, so make sure your companions are not in a hurry either.

A simple example of the idea which you might like to try involves an imaginary journey to a place that is quiet, peaceful, and calming, and where it is easy to sink into an altered state of awareness to commune with the 'inner you.' For this particular exercise, a beach scene has been chosen because it implies a holiday away from the everyday sights and tensions. If you prefer a woodland glade, a mountain path, the interior of a large and beautiful house, or a wild and lonely moor, then, using the same sort of pace and imagery, invent your own path.

Get yourself into a meditative frame of mind; make sure you will not be disturbed for about half an hour. If you are not able to record the narrative, read it through a number of times until you can recall the various stages and tell it to yourself without having actually to read the text. You need to be as relaxed and comfortable as possible, and work steadily through the images at your own pace.

Imagine you are walking along a path among short pine trees and sweet scented shrubs. It is a warm sunny afternoon and there is a light breeze carrying the smell of the sea. You stroll slowly, basking in the warmth. Soon the path turns a corner and begins to slope gently downwards, zigzagging along the face of a golden, sandy cliff. Below is a long beach of pale sand, here and there dotted with rounded boulders of a darker reddish colour. At the foot of the cliff path you pause, touching the rock and finding it warm and soothing under your fingers. The tide is coming in and there is a narrow belt of weed and shells rippling along the beach. No one is in sight. Turning to the left, you walk along the base of the cliffs, which rise and darken in colour to an almost russet red. You see where rain and tide have formed steep canyons or shallow caves in the soft sandstone. Along the top, like a green fringe, hang swathes of grasses and small weeds with white, red, or yellow flowers. It is very quiet and the small waves make a soft, swooshing sound as they run in over the firm sand.

After walking a distance from the cliff path you notice a rounded boulder which is just right to sit on, and with your back against the sandy cliff, you sit and look about you. In both directions, the beach curves inwards to form a large bay. In the distance, you can see small white houses clustering beneath red tiled roofs among deep green pines. It is very warm and you look out to sea. The water is clear and the small waves break translucent greeny-blue with white foam on the tawny shore. Although the sea is calm you can sense its power, which is shown by the deeply etched cliffs and the worn-down rocks. You can imagine it pounding the beach in a storm and tossing great ships about in a smother of foam. You can feel the pull of the tides, and you recall that man is made up largely of water. There is a natural ebb and flow of things in your life, and sometimes it has seemed as if a great wave has swept away things you did not want to lose. The tide of seasons works on land as it does in the oceans, but the earth tides are slower. For a while you pause and consider all this. . . .

Looking up into the clear blue sky you see the sun and feel again its heat upon your skin. Here it is mild, yet in a desert it can dry and wither all who stray beneath its rays. It has the power to bring forth life in spring, yet it can scorch and shrivel the life it calls forth. Without the sun's heat, this world would be a dead speck of ice in a sunless night. You think of heat as anger, power, or energy and remember the warmth of love, the fires of passion, and perhaps having a hot temper. It brings to mind all sorts of memories. . . .

Lowering your glance from the hot sky, you notice a small yacht, with white sails slanted against the wind. You feel the breeze on your cheek and scents of land and sea waft past you. Perhaps the smell of cooking awakens a memory of a past meal, or the scent of flowers a walk in a sunlit garden. Maybe there is a tang of seaweed or of flames quenched by rain from long ago. The wind may bring you the keys to many past experiences, for the scents can release long-forgotten incidents and call them to mind. The oily shrubs may smell like incense; mown grass or the sea itself may awaken dreams of childhood holidays. The store of memory is opened and many images and feelings flood over you. For a long moment you are enthralled and absorbed in these. . . .

On the wind comes the cry of a gull, and the distant murmur of traffic. A boat engine roars out to sea, and above you on the cliff, children's voices call and chatter. Their laughter reminds you of your youth, and the other sounds compel you to take notice of the present. You know that you cannot sit dreaming for too long, and that there are tasks and duties that need to be performed. Gradually, you rise and return along the beach. The tide has come in and the sand is narrowed at the foot of the cliff. You cannot prevent the tides of the sea or the land returning and must move with them.

Soon the foot of the path is reached and you walk lightly up its twisted track. You feel refreshed and filled with sunlight and a clean wind. You breathe deeply and freely, and feel as if you have cast off a heavy burden. You have regained a little of the childlike freedom of spirit. Slowly you return to your own room, your own place, opening your eyes to today's world.

Do not rush to get up but stretch and yawn. Have a good shake and perhaps a drink or snack to get you back into the here and now. You may be surprised how much time has passed during your 'holiday at the seaside.' You should feel good, both relaxed and calm, and you will be filled with energy. If you do not feel right you may need to try this exercise a few times to get the hang of it. No magical exercise should make you feel weary or tired or otherwise unpleasant. They are mostly based on relaxed and aware states, and so it is only your mind that has been working. Any feelings of strangeness are due to the fact that you are re-opening old channels between your imagination and your conscious mind. Each half of your brain is concerned with a different sort of perception, and these magical journeys are aimed at forging closer links and clearer channels along which information and perception may flow. If these paths of communication have become silted up, it may take a bit of work to free them. Do not give up if you didn't get a great deal the first time.

At each set of dots . . . there should be a pause in the narrative so that you can really study any images or feelings that come your way and get as much as possible from them. At first the pictures may be blurred and vague, but like remembering dreams, there is a knack to it which you will get with practice. Be patient.

You may find if you share this experience with a friend that he or she sees different things, or senses quite another place. That does not matter. Just as your memory of a shared event will differ, so do people's perception of the scenery of these inner journeys. The images must be based on memory, and if you have never been to the place in which this path was set, the Algarve coast of Portugal, you will have had to invent or recall the nearest thing you have seen. Nowhere in Britain are there cliffs of sandstone the colour of tomato soup, backing a white beach, where the sea, depending on the weather, is grey or blue or emerald green. Create what you can and revel in whatever images you can literally conjure up. That is what matters, for it is widening your own experience. It will also, through delving into memory, uncover aspects of your self that you may have forgotten, and it will brighten your dream life too!

A 'Place between the Worlds'

It is a good idea to make use of these techniques in ordinary life, for magic can be applied to mundane matters as well as being separate from everyday existence. If you cannot get to sleep, create a visual journey to take you to the Land of Nod. Imagine in great detail a peaceful place, warm and filled with lulling sounds and scents. Try to examine every flower, every object or person there, and you will find it works far better than sleeping tablets. It works on children too, so if they are hard to settle down at night give them a small drink of warm milk and honey, which is nature's own soporific, and tell them a tale of wonder and beauty. Get them to travel into the realms of dreamland, and soon they will be asleep, if you speak gently and lull them with your words.

You can also apply this to real places and discover where you left some lost item. Relive any good or bad experience silently in a peaceful place and you will learn a great deal more from it. Even the most unpleasant happenings can be reviewed calmly so that they do not become unhappy events to be left festering in your memory.

In magical lodges, the technique of pathworking is often used to lead the whole brotherhood into a shared experience of another place, a sacred temple or centre of the wisdom they seek. All will share the visions, each seeing his or her own interpretation of the images described, and it is in this 'Place between the Worlds' that a magic happening can be translated into a real event.

Reread old tales, science fiction novels, and historical tracts and see to what extent you can enter into the scenes described and participate in the events. You may in this way uncover consider-able amounts of fascinating information about different eras, or old heroes or out-of-this-world places. It is a very cheap form of entertainment, ideal for filling any spare moments, and there is no end to the material that can be turned into films to be shown in your personal 'inner theatre.' It will also release mental blockages and make clear the paths of awareness and intuition, which is what living is all about.

5

GETTING FIT FOR MAGIC

Magic, as you will have come to realize by now, requires certain training and certain disciplines which these days people are expected to be able to apply to their own lives. In the past, the magical schools were run pretty much on the lines of monasteries. Each student was committed from an early age to follow a discipline, rules, and patterns of conduct in common with the others. All rose together, worshipped at the same time, dressed alike, ate and worked in unison, and none of them needed to make any decisions at all. Now we are living in the wide world with all its choices and personal freedom. In order to get the best out of our magical abilities and grow into the most effective individuals we are capable of becoming, we need to learn self-discipline and control.

The methods of magical training presented here are designed to enlarge the percentage of your life that is under your own direct control and, as your magical skills advance, help you cope with more aspects of both your ordinary pursuits and the large area of your inner life that has been long overlooked. During all the activities in which your state of consciousness is altered, in meditation and the other exercises, you will always have total control. If there is an emergency or something that needs your immediate action, you will be ready to cope, not under the sway of some enchanter, spellbound and helpless. The various skills you gain from these occult studies should make you more able to deal with any situation, because you will have gained awareness, not only of the obvious, but of all the subtle aspects of any experience that are too often missed.

Not only should you find your powers of concentration increase and that you become more relaxed and at peace with the world, but by studying the various methods suggested here you should become totally well and be able to offer healing and comfort to those around you. When you began the exercises, you had to examine the state of your self, acknowledge any faults and failings, and see reflected in the mirror of reality the real you. Perhaps you admitted to habits or states of body or mind that were not totally pleasing, or stress situations which you can only deal with by taking drugs. It is important that you try to get your health under your own control too, as well as the inner workings of your mind.

If you suffer some kind of illness or disability, what are you doing about it? Have you consulted a doctor and what was his advice? Have you ever been told that 'Nothing can be done in a case like yours. You will have to live with it. Your problem is due to your age, lifestyle, etc.'? Did you take that advice seriously, and have you given up hope for ever being 100 per cent well? Read on!

Allopathic and Alternative Medicine

The human body is a wonderful creation. It is extremely complex both in design and operation, and the more that is known about its various functions, the more incredible it is seen to be. Like anything else, it can go wrong, break down, or be damaged. Left to itself, or given the right assistance, it can probably go a long way to putting itself right. We live in an age of 'miracle drugs,' 'wonder cures,' and so on, but there are lots of troubles that still have no certain cure. Things like the common cold, depression, certain cancers, and many other simple and serious complaints still cannot be innoculated against or prevented by drugs.

For over a hundred years, most people have been treated by allopathic medicine; that is, treatment, medical or surgical, which is based on the idea of alleviating the symptoms. If you have a fever, it is thought that a drug which brings your temperature down will speed your recovery. If you have a pain, it is to be eased with analgesics, and so on. Other forms of treatment have taken a different approach. For example, homoeopathy, which treats like with like, argues that if a body has a fever, it is that body's way of striving to throw off the illness, and so in homoeopathic treatment, a drug would be given that causes a fever in a healthy person. In this way, the body is aided to act in its own way of curing itself. Homoe-opathy and many of the other natural forms of healing use minute doses of drugs, so diluted that traces are hard or even impossible to detect, in the medicine actually taken of the healing substance. However, these tiny doses are as effective as ordinary medicines, and they seldom have any side effects, which are a common occurrence with allopathic drugs.

Many other forms of treatment do not follow the conventional lines of Western medicine. Acupuncture, for example, suggests that there are 'meridians' through which the life force flows. If a blockage is made in any one of the fourteen main channels, some imbalance and subsequently illness will result. By allowing the life energy to flow freely, often by inserting extremely fine silver or gold needles, or by massage, or by the application of heat, the balance is restored, the pain relieved, and the patient recovers. These, and many other forms of treatment, using herbs, diet, flower essences, and so on, are called 'alternative therapies,' because they are alternatives to conventional allopathic medicine.

If you have not been helped by the usual forms of treatment, or if you suffer from some ailment which is hard to define and describe to an ordinary doctor, you might well benefit from a visit to an alternative therapist. Apart from homoeopaths or herbalists, whose medicines are of herbal or natural elements, mineral or flower essences, there are a number of healers who treat by massage, manipulation of joints, bones, or the spine, or who use other methods of 'laying on of hands' or 'spiritual healing.'

Any form of healing that encourages the unwell body to heal itself rather than drugging it or cutting into it unnecessarily has advantages. Although many people dislike the idea of having needles stuck into them, the fine ones used in acupuncture should not hurt if the therapist is skilled. Osteopaths, who manipulate bones and ligaments, often offer help in cases of long-term backache, stiff necks, and 'frozen shoulders' and so on. Chiropractors work mainly on the spine, and they successfully treat many back, neck, and headache problems, as well as complaints which are caused by compression on nerves in the back.

There are also many less easily explained therapies, such as colour healing, where the individual or damaged area is flooded with light of a particular colour. Naturopaths rely on the natural abilities of a body to put itself right by recommending a simple, basic diet, plenty of water to bathe in, drink, and relax in, so that toxins or poisons in the system may be quickly eliminated. Radionics practitioners use a form of dowsing to pinpoint areas of infection and use various instruments from simple pendulums to elaborate 'black boxes' both to diagnose and to treat a patient. Although it is not easy to understand *how* such methods may work, they are certainly effective, and a great number of people from all walks of life, suffering from every possible kind of ill health, physical, mental, or spiritual, can be helped by some form of therapy. It is also often possible for many people to discover they have healing ability of their own, which can be used to cure their own minor ills and those of people about them. Everyone who seeks to practice magic should at least try to heal by whatever methods they can. Many of the more complicated systems have a simpler form, which can be learned in the way conventional first aid is learned. Common ailments like headaches, stiff muscles, bruises and minor tensions, and depressions can all be treated by application of alternative first-aid methods, and there are plenty of basic books on all the therapies mentioned above.

Bach Flower Remedies

When you have learned some of the techniques of magic for yourself, you may wish to apply them in the field of healing. Everyone has some abilities here, and there are always people in need of sympathetic treatment in your circle of acquaintances. You may study simple forms of herbal medicine; massage; reflexology, which concerns finding areas on a patient's feet which reflect inner blockages or troubles; shiatsu, which is a form of acupuncture without the needles; or any of the more magical treatments. Some of the most useful, because they work in areas which are not tackled by orthodox medicine, are the Bach Flower Remedies.

Dr. Edward Bach was a qualified bacteriologist, and one day he was sitting in his garden and noticed the petals of a flower had fallen into a glass of water. He wondered if some of the 'virtue,' or health-giving strength, of the flower could be transferred into the water and so act as a medicine. Over the years, he experimented and discovered thirty-eight different flowers, shrubs or trees which had some healing properties. These do not act directly on physical disorders like fevers or infections, but on 'subtle' mental states, like fear, anguish, nervousness or terror. He was convinced many people suffer on a mental level, and this prevents natural healing of bodily ills by their internal balance system.

The Bach Flower Remedies are made by blending flowers with pure spring water in sunshine. A small amount of brandy is added to preserve the virtue. These are effective in the case of many of the uncertainties of life, or where people have been injured or unwell for no particular reason. They help the inner self combat disturbing influences and bring calm and natural healing.

Because they are made of flower extracts, they are safe for children and work well on animals or the very old. Like many natural remedies, they do not always work immediately, but they are gentle and cannot cause any side effects. It is necessary to take the recommended dose for a few weeks in some cases, until it brings the inner self back into balance. More information about these remedies and how best to prescribe them comes in a later chapter.

Stop Smoking, by Magic

It is very much in your own interest to get yourself well and stay that way. Magic is not an easy matter; you will need to be strong and fit to carry the responsibility you take upon yourself when you begin to practice the arts of magic. When you began the survey of your self and the meditations on your name, did you consider any bad habits you have? If you smoke, you must know that inhaling carbon and nicotine and all the other harmful materials is likely to shorten your life, or make you reliant on medicines or surgery to keep you alive. Perhaps you are a tobacco addict, but YOU can cure yourself.

An addiction is the combination of a mental need and a physical desire. Smoking may be soothing, but it is actually numbing your reactions. Because you have poisoned a part of your system, it cannot work to get itself, and consequently your whole self, well. You can give it up because you are stronger than the part of you that is craving more of the harmful substances. You *can* decide that health is better than illness or early death. You *can* make up your mind that you are going to be in charge of your whole being and not let some chemical dictate what you do with your body and your money. No one wants to be controlled by anyone else, so why should you be ruled by a harmful craving which is making you less than you can be?

It is obviously hard to stop smoking, but it is within your grasp. Imagine yourself strong, healthy, and free of this (or any other) bad habit. You see yourself able to cope, as you can with any unpleasant cravings you may have. You do not need any expensive therapy; you simply throw away the cigarettes in your possession and join the ranks of the non-smokers. You can try cutting down, but that is not a magical act. It is too easy to slide back from thirty to forty, or ten to twenty without noticing. If you give it up, that is it. You will be able to really test your magical ability. If you can do this, tackle every unpleasant longing by meditating on getting the poisons out of your system, imagining every breath you take is bringing in healing oxygen and washing out dirty, black tars and harmful chemicals, it will enable you to get a greater hold on your health.

If you find your hands wish for something to play with instead of a cigarette, carry a lump of modelling clay with you to mould into various shapes, or even a nice round pebble to fondle. All the time imagine a breath of healing air filling you. It does not take long for you to discover the taste of foods again, or to smell flowers and sweet incenses. You will notice the unpleasant stench in bars or smokey rooms which never bothered you before, and come to realize why non-smokers dislike it! If you can achieve the freedom to select what you take in, you will also be able to help others. If you have a companion to share your magical exercises with, make sure he or she is smoke-free too. It can be a great relief when you discover you are in control again. Not only will your body appreciate the change, but your intuitive senses, which have also been numbed by addiction, will begin to come into play. If you have lived on nicotine and strong coffee or tea for a long time, you will be amazed how the subtler senses re-emerge from their drugged state.

Meditational Bathing

A simple and effective way of getting yourself to feel well is to take a meditational and medicinal bath. This is one time when you ought to be able to consider yourself and see if you are happy with the body you are at present occupying. Run a nice bathful of hot water, scented perhaps with some fragrant essence, or natural herbs, and without using soap, lie back and consider yourself. Relax and become still, lightly floating, undisturbed and warm, just as you were before you were born. Be honest: Are you too fat or too thin? Are you flabby or bulgy with overdeveloped areas? You are your own problem, but by considering what you are like, and what you might like to become, you can gradually change yourself.

For anyone who just cannot find time to meditate in a conventional way, this can often provide a suitable alternative. By going back into the water, in which element life may well have begun, it is easier to cast off the conventional ties and return to simpler, more basic thoughts and ideas. Allow yourself to be free and immersed in a warm relaxed state when new ideas may come to you. When you are ready to get on with real life, you can symbolically wash off all the problems and hindrances to achieving total awareness and control of your life. Watch them depart with the foam down the plug hole and arise, clean not only in body but in spirit. You can actually build a very effective ritual about something as basic as taking a bath, adding scented essence and heat, imagining the steam carrying aloft prayers and ambitions to a level where they can become 'real.'

Natural Eating

As you began by examining the way you felt about yourself and started to come to terms with the 'real' you, you must apply the same sort of examination to the way you eat, and the things you enjoy. If you live entirely on pre-packed 'instant' food, it may take a while to reeducate your palate and digestion to accept more natural foods. There are several reasons for suggesting that more attention should be given to eating unprocessed fruit and vegetables, one of which is the necessity of avoiding potentially harmful chemical additives. Another is that a piece of fruit or a raw green plant is probably still filled with its own life force. It will have all its vital vitamins and trace elements unspoiled and these minute natural chemical doses are valuable in balancing a diet.

Some people suggest all magicians should automatically be vegetarians, or better still vegans, who eat no animal products at all. In practice, most of the best-known occultists have eaten meat and other conventional things. What matters is your attitude to what you eat and how you see it as being good for you, not only as a body, but as an 'inner self' too. If you try to eat as many different things as you can, you will be increasing the chance of absorbing all the minute traces of minerals and vitamins you need from natural sources. It is not necessary to indulge in special vitamin supplements or other medicines, except occasionally as a tonic.

Do try to eat raw fruits and vegetables each day. Children will benefit far more from a slice of sweet apple, pear, or banana or a piece of carrot or celery than a chocolate bar. If you wish to lose weight, one of the best things you can do is to make a large bowl of mixed chopped vegetables and fruits and nibble it all day. Avocado pears are an excellent source of vegetable protein and often the small ones are cheap. Red and green peppers have plenty of vitamin C, fennel adds a spicy taste to a salad, kohl rabi makes a change from carrots as a hot vegetable. Aubergines, courgettes, and peppers stewed with some garlic or onions in tomato juice make an interesting thick soup or toast-topper, especially with a little cheese grilled until runny.

Be adventurous in eating, because it can be a real treat to discover you really like the taste of some strange objects which you had previously not dared to try. Ladies fingers added to stew give an oriental touch, kiwi fruits sliced over a mixture of sliced pears, bananas, and apples make a far healthier fruit salad than the sickly sweet tinned variety. Cut down on white sugar and if you need sweetness try dark brown natural sugar or thin honey.

You can exchange some of your cups of tea or coffee for either a glass of natural fruit juice or even one of the sparkling spring waters that are appearing on many supermarket shelves now. Change soft white bread for one of the wholemeal or granary-type loaves, for these are far more nutritious and contain fibre, which keeps your system in healthy order. Try plain boiled rice, white or brown, instead of chips, or fill up with wholewheat spaghetti or noodles. Again, go on a voyage of discovery around your local supermarket or healthfood shop. The different items need not be expensive and many of the beans, lentils, and varieties of rice or noodles prove cheaper, as you use less per portion because they are filling.

There is a traditional British dish called a Salmagundi, which is a huge dish covered with an elaborate design made up of all sorts of vegetables and fruits with slices of hardboiled eggs, anchovies, cooked meat or fish, and olives, etc. This makes an interesting centerpiece to a party and can keep a family fed for several days. The base is usually chopped white cabbage with patterns of sliced tomato, cooked potatoes, raw carrot, celery, beetroot, green and red peppers, chicory, watercress, raw spinach, and onion rings. This can also have slices of apple (dipped in lemon juice so they stay white,) peaches, mangoes, oranges, pineapple, and grapes scattered about. It may sound very strange, but the combination of fruits and vegetables is pleasing to the palate, and the various new items will add a sparkle.

Try to experiment every day. Greek humus or taramasalata eaten with flat pitta bread makes a change from beans on toast; try French ratatouille instead of soup as a starter; a half small melon filled with fresh strawberries is better than a tin of peaches in syrup. Open your eyes to interesting things and do not be put off because they look strange.

Do not ignore the wild fruits and herbs which grow all over the country too. The blackberries, whortles, and rosehips found in country lanes can provide a free basis for pies, jams, or wines. All contain valuable natural elements and the outdoor effort of collecting them brings you closer to nature and the seasons of the year. Many farms now have 'pick your own fruit' sessions and a sunny afternoon gathering fresh strawberries or raspberries or blackcurrants can be extremely rewarding.

You might think the above has very little to do with magic, yet by working hand in hand with nature, you will be experiencing the great rite of creation in all its season-long splendour. Magic is not something that has to be locked away in the dark. It lives under the sun and all around you where plants grow, where springs flow, and where stars dance in the zenith of heaven.

Magic is concerned with living to the full, and if you can strive to be well, to eat sensibly and adventurously, you will start to become a far more effective human being. Once you start to feel fitter, you will find your subtle senses or intuitions will begin to ,function. You will be able to 'feel' how things are, or what needs to be done. Your meditations will begin to fill you with ideas and inspiration, and each day you will feel more able to cope, more flexible, and more alive. It does take hard work, dedication, and patience, but surely such a gift is worth it. No one else can get you healthy and fit if you will not make the effort yourself, and in a changing world it is far better to be in charge and control of any changes that are happening to you. Look in the mirror, and then in the food cupboard, and see where you can change things now!

6

THE EXPERIENCE OF RELIGION

Every major religion once had its mysteries, its magical and secret side. In some cases this has been lost and with it the power of that faith to attract and hold adherents. This has done nothing to prevent new cults appearing, but the trouble with cults is that they interpose a leader, teacher, or guru between the seeker and that which he is seeking.

The view most practising occultists hold is that there is a Creator, that angelic forces or gods and goddesses can be contacted in a variety of ways, and that prayers or ritual invocations can bring real and genuine answers. The adherents of many religions look forward with the confidence of faith to some future state, but for those who cannot accept the idea of a deity there can be no concept of an afterlife: Their actions must be directed towards making the most of the here and now. The magician does not believe: He knows that his prayers can be answered. He has seen or sensed the presence of angels or the gods, and he has had a variety of real personal experiences. He is aware that direct contact can be made between himself and the powers he works with.

Because this experience is personal to the magician there can be no common formula that applies to everyone. There has to be complete freedom so that every student can come to terms with his own concept of God, the gods, or no God. Like experiments in other branches of magical practice, it will be necessary for you to meditate, consider, and perhaps walk a path of imagination that will lead you to have some religious experiences of your own. There can be no rights and wrongs of religious belief any more than there can be absolute rules about the job you have or the pattern of life you lead. You must seriously consider the question in the light of your current knowledge, experiment, and later experience things for yourself.

Some religions teach that suffering is a necessary part of life, that sacrifices have to be made, that sins will be punished. Certainly life does have the habit of throwing nasty experiences our way and from them we do indeed learn; but does that get us any closer to heaven? Probably not. On the other hand, there are some modern organizations with eastern leaders that teach another path: that life is joy, that we have freedom in order to be free, that we can love and live as well as possible. Life can be joyous; it can be filled with wonderful experiences and beautiful relationships, but we need to work at it. We need to cast off the shackles that have been laid upon us by the society in which we live, examine everything and judge things for ourselves. It is not necessary to cast away everything from the past, cut ourselves off from all the good and bad events we have experienced and the lessons they have taught us; we must simply examine each concept carefully and evaluate it for ourselves. Much of the information we have gathered about how we ought to live is valuable and still true, but when it has been held under the spotlight of new understanding it may be found to be even more valuable. It is wrong to cast out all teachings and religious attitudes and dismiss holy books and holy men as irrelevant, ineffective, or worse. Each should be studied, and then, perhaps, cast aside.

The Mother Figure

Many aspects of modern occult work, as seen from the outside, have a strong religious bias. Witchcraft, for example, is closely associated in many books with the Old Religion, the pagan faith of the people before Christianity took hold. The Old Religion is concerned with nature, with the changing seasons seen as the life story of a God and Goddess. Through the centuries these have had many names and different personalities. They have been publicly worshipped and held in awe in many parts of the world. The God and the Goddess appear disguised somewhat in most modern faiths. The Lady of the pagans is the Virgin Mary, the Bride which the Sabbath awaits in the Jewish faith.

The idea that there is a female aspect to God is a very ancient one. The earliest artefacts to be identified as having religious significance show a female figure, greatly pregnant and fat with milk. She is the Earth Mother, the bringer forth of new life, the symbol of fertility and generation. The function of the mother was known long before the part played by the father was recognised. Many ancient societies were ruled by women and the inheritance of land was through the mother.

The bearing of children must have seemed a magical act, and even today there are places women visit if they wish to bear a child. The Old Religion was concerned with fertility, because without an ample harvest of crops, livestock, and children, a primitive village would soon die. The need for a good supply of natural resources has been paramount to the evolution of any society, group, or country. It is still true, for if oil, coal, and natural gas all gave out, we would not survive long. All these things are the gifts of nature, long ago worshipped as Mother Nature, the great creatrix of all life.

Animus and Anima

Today people are dissatisfied with conventional religions because they do not appeal to the inner self. The soul is left hungry and this leads to yearnings that are hard to identify. People feel unloved, unfulfilled, and empty, even though they often have good homes, comfortable incomes, and all the benefits of twentieth-century living. Something is missing. Dr. Carl Jung, the psychologist who advanced the study of the human mind in far more ways than is usually appreciated, wrote a book called *Modern Man in Search of a Soul.* Jung was convinced that as well as satisfying our bodily needs, we had a soul that had to be tended as well. If this spirit is left alone and ignored, it has ways of making its presence felt, and perhaps lies at the root of many forms of 'mental illness.' Many of these seem to be sicknesses of the spirit, the depression, the divided-self of schizophrenia, the anger and confusion of manic depressives, the feeling of threat or danger felt by many phobics. Perhaps it is the forgotten spirit trying to make contact looking over the shoulder, leaning on the individual, and causing depression by its own sense of isolation.

Jung said that each individual has an inner self of the opposite sex. If we can come to terms with these inner parts of ourselves, we shall have a much better understanding of other people and what makes them act as they do. This is another subject that requires further reading, careful thought, and consideration. Many of Jung's ideas, based on his study of people, of alchemy, and the Eastern divination system called the *I Ching* (the Book of Changes), are accepted by open-minded occultists and magicians.

No one should feel it necessary to accept the idea of a goddess or a god as a personification of a super-human being if this concept has no appeal for them, but it is well worth studying some of the many books on ancient religions that tell the legends of Isis and Osiris, of the Indian Gods and Goddesses, and of the pantheons of Greek and Roman deities to see how you feel about them. In the past, instead of believing in a single male God, many cultures worshipped a variety of gods and goddesses, each of whom had a particular speciality or 'job.' There was a god of war and a goddess of wisdom, one god concerned with expansion and growth, another with communications, travel, and trickery. Many of the gods were linked with heavenly bodies, the Sun and Moon, and the planets, whose names are those of the Roman gods and goddesses: Venus, Mars, Jupiter, Saturn, and Mercury. Later discoveries, like Neptune, Pluto, and Uranus, still have the names of ancient gods.

Dion Fortune, who wrote many books on all aspects of magic, wrote in her occult novel *The Sea Priestess*: 'All Gods are One God, and All Goddesses are One Goddess, and there is One Initiator.' This is a useful way of understanding that there can be aspects of God that need a separate name or title, yet beneath all the variety there was one Creator, one source from which life, the universe, and everything sprang. The words of the Bible tell us that 'God created man in his own image'; yet another translation states that 'God created man in his imagination': again we are back to the magical power of image making. By imagining the gods and goddesses as they are described in classical literature or shown in

Egyptian wall paintings, you are recreating them. Like Tinkerbell, the fairy in J. M. Barrie's *Peter Pan,* they have to be believed in or experienced or they will fade away. If you believe in a Goddess of Love and create her in your heart, you must gain in the ability to give out love. If you create a God of Plenty, surely you will grow in benefits from that source. When you need a particular sort of help, you can either rediscover an old deity with an appropriate function, or design a new one—an up-to-date image to help you achieve your wish. It is a way in which man and the gods have worked in partnership for a long time, and is still effective.

The God and the Goddess

The most basic forms of the God and Goddess that occur in many modern rituals are concerned with the powers traditionally associated with the Sun and the Moon. The Sun God has many names like Helios, Apollo, and Sol, and the Goddess, who reflects the varying phases of the Moon, often has three different names: Diana, the new moon maiden, Artemis, the full moon mother, and Hecate, the waning moon crone. Most of the classical religions had this idea of three Goddesses and one God who took several roles during the course of the natural year. At one time he might be the lover of the Goddess, her father, or her son. In the West a complicated story is told and enacted each year about this relationship of Earth and Sky, or Sun and Moon.

Many of the legends of heroes and heroines are really versions of this annual myth, retold as if they were the actions of real historic people. Sometimes the stories of the Old Gods have become so interwoven into the legends that the characters are thought of as actual kings who lived in historic time. One familiar one is the story of King Arthur. History places him as a leader of a band of warriors who fought against the Saxon invaders in about the 6th century AD, but legends place him much earlier. His court and adventures mix real conflicts with traditional tasks that the Sun God as hero was called upon to undertake. The magical sword, the wizard Merlin, who directs and guides the young king until he is enchanted by a witch, the perfect knights, the beautiful ladies, and the quest for the Holy Grail blend history and myth.

The quest for the Holy Grail can also be seen as a quest for the true self, and the adventures the legendary knights encountered will be found to occur in the lives of all seekers. There is a Sun God, who is born at the dead of winter, soon after the solstice, who grows with each passing day, and who receives his sword and arrows from his Mother, the ever-virgin Goddess. Later, as the year turns, he becomes her lover, and when she is disguised as a deer, he chases her into the forest. At midsummer, he is at his height and fights the dark side of himself, the winter king. He loses, and later on, as the spirit of the corn, is laid low at harvest. The Earth Goddess receives him and takes him into her house. This is still symbolized by the corn dolly, made from the last sheaf of standing corn. Autumn brings the bonfires of Hallowe'en, Summer's End, when the whole family gathered and invited the Goddess and the God, who were their ancestors, to visit the house.

Traditionally, on this ghostly eve all the dead return to join the revels, and the unborn children meet their parents in spirit. As the king of winter, the God at his lowest ebb rules with the dark queen, Lady of Night, and at midwinter he is born again, a weak child, the star child, the bringer of hope in a time of darkness.

These legends form part of the ritual pattern of many of the modern covens of witches, with the high priest and priestess acting out the story of the God and Goddess. The Druids follow this cycle, and many other pagans, whose ceremonies are less well known, also work their way through the stories of the old gods, just as the Christian Church tells different stories from the Bible at each feast.

The Old Religion and its current adherents are all seekers after joy. It is a religion of personal experience and of ceremonies that bring companionship and happiness to the people who share them. They do not see the cakes and wine of their communion as the blood and body of a slain god, but as tokens of the harvest from the Earth Mother and her Lord. There should be no idea of sacrifice, for the corn is grown to be harvested, the fruit trees are cultivated to provide a store of winter food. No one can offer anything except himself, and it is his life of service to the cause of Life that is offered. Killing animals or offering cut flowers is a strange idea when it is to the Life Force that these are being offered.

It is hard to explain how a student of magic should go about coming to terms with the Lord and Lady of Life, and except by experiencing communion with them you cannot judge their reality for yourself. The best way to go about it is to devise a place that is not entirely in our world nor entirely in theirs, and in this half-way-house, meet them face to face. It is another application of imagination, but you will frequently be guided as to how the images or feelings should be shaped. Like the other exercises, you will need a quiet time and place, and if you already have some idea of symbols for the God and Goddess, it might be appropriate to place these where you can see them without effort.

You will need to build up an image of the sort of place you imagine them to inhabit. If you choose to meet one of the classical gods of ancient Greece or Egypt, you may wish to construct a temple after the manner of the area. If you feel the gods are part of nature, then you might imagine a wild moor, rocky mountain or deserted sea shore, a glade in a forest or an island at the centre of a sacred lake. If you find it hard to describe a setting, you may find some poems may inspire you, or perhaps descriptions of sacred places taken from books. If you cannot imagine gods in human form, visualize them as powers. For example, you could see a landscape in daytime. You could start from sunrise, in a bare winter landscape. As the sun rises, its life-giving power turns the fields green; the corn and other plants begin to grow. When the heat of noon has passed and the sun begins to set, the corn is ripened and is ready for harvest. Here you will be seeing the real effect of sunlight on growing things without personifying the power of the sun.

The same applies to the moon. Her light can guide the lost in midnight's darkness. She also reflects the changing nature of women and, as she rules the sea, she affects the body, which contains a great deal of water. The moon actually alters the moods of many people, bringing periods of lucid dreams, visions, or greater psychic sensitivity. You can imagine the three separate Goddesses, the maid, mother, and old woman, each teaching you things; or just see her as a barren globe, circling our home planet. If you imagine a dark night with the sky lit by many stars, and then allow whichever phase of the moon you wish to work with to flood that darkness with silvery light, you will begin to sense her effect upon you.

In each case, create a flexible image through which the God or Goddess can show aspects of themselves to you. Some people are rather frightened by the idea of seeing these great powers face to face; yet it is an experience which ought to be sought out, since it adds a new dimension to your understanding of life. Any fears you may have are reflections of your own inner uncertainty. The gods will not harm us, and often a closer understanding of the powers which they represent can result from exercises or meditations. These powers can help us in many aspects of our daily lives, and there is nothing to fear from them. Do not be afraid to venture into the realm of the gods, or draw back from creating a safe place in which to meet them, for they represent a great power for creativity and growth, and through understanding them we can rediscover innate inner strengths. In the Gnostic Mass, each communicant, taking the cake and wine, says: 'There is no part of me which is not of the Gods.' That, too, is worth thinking about. We are parts of creation just as the trees or the stars are; but we are able to grow and set ourselves free to experience a wide range of things, if we so wish.

Perhaps the easiest way to think about the God and the Goddess is to see them as forces for CHANGE. They change the weather from cold spring rain to hot midsummer sunshine, the growth of plants from dead-seeming seeds to flowering, fruiting, and seeding trees and shrubs. It is the power of change which turns the tiny, helpless baby gradually into the full-grown, competent adult. Change, too, has led to the evolution of dust into planets, chemical elements into simple life forms, and, aided by the Great Initiator, has changed lifeless matter into all the variety of species of plants, animals, birds, and insects that inhabit our planet. There is some tiny spark of the Creator in every part of creation, from the simplest amoeba to the largest tree, from the most complicated animal to the loftiest mountain. Nothing is without its own God-given life force, and through our sharing of this tiny spark of the eternal, we are able to work with it through magic making, healing, and understanding far beyond our own abilities.

Reincarnation

Another aspect of this divine spark in man is that it is immortal and does not die when our body does. The doctrine of reincarnation holds that each soul lives through many human lifetimes, gradually gaining skills and strengthening its power to evolve. We recognize this eternal factor within us and probably think of it as our 'selves.' As the soul lives each life on earth, it gains new experiences and balances the pattern, becoming more complete. Between lives it rests, in a state which might be thought of as 'heaven.' Here it can assess its own progress and is not 'judged' or made to account for 'sins' but can see dispassionately how it has done in life. If a certain part of its development has been overlooked it will come back into life to learn the lessons so far omitted. This may account for geniuses, young children who can 'remember being someone else,' and early skills.

There is a good deal of research going on into this subject at the present time, and there are large numbers of books being published, both about the concept of reincarnation and the methods by which anyone can explore their own past. It is important to recognize that though a soul may have experienced many lives and deaths, these would not always be among the privileged classes of the time. There are many accounts of people recalling being pharaohs, priests, kings, people of high rank or historical significance, rather than humble servants, farmhands, soldiers, and slaves. They seem to forget that a simple life can teach lessons that are just as important—being a parent, coping in hard times, being persecuted, ill-used, and suffering disease and neglect. Most of humanity has had periods of striving to raise itself up, and times when nature was against it—times of drought, plague, and famine. Although suffering is not thought to be necessary, as is taught in some major faiths, it does bring out aspects of the human soul which might otherwise lie unexploited.

If you do want to explore your own past lives, do go about it sensibly, because it can be an unsettling experience. It is vital to have a reliable companion, plenty of time, and to make detailed records. You may be very frightened, for by accepting reincarnation you already acknowledge that you have died and been reborn. Death is not an easy subject to deal with and many deaths in earlier centuries are likely to have been violent, painful, and nasty! Do not take everything you learn without checking the facts—there are plenty of accurate historical accounts of most times and places, and the research can help confirm whether what you recall is valid and 'real', or just fantasy or imagination, or worst of all, created to flatter your ego!

Karma

Central to the idea of reincarnation is the doctrine of Karma, which is a cyclical concept of action and reaction. It is sometimes thought that it is simply a way for one individual to pay another back for harm done in a past lifetime, but it is far more complex than that. If you were killed by A in a past life and encounter him again in another incarnation, it does not mean that you have to kill him in order to get the balance right. Often there is some other way in which you and he work out the karma you share. Perhaps he repays the debt in some other way, for his death at this time might not be right. Sometimes it can be seen that your previous death was 'due', and that there was no blame to be dispensed; there could even have been an earlier life in which you caused A's death. Without a great deal of digging, it is hard to get to the bottom of a single event, and life is full of the effect of karma.

It is sometimes thought that crippling diseases are karmic debts being paid off, for individuals may have maimed, tortured, or crippled others in the past and are now suffering for their cruelty. No one knows if this is true, but karma does teach lessons, and good and bad deeds may well be balanced out. You must remember, though, that it is the soul that chooses the conditions into which it will be born each time. No other being directs the pattern of reincarnation. It is also possible that longlasting relationships can continue from one life to the next. Often you will meet people for the first time, yet you recognize them and even find you become close friends; you feel as if you have 'been there before' when visiting somewhere new, or occasionally take an instant dislike to someone for no reason. You feel sympathy or antipathy towards strangers, sense bonds of love or hate which seem to linger beyond death and through great spans of time.

It is important that the bonds of love should outlive the grave, and it is these that all religions should teach their followers to construct. If you can give out love, to God or the gods, to mankind, to those closely related to you, as well as to casual acquaintances, it will be reflected back on you and you will be loved. Be prepared to show love, not in a 'sloppy' way, but genuinely from the heart. Touch people lovingly, cuddle those closest to you, put your arm around someone in sympathy, support the elderly. Be open, unembarrassed, and easy with those around you, and it will be repaid immediately by a happier, more loving atmosphere. 'God is Love,' it is written, and all of us have a spark of God in us. Let it shine as a flame of love, warming all our relationships. You will be surprised what a little love can do.

7

DIVINATION
STRETCHING YOUR SENSES

If you have made a serious effort to master the earlier exercises, you will have begun to realize that there is a great deal that you had not known about yourself before, and perhaps you are also finding new skills. Divination is another magical art requiring study and practice, but there are forms of it anyone can learn. Technically, 'divination' means communing with the Divinity, and thus receiving information that would otherwise be unavailable. There are all sorts of methods of divination using symbols, like the Tarot cards; there are the hexagrams of the *I Ching;* the configurations of the astrological birth chart; the visions 'seen' in a crystal ball; the interpretation of tea leaves; palmistry; graphology (the art of analysing handwriting). Some methods are very simple—for example, using the nine symbols of divining stones, sometimes called rune stones. Originally, rune stones had characters from the old Scandinavian alphabets on them.

Again, there are dozens of excellent books dealing with each of these methods. Always consult several books on the same subject of divination because every author has his own ideas and interpretations, and there is no 'one' correct way. Do look at a number of different methods, as you will find some immediately 'click' and make sense; others take longer to reveal what they can tell you.

The Tarot

Each of the 78 cards of the traditional Tarot pack has a specific meaning, and every combination with the other cards around it tells a different story. It is only by becoming familiar with the images on the deck you use, and letting it 'speak' to you, that you become able to turn a bare mechanical reading of what a book on Tarot says into a valid and thorough reading. This does come with practice. It is also helped by the methods of meditation and visualization which, with the altered state of consciousness that is a part of those techniques, provide a frame of mind that is open to subtle impressions. If you go about any sort of reading coldly and using only the intellect, the result will be shallow and vague. If you relax, you will sink into a perceptive state and open your inner self to receive guidance. This is not a trance state, and trances (when you are no longer in control) are never used in modern occult work of any sort. You simply attend to what the symbols have to say rather than to what is going on in the room about you.

Often you are giving a reading for another person and to some extent you will be turning your attention to their life. It is possible, whilst in a meditative state, to perceive clearly the way that the symbols explain themselves. A Tarot card depicting a scene of struggle might be seen in terms of a person striving to gain a better understanding of the question, or it could be his attempts to succeed in his job, or even an actual quarrel among his companions. The same applies to the positions of planets in a person's horoscope: Read in one way, they could mean strengths and successes in the world; in another, difficulties and conflicts inside the individual.

One of the easiest ways to learn what the Tarot cards mean to you is to take cards at random and simply relax, allowing the image to flow through your mind. Jot down what it seems to be saying to YOU—which is far more important than what the same image may have said to the writer of a book. Work through the whole pack until they are all familiar. This method of building your own interpretation is far quicker than trying to learn, parrot fashion, the meanings of cards given by someone else. Everyone is different, everyone has a unique understanding of the world, and that is what is important. Carry the cards about with you, glancing at the odd one whenever you get a chance so that they become easy to recognize. Sometimes they will speak to you, giving information as to what is about to occur.

It is important to realize that divination, no matter what form you may be using, can only indicate one of many possible futures.

Life is like a chess game. Each time a move is made, all sorts of other possible moves become available. Life is the same: Change one tiny aspect and the whole future pattern could be radically altered. It is in this way that will can be used to overcome or avoid ill luck. If you make up your mind that you will cope with any problem, or change yourself so that the person to whom the misfortune would have befallen is now no longer you, it can be avoided. Remember, man has free will; he can choose what path he takes, and if he learns to use common sense, looking ahead at what may befall, he can walk a much straighter, safer path through life. He has the ability to make decisions about what he wants to happen and mould himself into the person to whom those things will happen.

Do not be afraid to face all the images of the Tarot. Just because there is a card called DEATH, it does not imply the immediate demise of either you or the person you are reading for. It stands for a change, and any change can be for the better. It signifies the end of an era and the start of a new one. The other so-called unlucky cards are generally thought to be the Lightning-Struck Tower and the Devil, but both of these offer a choice. On the one hand, God is striking the tower, and as we are all well aware, there are many situations over which we have little control; but usually there is a benefit when the upheaval is over and things look brighter. Do not be afraid to face losing things; it is only a form of growing up when the 'toys' of your previous self are outgrown and put aside. The Devil can often refer to the inner side of your nature, which is wild and uncontrolled. It may be the 'psychic dustbin' of repressed fears and bad habits that has not been tackled and cleared out. It can suggest ill health, but it can equally act as a warning and tell you to do something about the state of your body in time to prevent the trouble actually affecting you. Most cards, and the hexagrams of the I Ching, are concerned with changes because that is when we get opportunities to make things better and alter them to suit our own purposes. As you grow magically, you will be better able to enjoy and control changes in your life, and gain more than you lose. Like most magical arts, this is a complicated and lengthy study, but the sooner you begin, the quicker you will be able to get results that give you valuable guidance or information. Be patient; get used to the system you have chosen and work hard to master it. You can apply the techniques of magical ritual to divination as well.

When you go on to the techniques of setting up an altar and a magical circle, which provides a still area free from distractions to mind or spirit, you can make a greater use of the Tarot. To begin with you may feel rather embarrassed when trying to explain the meanings of cards to other people, and it is a good idea to get used to this before you set up as a Monsieur Magicko or Madame Mysterioso who 'Sees all, tells all.' Practise explaining the cards or what they point to on tape until it is easy to give a clear picture of what is going through your head. Draw cards at random and explain the meanings and implications of them until you can make a story that hangs together and that is coherent and informative. If the cards say nothing, which they do from time to time, say so. Honesty is the most important aspect of divination. If the Gods choose to tell you anything it is up to you, on your honour, to pass it on intact and unaltered. If the indications are unlucky, find a way of explaining them so that the questioner understands that things may not go well; but do not send him away quaking in his shoes, certain that the end of the world is nigh.

Never boast about your abilities to divine, or claim to be a fortune teller. If you are asked to predict the outcome of some action, or how a certain plan is likely to work out, be humble. Offer to try to see what might happen, but do not be dogmatic or promise 100 per cent results. No one can do that, for sometimes the voices are dumb, the cards dead, and the symbols meaningless. You will only gain a good reputation in this field if you are discreet; do not tell one questioner what you have divined for another, and do not brag about your successes, or these may be the last you enjoy.

Dowsing

Although dowsing is a very ancient art, many people do not realize that it is something most of them can learn. Like playing a musical instrument, it takes understanding and practice. In the old days it was usual to use a twig cut from a hazel tree or willow in the shape of a 'Y'. This was held in a rather awkward-seeming grip by the ends of the top of the Y, so that the hands were held palm up, with the thumbs facing outwards. The fingers were lightly curled round the ends of the twig and slight tension was put upon it by tucking in the elbows to the sides and getting the finger knuckles to point forwards. Because the twig was under strain, any tiny movement made by the muscles of the hands or arms would be magnified and the ends of the twig would point sharply up or down. A dowser would walk over a field and when he crossed an underground spring the twig would react. Something in him recognized the unseen water; this made his muscles twitch and the stick showed this clearly. No one is sure how this reaction comes about, but many dowsers make a reliable living, finding not only water, either as a spring or in a pipe, but also tracing electrical wires, gas pipes, sewers, buried treasure, and archaeological artefacts.

Nowadays, instead of the twig, many dowsers use two metal rods, often made from wire coat hangers. These are cut to give a short end, usually inserted into some sort of tube, and a long arm, about twelve to fifteen inches long. The rods are bent into a right angle and held so that they can swing freely inside the tubes. By gripping the tubes lightly and holding the long arms parallel with the ground, it is possible to walk slowly forwards over an area where hidden minerals or water is suspected. The rods will swing gently in and out but as the dowser crosses the hidden object they will usually swing firmly across one another, and will only uncross when the far side of the stream or pipeline is crossed. This feels very weird at first, and it often seems that the dowser must be cheating; but experiments have been carried out under controlled conditions that clearly demonstrate the dowser is reacting to something he cannot 'know' is there. You can make some of these rods or even buy some specially made ones, and try walking about in your own garden. If you relax and allow the rods to swing freely you will soon begin to notice they seem to react to something. You can help by running a tap to ensure a flow of water, or even walk up to a bucket of water, until you get the hang of it. Like meditation, there is a definite 'knack' which has to be learned. Once you can do it, you only need practice to become adept.

The Pendulum

Another application of the dowsing principle is divination with a pendulum. For this you will need a large bead, small plumb-bob, or similar symmetrical object with a hole through it, and about eighteen inches of thin cord, twine, or thread. The best sort is woven rather than twisted, as it will not unravel as you use it. Picture cord is ideal as it is thin, cheap and, being an artificial fibre, will not wear out quickly. Once you have threaded the weight onto the cord hold it lightly over the top of your finger so that the pendulum can swing freely in all directions. Just relax your hand and do not make any deliberate movements with it. The first objective is to establish a code which is personal to you. Some books suggest a particular swing means a particular thing but this does not work for everyone, so establish your own signs. Ask yourself a question to which the answer is 'Yes'—anything simple, like 'Is my name . . . ?' You will soon find the bob begins to move, either in a straight line towards you and away, or left-right, or perhaps in a circle. Ask it to indicate more clearly if the movement is faint and unclear. Keep on with positive questioning until you have a definite movement, than ask a question to which the answer is 'No.' See what the pendulum does then. It ought to be different from the first answer. Again keep on until you have a clear movement which is easily distinguishable from the 'Yes' answer. Ask another 'Yes' question to test the method and then another 'No' question, alternating and allowing the pendulum to swing at least a couple of inches to make its answer clear. Everyone can get some sort of swing going, but sometimes it is a very weak response. You can improve this by changing to the hand you use least. Often the left hand of right- handed people will give very large swings. Unless you get a definite 'Yes' and 'No' swing, which you can tell apart, you will not be able to use the pendulum for some of the magical methods.

Your code for yes and no, or positive and negative, is a way in which the inner you can make a simple communication with the outer self. The inner you has a great many more 'senses' than your outer five. It can detect underground water, lost objects, metal pipes, and less obvious things like 'ley lines,' which are ancient power lines apparently linking ancient monuments, stone circles, and megalithic structures. (These places are thought to have beneficial magical connections, and are often used for rituals and seasonal festival celebrations where possible.) The use of a pendulum also has many magical applications. For example, if you were reading the Tarot cards for someone and could not decide if a card was relevant or not, by holding a pendulum over it you would get a positive or negative decision. You can use this method to select cards for a reading for yourself, looking at those over which the bob gives a 'Yes' swing. You may use the pendulum as a way of answering any questions to which the answer is yes or no, or if you can develop some sort of binary code with it, for any other purpose. You can sometimes get answers from your inner self to questions your outer self cannot answer.

Healing with the Pendulum

Probably the most important area of divination with a pendulum is that of healing. There might seem to be no obvious connection, but once you realize that everyone has some sort of healing skill, even if they are not yet trained, you will see how the pendulum can be used both to help in diagnosis and in treatment. There is a field of healing called 'Radionics,' which uses the same idea as divination to treat all sorts of health problems, both physical and mental, and even things which affect the subtle aspects of the individual, his psychological state or soul. By divining with a 'Black Box,' which has dials and magnets inside, it is possible to discover a 'rate' for an illness. Each dial has numbers around it and by slowly turning these in a set fashion whilst stroking a pad of soft rubber it has been found by diviners that the finger will suddenly stick to the pad when a certain number is reached. A similar method of rubbing to

reach an answer has been used by wise men in Africa for generations. There, a wooden carved figure, damped with water or spittal,
is rubbed with a special block whilst questions are asked. When a
particular answer is relevant the block will stick quite definitely to
the rubbing figure. The same happens with the Radionics machine.
It will suddenly stick and indicate a specific number for each illness.

A more simple method can be used by anyone who has the
desire to try to heal or give help to people. First it is necessary to
establish if you can actually offer them help, which is done by asking the pendulum 'Can I help this person?' You should get a clear
'Yes,' or 'No.' If the answer is negative, then you should suggest the
person goes elsewhere for help, rather than try something and get
out of your depth. If the answer is 'Yes,' you can begin a series of
questions. (It is worth bearing in mind that a pendulum can suddenly change the code it is using, especially if you are dealing with
a person of the opposite sex, so ask a check question before you go
on to lengthy answers.)

Ask things like 'Could an ordinary doctor help?' 'Should this
person go into hospital?' 'Is the illness in his/her body, mind, or
spirit?' 'Does he/she need magical healing?' 'Can he/she cure himself?' 'If so, how?' and so on. Try to find out from the person what
sort of treatment he has tried before, how effective it was, and
whether he has sought professional advice.

If you have studied herbal, homoeopathic, or even the Bach
remedies (which work to alleviate many mental and anxiety states
better than anything), you can dowse down a list of methods of
treatment. This will help you tune in to the best way of treating
the individual. Often a person can go a long way to getting himself
right with a little help or guidance from a friend. A change of diet,
reduction of bad habits, more controlled relaxation, or exercise
can often go a long way towards a total cure and involves no drugs
or other treatment at all. Foot massage ('Reflexology' or 'Zone
Therapy') might be worth learning because it is fairly simple and
very effective in all sorts of troubles.

There are thirty-eight Bach remedies, made from the flowers,
buds, or leaves of various plants or trees, all but one native to Brit-

ain. Each treats a particular fear, anxiety, or nervous state. Even long-standing problems can be gradually alleviated by these gentle medicines. It is sometimes difficult to obtain a complete picture, and thus prescribe the best remedy. When this happens it is best to consult your pendulum. First make sure that it is in your power to help the person, and (just as importantly) that the person wishes you to help. If he is at a distance you can still help him, so long as he wishes it. If you can get a clipping of hair, or his signature on a letter, or even a clean tissue to which he has put his tongue, you will have a 'witness,' a link. This is very important, as you are using a magical art, and links between the magician/healer and patient are vital to the work. You can use herbal methods to treat animals in the same way.

Often dowsing will show aspects of the case that are not apparent to a non-magical approach. Illnesses are seldom simply caused by a single factor; rather, they are the cumulation of a variety of conditions and diseases. We are all surrounded by bacteria and viruses, some of which live inside us and cause no trouble, but when some part of our protective system of health breaks down, for whatever reason, we become susceptible to illness. The less orthodox methods can often reveal the true causes of illness and disease, which may be psychological as much as physical. By treating the *individual* rather than the disease, it is more likely a permanent cure can be found.

Dowsing can help pinpoint allergic reactions to foods or to environmental factors such as pollen. You can often dowse over the body of an unwell person, allowing the pendulum to answer the question: 'Is there anything wrong with this part?' You will sometimes find the area indicated by the pendulum is quite separate from the painful place or the apparent seat of infection; but by looking at the meridians along which acupuncture points lie, you may well find that the pendulum is indicating an unbalanced meridian. Use common sense and build up your skill with a pendulum, or any other form of divination equipment by becoming certain that the answers you perceive are correct at that moment. If you get vague answers, or no clear indications, go back to the basic exercises, play 'treasure hunt' with coins hidden under a carpet by a friend, or work with lists of appropriate questions with answers that can easily be checked.

Most children can dowse and they enjoy playing at finding hidden treasure, or identifying a series of different metals, etc., hidden under a blanket. It makes an original party game to get them searching for concealed prizes. It is possible to hold the pendulum in one hand and point with the other, asking 'Is it hidden in this direction?' The swing will become positive when you point in the right direction. This can also be used out of doors, to locate an underground stream, some lost object or the layout of an archaeological site, for example. Try out as many of these applications of practical divination as you can, for they stretch your senses and improve your magical skills.

Crystal Gazing

Crystal gazing, or scrying, is basically an extension of the art of meditation, but instead of a phrase or subject on which you meditate, you use something on which to concentrate your eyes, leaving your mind to range freely. Although a glass or a real crystal ball (very rare these days) is an ideal speculum, a bowl of water, a mirror, or a piece of polished black glass, jet, or even coal, will do just as well. A simple and effective 'black mirror' can be made from the glass face from an old alarm clock painted with several coats of matt black paint on the convex side. This should be set in a shallow tin or box, lined with velvet, to make a dull frame around the dark glass. Relax, as you would for meditation, but keep your eyes focused just below the surface of the glass. After a while, when you get into the properly relaxed and altered state, you will find what looks like drifts of mist or smoke begin to form, which gradually thicken and swirl. From this stage, if you remain alert yet very still, you will find the mist begins to clear and pictures, letters, symbols, or figures may be seen in the space. It takes a good deal of practise to get to this stage, for it often happens that the surprise of seeing the formation of the mist or smoke disturbs the relaxed state. Keep on trying, a little each day, until you can regularly see something. Later on, this skill will develop into a valid form of far-seeing, both in physical distance or through time.

All these divinatory arts need much serious study and practice, and it is no use giving up a technique just because you do not get instantly spectacular results. Like all worthwhile abilities, you will need to keep on with the basic exercises until you find they suddenly become easy. There are other applications of all these magical arts that you will discover as your expertise progresses, but they also have ordinary benefits. You will find you get useful 'hunches' more often, and that you can sense things about situations or people you would have missed before. You should be able to understand your own life and its ups and downs better, and through this, be of help to those around you. Be patient and ask the God or Goddess to help you see clearly and speak 'sooth.'

8

THE EQUIPMENT OF RITUAL

Ritual magic has a great appeal to many people who have come across some of the most imaginative works of fiction writers, but in reality it involves dedication, hard work, patience, and attention to detail. Certainly there are 'words of power,' great invocations, and elaborate settings of candle-lit altars, exotic regalia, and complicated ceremoniesl which vary from lodge to lodge, or group to group, and even from individual to individual. Some of these rituals are concerned with magical work, like uncovering new information, creating talismans for various purposes, or healing; others are concerned with celebrating certain seasonal festivals or ritual occasions. Depending on which system the rites are based on, some ceremonies will involve initiation or the recognition of magical advancement to a higher degree; or they might be more pagan in nature, the rituals of witches following the Old Religion with all its feasts and moon-orientated gatherings. Some rites are communions, like the Christian Mass, but older by many centuries, in which all participants join in sharing wine and special bread or cakes.

If you are working alone, some of these major ceremonial occasions may be beyond you until you find the right sort of group to join; but many of them can be quite successfully worked by an individual or a small group of novices. No matter how basic your level of magical working is, ritual must always be undertaken with a conscious purpose and with regard to common sense. Often, in books based on the magical grammars or 'grimoires' of the middle ages, all sorts of weird and wonderful things are suggested. Sacrifices of animals or strange substances are written about, but quite often these are nothing more than a kind of code. Many of the supposed 'animal sacrifices' are in fact common names for herbs, and the resulting substance was actually an incense. Many medicinal plants were called after animals—dog's mercury, horehound, cat's paw, foxtail grass, colt's foot, harebells, and so on. There is no valid modern ritual that requires blood, the death of any creature, or the harming of any person. If you read that these sort of things are necessary, discard that book, for it is either very out of date, or written by someone who is not a trained magician or occultist.

For every ritual, these things must be considered: What is it for? Where and when can it be done? What equipment, regalia, symbols, and other material (such as appropriate incenses, candles, and so on) will be needed? How many people are necessary/available to do it?

You will need to begin fairly simply and then build up more and more complicated ritual patterns, to whatever level of complexity appeals to you and your companions. If you are all novices, you must go slowly because it can be very strange when things begin to happen in accordance with your ritual purpose. You will need to understand that a ritual is like a telephone number: If you get the codes right and dial it properly, you will get through to the individual, or in this case to the 'power' or angelic force or god/goddess you have called upon. Of course, they can still be out, or the line can be engaged and so you do not get through. In a magical rite, just as in making a telephone call, you will know when the line is engaged or the call unanswered, for there is a definite feeling.

Correspondences

To work ritual you will be using a pattern of colours, numbers, metals, incenses, instruments, and so on called 'correspondences.' Magical correspondences are the equivalent of the telephone codes; you will need all of them to get the message through to where you wish it to go. You will have to build up lists of correspondence and gradually acquire the various items which these tell you are relevant to your purpose. For example, if you wish to work for a new job, the correspondences you would need are those of Jupiter. This planet is named after the god concerned with material growth. His colour is usually royal blue and his number is four. His day is Thursday (Thor's Day, the same god/power in the Norse pantheon). The metal of Jupiter is tin, or sometimes brass, which is a mixture of tin and copper. From this information it might be clear to you that you could make a square (foursided) blue talisman on a Thursday, call upon Jupiter to answer your plea, and light four royal blue candles, set in tin or brass holders. Alternatively, you and three others, on Thursday, dressed in royal blue and holding wands made of tin, could walk four times round a square altar on which is an incense burner filled with cedar, a talisman of tin painted with the sigil of Jupiter in blue, and invoke for a new job.

For any kind of magical activity, you will need a room large enough to set up a small table for an altar, either at the eastern side (or one side which for magical purposes becomes the east) or better still, in the centre. Ideally, you should have a large, square room with several cupboards, but it is possible to manage in a bed-sitter with a suitcase or small box, which contains all your magical gear and can be used as an altar when necessary. Magical robes, equipment, and ritual books should always be kept under lock and key, as power is built up in and around them and this becomes dissipated if things are just left about. You will save money if you make as much of your equipment as you can; it will also be magically much more powerful. An object bought from a shop is in no way linked with you, but a pot lovingly, even if badly, made by your own hand is a clear link between you and your magic. Much of the traditional equipment of magic is very old and might seem out of date on the verge of the Aquarian Age, but its symbolism is very powerful. Magic does not discard something unless it is found to be useless and the traditional items of wear, the four instruments and elements of earth, water, fire, and air still have their parts to play.

Basic Preparation for Ritual

Having tried successfully some meditation, visualisation, and perhaps divination exercises, you will first need something to wear. The most comfortable, practical, and traditional garment is a floor-length robe, sometimes with a hood, or else worn with a hooded cloak. If you wish to make your own robe, which is really best of all, you can do so quite simply, for modern fabrics offer a wide range of colours, textures, and weights.

First of all you must measure your height from the floor to the top of your shoulder. You will need a piece of material twice this length by about 48 inches, or 1.2 metres, wide. Choose dark blue, brown, green, or black as a basic colour to begin with, and look at fabrics which are easy to wash and drip dry.

You can buy a shop pattern for a kaftan or dressing gown if you wish to make an elaborate robe, or you can buy something of this nature; but a magical robe is easy to make to the following pattern and requires very little sewing (experts can add details and embroidery to the basic shape). You will need the measurement from your shoulder to the ground, and your chest/bust measurement. Fold your piece of material in half so that it is exactly your height (A in Figure 1) and cut off any extra. Fold the double material in half longways so you have a strip half the material wide by your height. At the centre cut a quarter circle C (Figure 2) to make neck hole, with a short slit on front side. At the edge measure 14 inches from top fold and place a pin there. Add 10 inches to your chest measurement and divide by four. Twelve inches down from the fold place a pin; from there go in this distance. That gives you the position of the armpit of the robe. Cut from the pin in the edge to this pin in a sloping line, then cut down to the bottom so that the hem is about 36–40 inches on each half. When you are sure you have sorted this out unfold the piece of cloth, which ought now to look like the letter T. Turn it wrong side out and sew from cuff to armpit to hem. Neaten the neck opening, perhaps insert a pocket into the side seam (invaluable for ritual handkerchief or a box of matches!). If the sleeves are not quite long enough, add a strip from the spare material. You can cover the join with a length of braid, which can also be used around the neck or hem if you wish. The seams can be sewn by hand or machine. Before turning up a hem, do try the robe on for length. You may need help to get it just right, but it can be done in an evening, even by a complete novice. (Needlework is another skill you have gained!)

The other very simple thing to make is a cloak, and if you really cannot manage the robe, then this is a necessity. Get a wide piece of fabric with a length from your heels to your shoulders and either turn over a hem or thread a ribbon in and out to gather up the top edge. You will need the ends of the gathering ribbon to tie it on with. You ought to try to make a hood, too, as this helps keep you warm and cuts out distracting objects from the sides of your eyes.

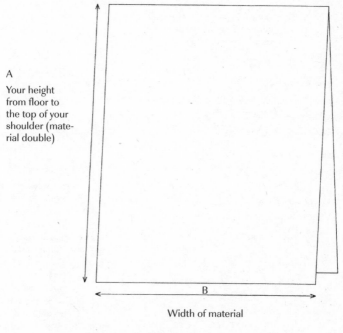

A

Your height from floor to the top of your shoulder (material double)

B

Width of material

Figure 1

As well as the robe, you will need a cord or belt to go round your waist, some soft slippers or sandals for your feet, and possibly a hat, biretta, nemyss, or coronet, according to taste. Refer to books of historical stage costumes to discover something appropriate. A simple headband may be made of strands of silver or gold elastic, available at Christmas time, plaited loosely and joined into a circle. This circlet will always fit, and will keep long hair out of your eyes and away from the hot incense burner! See what you can design. The waist cord may be any colour, and it is quite an inexpensive way of having something of the correct colour for a specific planetary ritual. You can buy plain silk cord or dressing gown belts with tassels in many colours, and often market stalls sell coloured braids, sew-on patches, and embroidery silks.

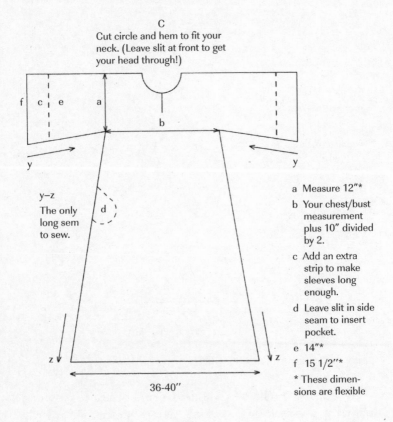

C
Cut circle and hem to fit your neck. (Leave slit at front to get your head through!)

f c e a

b

y   y

y–z
The only long sem to sew.

d

z   z

36-40"

a Measure 12"*
b Your chest/bust measurement plus 10" divided by 2.
c Add an extra strip to make sleeves long enough.
d Leave slit in side seam to insert pocket.
e 14"*
f 15 1/2"*
* These dimensions are flexible

Figure 2

As you progress with your practical work, you will probably find you need other items of wear for special ceremonies, or if you become a member of a lodge, you may be expected to devise different coloured items for particular ceremonies. These can be cloaks, made of brightly coloured cloth, or sashes, or tabards (made out of a strip of material the width of your shoulders and usually about knee length, often with heavy fringes to make it hang well), or an over-robe, which may be sleeveless.

If you wish to celebrate rituals in public places, or out of doors, or if you like to work naked, there is one very simple piece of regalia you could find useful. This is a ritual ribbon. Take about two yards (or two metres) of wide ribbon, fold it in half and across the fold, sew a seam at 45 degrees. Cut off the excess triangle of material. This makes a point which hangs down your back and may have a tassel if you wish. The ends may be turned up to form pockets into which a book of words, talismans, or ritual objects may be placed. The ribbon can be embroidered, have applique designs or even painted symbols on it.

Ritual ribbons are cheap to make from offcuts of ribbon or cloth; they can be carried about in a pocket or handbag, so that you always have your magical robe about you, and they can be any colour or material to suit the purpose of every ritual. They can be offered at initiation or to mark the gaining of specific grades and so on.

Once you have made a robe or similar item of ritual clothing it should be kept aside and not worn to fancy dress parties or just to show off. You will find that any object used for ritual purposes will build up an atmosphere about itself, and this should be preserved by keeping all magical materials in a closed cupboard, box, or suitcase, well out of the way of the curious. At a later stage you will probably be able to dispense with some regalia or ritual instruments, but while still a novice these 'props' are very valuable.

The Four Elements

Traditionally, a magician has a wand, a pentacle, a cup, and a sword. If you have studied the Tarot, you will have come across these symbols already and some of their correspondences. Today, although a fully set-up ritual magician will have these instruments, they have to be made, acquired, or altered to suit a special purpose. For a novice, simpler alternatives are possible. The basis of Western magic, whichever system you may choose to follow, is that of the four elements. Earth, Water, Fire, and Air are each symbolized by something on the altar, which may be shared during a communion ceremony, or by an instrument, or by some item which is magically seen to represent each element. By meditating on each element in turn and choosing something which seems to you to be representative, you can build up sets of items to use. Obviously, you can go for the Pentacle of Earth, the Cup of Water, the Sword of Fire, and the Wand of Air if you have access to such traditional symbols, or you can find other things that seem more appropriate to you. Usually there are the four weapons and four items on the altar which are also symbolic of the elements. These may be a rock or stone, some bread or salt for Earth, a dish or shell containing water or a cup of wine for Water, a candle or lantern for Fire, and an incense burner or joss sticks or a scented flower or even a fan to represent Air.

The four elements are very important because they form the key that links the inner workings of magic with the outer ones. When you begin to examine your character, perhaps with the aid of your horoscope, you will find that you had certain planets in the signs ruled by the different elements. Earth signs are Taurus, Virgo, and Capricorn; Water rules Cancer, Pisces, and Scorpio; Fire is Aries, Leo, and Sagittarius; and the Air signs are Gemini, Libra, and Aquarius. Each makes a kind of filter, like colour filters in photography, so that it colours the effect that the planets have upon the individual character. You will probably have come to see that you have an earthy nature, a watery or emotional side, a fiery temper, or an airy-fairy imagination. By working with the symbol you choose to use in ritual magic, you will strengthen any aspects of your character which seem weak in that respect.

Obviously you will have to work within your own circumstances, but buying expensive equipment is no substitute for putting effort into making things yourself, even badly, for use in magic. If you are hard up, you will have to adapt things you already have, or hunt for bargains. The most important thing is a table or the top of a bookcase, a chest of drawers, or a large box which serves as your altar. This may have religious connotations, but it is really a work bench. It will need a cover, perhaps a white table cloth, or a black square of material on which different coloured cloths or paper can be placed to harmonize with your ritual purpose. Make sure that the basic cloth is clean and pleasant to look at and that everything is kept away from lighted candles. Incidentally, you will need at least five candle holders. These can be made out of lumps of modelling clay, or from crack-filling plaster, moulded in a yogurt pot. It is best to use the mould upside-down so that they are wider at the base and less likely to fall over. Simple candle holders can often be bought around Christmas from chain stores, but whatever type you decide on, make sure they will take a tall candle without falling over easily. Although various coloured candles may be required for specific rituals it is better to buy a stock of ordinary white household candles, as these are fairly cheap, will give a good light and can be dipped in melted colouring crayon to give them a coat of whatever colour is required. To make a lantern for the centre of the altar you can take a small jar, dip the bottom of a candle in petroleum jelly, support this in the centre of the base with strips of card, and then fill the jar with about an inch of small pebbles and then fairly runny plaster. Let this set firm over night and lift out the candle. You should have a safe lantern in which short pieces of candle can be safely burned. This design can also be used for candle holders intended for outdoor use.

You need five lights because traditionally you always have one in the centre of the altar to represent the Light of the Universe, or the spark of God at the centre of your working, and one candle at each point of the compass. If you are not able to actually place one light at each quarter, don't worry; but you will probably need at least five or six candles for specific sorts of rituals. Use your imagination to design safe and pleasant looking items, even if they cost very little. An hour of work and effort put into making the equipment you need will pay dividends, for the power of the object is much greater than a new, bought object. Do not be afraid to experiment.

You will need to find containers for water, salt, oil, and incense because in order to consecrate and make everything you use magically powerful, these things will be needed. Small dishes, tiny jam jars, or other glass pots are well worth keeping for storing consecrated materials, incenses, herbs, and so on. You will begin to examine many things you have about the house to see if they can be adapted for magical use, and searches round secondhand shops may turn up useful items. Whatever you do choose (even natural objects, like stones, seashells, flowers, pieces of wood) will need to be consecrated before they are used in magical work. Consecration 'washes away' any unpleasant connections an object might have; without this, the atmosphere of a ritual can be disturbed.

Incense

Most rituals require incense and as this is something you might not have had to deal with before, here are a few hints. Although joss sticks can be used, the gums and resins associated with the planets and powers in Western magic are not usually made into joss sticks. Joss sticks produce pleasant scents, but they do not give the clear smoke nor the subtle 'psychic' atmosphere which is so important in ritual work. You will find it is worth the trouble to get some real incense, which comes in the form of grains in various brownish shades. It is necessary to get some blocks of charcoal, usually containing a little nitre which makes them light quickly. Barbecue charcoal can be used, but it may be difficult to light and it does not burn steadily. Incenses can be bought as blends, such as 'Basilica' or 'Glastonbury,' from church suppliers, or as pure gums and resins which you mix yourself. Again, the specialist suppliers will help you. Some make planetary incenses, or ones suitable for particular gods or festivals. To burn incense you will need either a proper thurible on chains, or a heat-proof ceramic dish. You can use a fireproof bowl part filled with clean sand, but you must be careful, as incense gets very hot indeed and can take the varnish off a table if the burner is not insulated. If you intend to carry the burner about during a ritual, to cense the room or make magical gestures with, make sure the container cannot fall over and burn you. A small metal tray or baking tin can be used. For standing an incense burner on the altar, a tile or section of roof slate or wood, painted dull black, can be used to prevent scorching the altar cloth. This is particularly important if you are using a paper cover to accord with the correspondences for a particular power. Ideally, a sheet of plate glass can be used to cover anything inflammable.

Holy oil is occasionally needed, and though this can be bought from specialist suppliers, it is possible to buy a small bottle of almond or olive oil from a chemist and decant a little into another bottle, to which chips of cedar, pine, or ground resin can be added to scent the oil. This is used to consecrate metal or pottery.

If there are several of you trying to work magic together, you will be able to share the work of finding, making, or adapting all the equipment you will require. Some items can be used by anyone, but each of you should have your own robe, cloak, or tabard and other regalia, and each of you should have a pentacle, a cup, and a wand. If you use a sword in ritual, this can belong to the group, although, of course, if each person achieves one of his or her own, it can be used when necessary. A small, sharp knife each is useful.

The Pentacle and Chalice

The pentacle is an Earth symbol so should be made of wood, clay, slate, or stone. It is a magical shield; it is the floor upon which you stand and the top of your altar, although in practical terms pentacles are usually made about six to twelve inches across. You must design the pattern upon it yourself, because it symbolizes your own position on the Earth, and no one can tell you what that is. It may be carved, painted, decorated with other materials, engraved, or etched, depending on your skill. During your original meditations you should have discovered something about yourself and the Earth and the Universe, so by looking at your magical diary, you may get valuable clues which will help with the design. Even if you cannot paint or draw, it is better to make the pentacle yourself, imaging as you do so the link that you have with the Earth, with Mother Nature, or God the Creator.

The next item is the magical cup or chalice. This should be a gift, given in love, not something simply bought to use. It symbolizes the emotional part of you which, like the cup, controls the shape of the liquid within, and directs your feelings and imagination. If no one cares for you enough to give you this unsought gift, then you will need to work on the emotional part of yourself. Try loving those about you, sending out good thoughts rather than acting selfishly. Give and you *WILL* receive. Suddenly you will discover a coffee mug turns up for your birthday, or perhaps a tea service arrives as a Christmas gift. Once you have received a cup, you can buy or adapt a goblet of glass, a silver chalice, or pewter wine cup for ritual use.

The Sword and the Wand

A ritual sword stands for determination and is often used to set a magical seal of protection about the working place. It may be placed to guard the door during a working, or else it lies upon the altar as a symbol of the strength of unity among the members. Although it is a weapon, it should not be thought of as something used to attack others or that cuts away connections, except in very rare circumstances. The traditional ritual sword is about 33 inches long, with a cross-shaped hilt. Many of these are now decorative daggers or stage props rather than ancient fighting blades. It is better to use a symbolic sword than a real one, for any traces of battle or fighting can be very hard for a novice to banish completely, and the feeling of fear, pain, or combat can linger a long time and will be picked up during the raised levels of awareness used in magical working. From an occult point of view, a sword bejewelled with fake stones and with a blunt, etched blade is a far safer thing to have about than a real battle weapon, with all its gory history.

The last item of ritual equipment is a wand. This again must be made by the individual and can be painted, carved, or polished natural wood. It ought not to be too long, especially if you are working in a small space. You will have to consider what it represents, having been derived from the arrow or lance of the soldier of old. It flies through the air, carrying with it your intention; in many workings, it is used to seal the lodge and conjure up the guardian spirits. Think hard about what it means to you before launching into a lot of hard work. You can buy a piece of dowelling or cut a stick from a tree. You can carve spirals, or wind it with ribbons. At the ends you can have spheres, lance heads, or metal ferrules, carved terminals or painted designs—so long as you understand the symbolism and it makes sense to you.

If you are uncertain about making these pieces of equipment, you can meditate upon the four Tarot suit aces, or visualize pictures of the magical work you wish to do, seeing what sort of equipment you would find most useful. As you work on each item, think of how it is an extension of a part of your inner self. The pentacle is your shield of self-sufficiency; the cup your ability to feel and sympathize; your sword or knife is the part of you that can make a way clear ahead and get round obstacles; the wand is your purpose, your will to succeed, and the application of your inner strength. Even if collecting, making, and perfecting this equipment seems a laborious process, it is time well spent, for like any other exercise intended to build up your physical muscles, gradual work brings greater strength and longer powers of endurance.

When you have made everything, find a safe place to keep it all. A robe and other regalia, and the four elemental weapons, and the objects to contain the elements on the altar, the candle holders, and so on will need a special place. These things are not toys and should always be treated with respect and care, and kept clean and ready for use. Once they have been consecrated and dedicated to a magical purpose they will take on a life of their own.

While you are making these pieces of occult hardware, you can be working on building up tables of correspondences for each. Divide a page in your magical notebook vertically into five columns. Across the tops of columns one to four write the names of the instruments—Pentacle, Cup, Sword, and Wand. In the fifth column write 'Instrument' and underneath that write 'Element,' 'Colour,' 'Point of the Compass' and so on down the fifth column. Then fill in the relevant information.

9

THE RITE WAY TO WORK

Ritual magic is usually thought of as the art of commanding spirits to obey your will, or changing base metal into gold by using strange 'words of power.' Fiction writers describe nameless rituals held in deserted ruined abbeys, where anyone coming across the magical work is immediately struck dumb or mad or both. In reality, ritual is the highest form of use of a trained imagination and will. It requires skill, patience, and a great deal of hard work. It may produce instant results but these will be the culmination of a long hard slog, gaining the basic knowledge, collecting the correct equipment, discovering the appropriate astrological moment, and so on.

Magic can only be safely and effectively worked if you are fully in control of your own self. It is no good frivolously trying a rite from some ancient book of magic. The results are likely to be very frightening, uncontrolled, and long-lasting. It is like driving a racing car in a Grand Prix race the day after passing your driving test. You may have heard of black and white magic; in fact there is no such thing as black or white magic, only black or white magicians. If you set out to work magic for selfish reasons, using cruel or ancient methods, that is black magic. If you work for the benefit of others, using your knowledge and skills wisely, trying to make the world a better place, albeit in a small way, that is white magic. For selfishness, you will pay dearly in the karmic balance, throughout this life, and several to come.

On the other hand, a student who acts sensibly and learns the different ways to make use of the skills he is gaining will gradually discover just what he is able to do. Although magic is normally applied as a last resort, when all the 'ordinary' things have been tried, it can be used in mundane situations just as effectively as in the specifically occult setting. You can use magical divination to track down a new magical instrument, or find your lost dog.

Once you have mastered the basic techniques, you will find uses for them in every area of your life.

Treat magic and the knowledge of its methods with discretion. Even in this day and age anyone who admits to being a magician or a witch is likely to be laughed at, at the very least. There are still people who think anything connected with the occult is evil and harmful. If you study magic seriously it will be part of your undertaking to see that this misinformation is put right, not by bragging, but by explanation. Many things that people do not understand are seen as dangerous, destructive, or just plain nasty. Magic is none of these, but because it is not easy to explain the philosophy behind it or the way it works, it remains hidden and therefore distrusted by many people. The occult schools taught discretion and silence for these very reasons, and if you become actively involved you should keep very quiet about your doings. Do not show off your regalia at parties, nor display your magical instruments to curious friends. If you do, these will become magically useless.

The Ritual of Consecration

The act of consecration is one in which a person, garment, or piece of equipment casts off its ties with ordinary life and becomes cleansed, blessed, and sacred. Most religions have a form of self-blessing, the most obvious being the way a Catholic will cross himself in a holy place or during mass. The cross is a very ancient, pre-Christian symbol and a similar gesture is used by magicians, and by students of the Qabalah in particular. What you are doing by making this gesture is to set an invisible seal about yourself, which can be seen by the powers with which magicians work and by clairvoyant people as a circle of bluish-white light. This helps raise the magician's level of consciousness by sealing him off from the ordinary world and its distractions. Usually there are a set of words said silently as you make the gesture, sometimes in English, sometimes in Hebrew, but there is nothing to stop you making up your own words and gestures.

The magical cross is made by touching your forehead with your first and second fingers (the other fingers and the thumb are tucked into your palm) and saying: '*May the Lord of light be with me.*' You then touch your solar plexus and say: '*And take the Darkness from me.*' Touching your right shoulder you say: '*Be your strength upon me.*' Touch your left shoulder, saying: '*And your wisdom guide me.*' You then make a circle, touching forehead, left shoulder, solar plexus, and right shoulder and say: '*So may this be.*' '*So mote it be*' (which means the same in Old English), or '*Amen,*' which is the same in Hebrew. Think about what you are saying and analyse your feelings afterwards.

Alternatively, you can describe a pentagram, the five pointed star, or a hexagram, with six places to touch and say something; but in both cases it is wise to complete the gesture with a circle. At the end of a meditation or ritual, you make the same gesture, but you can 'unwind' the circle if you wish, to brush it away.

Once you and the others with you have sealed yourselves, you will need to apply the same treatment to the place in which you intend to work your rituals. (Obviously, before you begin, you will have gathered together all the necessary equipment, robes, and so on, and decided the specific purpose of the ritual.)

It is traditional also to seal the working place, be it coven circle, or magical lodge, or private meditation room. The methods used differ, along with the prayers, instruments, and participants; but in general, the four elements are used. You will need portable symbols of Earth, Water, Fire, and Air, usually represented by a stone, a bowl of water, a lighted candle, and a burner of incense. If you are planning a communion, you will need a chalice of wine or fruit juice, some bread, cake, or biscuit, and usually salt (*not* sea salt). If there is more than one person and sufficient space, the carrying round of the elements can be shared out, preferably one person per element.

The elements are generally presented with Earth first, then Water, Fire, and Air. Each is either carried round the room, with an altar in the centre, or offered up and presented to each point of the compass in turn, beginning with North, then West, then South, and finally East. If you have room, the presented element is placed on the altar in the same quarter. If salt is used to represent Earth, it may be sprinkled about the room and drops of water also. As you carry each element around say something like: 'Power of Earth (Water, Fire, Air), bless this place; cleanse it and make it sacred. In the name of . . . help my (our) work.' Again, you can make up your own invocations or prayers, calling on assistance from the Unseen to suit your ideas. This is better than slavishly following some old book, especially if it has 'sonorous names' and 'words of power' that you do not understand. You can be far more specific in your every-day language than in mispronounced Greek or Enochian. If you do not know the name of a particular deity, make up a title or description to define exactly what sort of assistance you need.

After you have carried round each element, or raised it to each quarter, you can prepare to consecrate items on the altar. In theory you will have blessed each of the elements as you picked them up and carried them round, saying the blessing as you did so, but you can cup your hands over each in turn and ask a special one as you wish. Say: 'Lord of Air (or Lady of Earth), bless this thy creature, in thy Holy Name.' When you are ready to consecrate your pentacle, cup, dagger, and wand, you will need to bless the elements, and then either sprinkle or pass the object carefully through the smoke or flame of each element in turn. As you do this you say: 'I bless, consecrate, and set apart this . . . in the name of the spirit of Earth (Water, Fire, Air).' When it has been blessed, keep it away from prying eyes. Once you have consecrated your four instruments, your robes, regalia, and any other equipment, you should be able to feel the difference between a blessed and unblessed thing. There should be a distinct 'feel' to consecrated items.

You can use the same method of consecration for talismans. You will also be able to go on to the next phase of the ritual, which may be a pathworking, a meditation, healing, scrying, divination, or simply a blessing on the work you aim to do in future.

After this, you can go on to the Communion. This is not a dese-cration of the Christian Mass but a celebration of the magical prin-ciples expressed symbolically by the bread, salt, and wine, which are ritually shared with all other magicians and occultists. Even if you are alone, you will be sharing the wine and bread symbolically with all others, and it is customary to pour a drop or two of wine and sprinkle a crumb of bread and salt on the earth as a symbol of this mutual sharing.

Choose words which have a meaning for you. If you associate the bread with the Earth Mother, dedicate it to her; if you associate it with the Lord of Harvest, bless it in his name. The same applies to wine or fruit juice or even spring water: See with whom it seems to link you, and then bless the salt. When these are shared, the bread and salt is offered first, and the recipient dips a morsel of bread or biscuit into the salt and eats it. You then offer the wine goblet in both hands and it should be taken with both hands, never just one; this signifies unity and friendship, both among those present and the unseen companions on the path. Together you can sprinkle a little more incense, sniff the scented flower, and warm your hands over the candle flame, or even pass these round, if there are enough of you, so that all participate in every element.

When the communion is finished, the cup should be emptied by the last to receive it and it should be turned upside-down on the plate on which the bread and salt were placed. This should afterwards be tipped on the earth to scatter any dregs of wine and crumbs to the creatures of Nature. (It is best to do this after a rite as it brings you right back to earth.)

The next part of the ritual is the Thanksgiving, during which prayers are said for peace in the world, for healing of the sick, for fertility and success of the Earth herself, and to the strengthening of the Lord of Life in the world. You can each say one of these in turn, or choose poems, songs, or prayers to fit the occasion, or whatever you feel is right. You should then collect the four elements and walk them round in the reverse direction to 'un-wind' the barrier that surrounds the place of ritual, as you do so saying 'Thank you' to the powers that you may not yet sense. There is no hurry but everything should be dealt with neatly and thoroughly. When you have finished, take off your robe and put it away. Wash up the cup and platter and tidy away all your equipment, especially now it has been consecrated, into its box or cupboard. You may feel very strange if you have never done anything like this before, and it is a good idea to have a warm drink and some fruit afterwards. You should also immediately write up your journal with all the details of the type of ritual, the people or their 'magical names,' and anything that occurred to you during the meditation or pathworking.

All incense should be allowed to burn out, but if you wish to quench candles, these must always be pinched out or snuffed with an old-fashioned snuffer. They should not be blown out because, magically, breath is life and even a flame is a living thing.

Practice the actions of handling round the goblet and bread/salt with your companions. Get used to walking about in a long skirt, and learn to move smoothly in it. See how much room you have for extravagant gestures, especially once you start waving your wand and sword about. If you cannot remember or make up the words of the prayers, invocations, and blessings, you will need a book to write out your rituals in, remembering it will probably have to be read in candlelight.

If you look back through this chapter, you will find all the stages of a traditional ritual set out. It is worth making a list of these so that you can gradually collect prayers and invocations which seem apt to you for each part. You and your companions can decide what you wish to do, and who should do what. It is a good idea to circulate all the parts so that different people get the experience of working in each place.

Initiation

Ideally, people should only work ritual once they have been properly accepted and initiated into a coven or ritual lodge. In today's world, however, at the brink of the Aquarian Age, this is not always possible. There are valid training groups, but these are few in number and they cannot between them cope with all the people who seriously wish to participate in magical work. If you are fortunate enough to come across such a group and be accepted by them, you will have many advantages over the lone student or the group of beginners who have to learn from books such as this; but all is not lost. Once you are certain that the path of magic is the one you earnestly wish to pursue, then you will have to set about the process of self-initiation. This is a very serious undertaking and not something to rush into after a month or so of meditation exercises; but if you have been working on these techniques for about a year, you *MAY* be ready to consider the matter.

As this book is written in the manner of a 'Do-it-yourself' manual, it is not a matter of simply providing a list of rituals to perform, prayers to say, and actions to make. The Age of Aquarius is the age of the individual, selecting his or her own path from the many offered. It is up to you to see what sort of religious commitment you wish to make, what gods or goddesses or conventional religious deities you wish to call upon for aid and guidance—only you can choose. You must decide if you want to commit yourself to the magical path from now on, or if you are ready to offer healing, divination, or guidance to other people as a result of your studies so far. Magical commitment is no light undertaking. In the old days the magical schools were run like monasteries and once you had taken your final vows you were under the abbot's bidding for the rest of your days. A magical initiation is just as serious and important a step to take today, and the vows you make, even if you are not being taken into a group; are just as binding. They may even be more so, for it seems that those who have followed the paths of magic in one life tend to return to it in subsequent incarnations. This fact is often recognized by wise teachers of the hidden arts, so that even a young novice may be acknowledged as having been a skilled and well-trained magician in a previous life.

If you are determined to follow this difficult and exciting way, which can lead from your own doorstep to heights you cannot yet dream of, you will need to prepare yourself and all the equipment you will require over a period of time. Look forward and see if it is coming up to a New Year, calendar or solar (21 March), your birthday, or some ancient festival which seems appropriate for your 're-birth day.' If such a date is a few weeks or months ahead, make that a time to work towards. Otherwise, examine your horoscope, find out which sign is specially good for commencing things—an astrologer will help you with this if you haven't the skill to decide. Give yourself time to prepare, for far too often magic is an art in which 'fools rush in where angels fear to tread.'

Any magical initiation consists of a number of parts that vary from tradition to tradition, but in most cases the circle or lodge is prepared by the group of initiates and then the candidate is brought in by one of them. He may be asked some questions, which he either answers from his own knowledge or they may be answered for him; he may be blindfolded or restrained in some other way. He will be asked if he agrees with the ideals of the group and will probably be expected to swear an oath of secrecy, honour, and commitment to the work of the group.

Various tools or symbols will be shown and their use explained to him and he will eventually take his place among his fellows. Perhaps some sort of communion will follow and all that is necessary will be explained as the ritual progresses. Details of various sorts of rituals of this nature have been written about widely, so if you wish, you can build up your own knowledge before getting directly involved. Often a candidate is given or chooses a new name or motto by which he is known in the circle, and there is often a 'death-and-rebirth' scene enacted during the ceremony; there may also be cleansing or banishing rites, depending on the tradition concerned. Should you be joining an established group, do ask what is likely to happen, what you might be expected to swear to, and anything else you can think of. If the group is a valid one, someone will explain as much as possible without breaking any rules, and you will feel welcomed and wanted. If this is not the case, think very carefully about it before you commit yourself to some unknown fate!

Any oath that threatens unpleasant penalties to anyone who chooses to leave the group later on, or suggests that it is impossible to break away, should be taken with a pinch of salt. No genuine group will bind its members by anything stronger than their desire to continue with it, and should they wish to leave, they will only be asked not to talk about what they learned or where. Fiendish oaths and threats make dramatic reading in novels but have little basis in fact. No one can carry them out and so they cannot be binding. If you do promise to be discreet, to hold with honour to what you have been taught, and use your skills to benefit others, try to do so. Promises made under threat of being eaten by demons, or being cut into a thousand pieces and scattered all over the globe, should be treated with the scorn they deserve—and the groups which make such threats avoided like the plague! If you do make a reasonable promise to behave and get on with your fellows and don't keep your word, the gods can find plenty of ways of reminding you, without resorting to horrible penalties!

When you feel ready to take such a step as magical self-initiation you will need to decide exactly what you can reasonably do without upsetting the family. A group of people who are all going to undergo a self-initiation at the same time will also have to select a time and place that is convenient to all. This might prove impossible, so that everyone has to do his or her own thing separately—often this is the best course of action. Because it is going to be a 'do-it-yourself' rite, you cannot expect the surprises which are normally arranged by any initiating group, but you will probably encounter one or two strange moments if you go about the matter seriously. (You will probably get worse shocks if you set about it without considering the consequences!)

The first part of many initiations, and especially self-initiations, is the vigil. In earlier times a squire who was to be dubbed a knight would spend the night in a chapel, keeping vigil over his sword and armour placed upon the altar. During the hours of darkness, he would examine his conscience, understand what he was letting himself in for, and perhaps his friends or teachers would whisper from the dark corners of the church sins or failings he hoped everyone had forgotten. In the morning he would be bathed by other young knights, his hair would be cut short, and he would be dressed in new clothes. His mother would present his sword, spurs, and helmet, and he would be dubbed by the king or some senior knight. There was then usually a service of blessing. A magical novice should go through a similar process.

Anyone living alone can arrange a proper vigil, ritual, celebration, and consecration of him or herself, but if you have a family, you will need to consider them also. It might be possible to perform your ceremony at the home of a friend or magical companion. You may not be able to spend all night watching over your collection of regalia and equipment, but you might be able to take a long walk through a wild or lonely place and during that time think seriously about your commitment to the magical way. No matter how you go about it, once you have committed yourself, it is forever. You will also have to choose a magical name: Even lone workers need an inner name to call to the gods, and sometimes they will call it back! This can be a thing, a plant, a motto like 'Sister Seeker of Truth' or 'Brother Bring Hope to the Earth.' Whatever you select, try to live up to it.

If you can spend a whole night meditating, thinking, and considering your future course, in or out of doors, in a mundane or sacred place, you will certainly be guided on your path from then on. It is possible to be alone at an ancient sacred site, and novices have stayed in longbarrows, on top of magical hills, or alone on a deserted beach—anywhere, in fact, where you can really think what you are doing in peace and quiet. It is possible that you do not really yet understand what such commitment will actually mean, and this is equally true of a novice who is being initiated into a group or coven. A wise leader will ensure that the newcomer is instructed and any queries or doubts ironed out before he gets as far as an initiation rite; but when you are walking this path alone, you can only rely on that inner certainty that it is right to proceed, and be patient if you are not sure.

When you are convinced you are making the right move, you will need to make a promise. If you are doing this alone, you obviously cannot swear to anyone else, but any promise you make is between you and the God/Goddesses you wish to serve. You cannot ignore this aspect of initiation: If you do not set yourself some sort of limit, you may find you have to undertake things which are beyond you. Do not make endless vows to work with a specific person, nor to support only one idea: You are growing in your magical knowledge and what lies ahead may change your direction. Make a serious promise to try to learn as much as you can, to apply your knowledge for the benefit of others rather than selfishly to honour the beliefs and practices of others, no matter how odd they may seem to you, to act responsibly with any skills you develop. If you have decided which God or Goddesses, power, angelic force, or humanitarian view you wish to support, you can make your vow in their name. You may make your promises with your hand upon symbols of Earth, Water, Fire, and Air in turn, or just touch bare earth, and swear by the power of the earth and the sky above to be true to whatever you have vowed. Work all this out well in advance.

Many people do not understand the principle of magical commitment or responsibility, but you soon learn it in practice. Whenever you make a magical act you are, as it were, making a move in the chess game of life. If you make a change that is anti-evolutionary, selfish, or simply very stupid, you will have to settle the karmic debt later on. This is especially important if you insist on using your newly gained magical abilities to meddle in the lives of other folk.

It might seem a good idea to try to bring together parted lovers or to perform a ritual to make yourself some money; but you will nearly always find that either the ritual goes wrong or that you just cannot do it. The reason is that sometimes people have to learn that their path is a lonely one, or that it is possible to cope with less money than they would like. These situations teach valuable lessons and if you try to avoid them, or make other people avoid similar experiences, they will only have to be faced at some other time. You may be tempted to use your magical skills to interfere with the activities of other people, and you may even be asked to act in various ways to help them. You must be very careful at not becoming involved in these situations, because when you start to change the pattern of somebody else's life, it will reflect on your own. Think very carefully, especially now, before you commit yourself to the magical way forever. Are you ready to advise, to guide and help those who may come to you, and are you wise enough to say 'No!'

from time to time? It is very important to understand that your responsibility will extend to all areas in which you use magical methods.

When you have decided what you are prepared to swear upon, you must draft what you intend to promise—to hold in honour the magical arts, to strive for peace in the world, to try to learn more and so help people more effectively, to grow into the best person you can possibly be, and to build your own contacts with the God and Goddesses, in whatever form you perceive them. Work it all out, and write it down so you can say exactly what you feel to be right. Perhaps there will be no other human to hear your words, but you can be certain that the Guardians of the Mysteries will hear and take note of your promise. After this you could lay out all your tools and equipment, and, as if you were teaching a novice, go over each item, saying what it is for, how you intend to use it, what it seems to symbolize. You can then have a few moments of meditation to see if all is going well. Next you might have your communion of bread and salt and a cup of wine. It is traditional to pour a small libation at this time, and if you are indoors, a bowl of earth from your garden, or from a sacred place, can be used to represent the Earth upon which you make your offering. Imagine that as you eat the bread dipped in salt that you are sharing with the Great Brotherhood of initiates all over the world. You may well even see them about your room, within the circle. Scatter a few crumbs upon the Earth, sip the wine, pouring a few drops for the Lord of Creation. Again, wait a little while, perhaps savouring your drink and consecrated bread, waiting for a feeling of companionship.

You can now add a little more incense to the charcoal, giving thanks for inspiration and guidance, for warmth of the sun and for friendships. You may have a new piece of regalia which you have not worn, or a cord which you can put on to show that you are binding yourself to the path you have chosen. In fact you can symbolically adopt the dress of the robed orders. The robe symbolizes the perfected you which you are striving to become, the sandals or slippers the path you intend to walk in the Mysteries. The headdress or circlet is your higher, inner self which guards and guides.

The girdle, cord, or belt binds you to the promise you have made, so that you do not forget what you have sworn. The talisman you may wear about your neck on a ribbon is the symbol of the tradition you wish to follow—the Christian cross, the Egyptian ankh, the witch's pentacle, the equal-armed, circled cross of the oldest magical schools, or any other symbol which is sacred to you.

After you have ceremonially adopted the robes and regalia you have chosen, you should say a prayer to each quarter, one for peace in the world, one for enlightenment and understanding, one for healing the sick, and another blessing the land for its gifts, fertility, and the fruits of field and orchard. Work these out for yourself and use them in your own ceremonies of communion or magic.

You may like yet another period of assimilation and meditation before you finally close the circle. When you are ready (and this ritual can have a very profound effect on you, even if you are thoroughly prepared), close the circle by collecting the symbols of the elements and walking them round anti-clockwise to bring the power down to its ordinary level. Place each in turn on the altar, say a formal thank you to all the invisible (or theoretically invisible) deities and powers who have attended your work. These are never dismissed, as you do not have the right to command them or order them about. Make sure you feel yourself to be back to normal before finally pinching out any candles and completely unwinding whatever symbols you used to seal the place.

You will probably need a good night's sleep after all this, so avoid a day of wild activity immediately after a self-initiation ritual. The effects on you may be felt during the actual ceremony, immediately afterwards, or even several days or weeks later. Do not expect ten-foot high angels to appear and offer you a crown of gold or a signed charter from God; the feeling will be intensely personal, inward, and uplifting. It can be a frightening experience unless you are really ready to take this step, and there is never a reason to rush into any magical activity until you know enough to undertake it safely.

Again, the course of this first ritual is not set out for you to simply copy and perform. You will need to read and reread this chapter, sorting out the various stages, deciding exactly what you can do and what you want to do, how it can be arranged, when and where. Plan, rehearse, and prepare everything well in advance, as this will all help to ensure the actual day goes smoothly and nothing is forgotten. If you do miss something out, mime it, or quickly re-think what you are doing. Once you have made your circle, you are committed.

10

A WEEK OF MAGICAL WORK

Although there are many applications of magical work, you will need to become used to ritual, divination, and all the other arts at your own pace before undertaking any ceremonies which may occur to you. One thing you will need to do is to build up a table of correspondences for the seven planets of traditional systems of astrology, etc. As each one of these applies to a day of the week, it is worth taking this concept as a starting point. Make another chart with the days of the week across the top and enter under each one the appropriate planet, the metal, the number, the gem, the colour and incense, and so on. Perhaps it is best to begin with Sunday. On the Saturday you can decide what the main purpose of your week's work is to be—this could be the search for a new occupation, some aspect of personal development, a quest for knowledge, mastering a new occult skill, or the healing of a sick friend. In general, the stages would be the same, but the symbols and so on would be different, and you might like to use your own symbol of the god/goddess/deity/power which is relevant to the objective. Think everything out and write a list of your requirements, the purpose of the working, and any other important information in your magical book.

It is not necessary to go to elaborate lengths to make use of the relevant correspondences, but if you have a robe you can also wear a coloured girdle, or a charm on a ribbon about your neck. Another way to match the colours to the ritual is to have a sheet of plate glass on your altar top and underneath it lay sheets of paper, foil, or cloth of the appropriate hue for your purpose; if you are using real candles and hot incense, do take precautions against setting fire to something—or someone. Sheets of wrapping paper can often be found in various metallic colours, like silver, gold, scarlet, green, blue, purple, yellow, and so on, and these will be very useful for ceremonies associated with a particular planetary purpose.

Use your imagination and commonsense when choosing things to wear or display on your altar for any ritual.

Sunday and Monday

Sunday is of course the day of the Sun. It is a day to work for healing, as the Sun is the life-bringer and its light is beneficial to anyone who is ill. It is also the 'planet' concerned with the personality, the self, and, magically, with the inner light of occult knowledge. Bear all this in your mind as you begin to set up your week's work. You may carry out your Sunday rite during the day, when the actual Sun is above the horizon. The number of the Sun is one; the colour/metal gold. The wand should be almond wood; the incense is galbanum. You can work out how you go about incorporating these into your own working. If you are making a talisman, it could be written in gold or yellow on a circular base by the light of one candle and you wear something gold/yellow as you do it; more expensively, a healing talisman could be inscribed on a gold disc, studded with diamonds and perfumed with frankincense.

Monday is the day of the moon and is more concerned with matters of a psychic nature, women (whose lives are to some extent ruled by the moon's phases), and visions.

You will need to work when the moon is above the horizon (which can be during the day). A study of the phase of the moon, her position, and rising and setting times is valuable to any magician because she has a powerful effect on any magical enterprise. You may wear white or silver, or even dark purple, and the number of the moon is two, so you will need two candles. A talisman ought to be made of silver and should be a crescent shape. Recognize the difference between a waxing and waning shape as these have different magical significances. The waxing, growing moon is concerned with increase and the outward showing of psychic or inspirational matters; the full moon is the date of pagan celebrations concerned with the Goddess as Mother; and the waning, fading moon takes away things—for instance ill health, bad luck, or nightmares. You will need to select the correct phase for the moon to work with you.

The perfume of the moon is jasmine, and as a drink for moon rites you can try jasmine tea, white wine, or the juice of white fruits. Gems include moonstones, crystals, or white quartz, and often cheap tumble-polished stones can be found to incorporate into any talisman of the moon. Silver foil can be used instead of the metal silver; again, use your imagination as to what is appropriate.

As the moon is concerned with psychism, Monday is a good time for any sort of divination, particularly scrying, or crystal gazing. This is a skill (see page 70) requiring patience and the ability, gained through meditation and similar exercises, to switch to a different mode of consciousness where physical relaxation combines with mental alertness and psychic perception. The sealing of a circle magically will go a long way to cutting down your perception of disturbing external noises or thoughts. You should bless your crystal or glass ball or dark mirror in the name of the Lady of the Moon in her guise as Goddess of inspiration. You can sprinkle it with blessed water, and any scrying glass or speculum should always be kept wrapped up in a dark cloth—velvet or silk are usual as these keep the magical charge inside and make the exercise easier.

Once you have shifted your level of awareness into an inner mode of perception, you will need to concentrate on any images, symbols, or pictures that drift into view. This is not easy and takes a while to master, but any form of scrying is a valuable adjunct to magical ability, for it is in this way that you are able to perceive the forces around your circle, and the way in which your spell will come into effect. You will also quickly be certain when your working is going to fail, and you will also realize why. Scrying can take quite a while, as you tend to lose awareness of time, and if you get into an informative session you must be prepared to see it through; so do not try to fit your Monday rite into the time before some other activity. Often a short spell of meditation using the moon as a focus will bring surprising insights into the problem or matter on which you are working and it may indicate a direction in which to continue your work that had not previously occurred to you. Be prepared for unexpected hints—even after your set time, because the faculty of inspiration may not work on your ordinary time scale. Do act on any information gained this way, as it is advice from your inner self.

Tuesday and Wednesday

Tuesday is ruled by Mars, the planet usually associated with fighting and soldiers. Mars is also concerned with courage, strength, and determination. His number is eight, the colour blood red, the metal iron, and his incense is tobacco. Often Dragon's Blood resin is used in rituals of Mars as it is dark red and has a sharp martial scent. If you are working a week of magic, now is the time to stress your determination and to call upon the God of Strength and Success to aid you in the battle for your aim. It also is the day to bless or consecrate your dagger or sword, whilst wearing something fiery red, on an altar covered with scarlet and iron or stainless steel dishes for salt and water.

The Tuesday ritual can be tough going because you may come face to face with your own weaknesses, anger, and with memories of these times when you lacked the courage of your convictions. You must demonstrate the qualities of Mars in your own nature, preferring the constructive strengths to the cruelty and overbearing nature of the warrior. You should recognize that mercy is a virtue shown by the greatest warriors.

Magic requires courage, for every ritual is an experiment in which you are working with forces far greater than you can imagine. You will be required to show both strength and humility. You will need willpower to go through with some activities and, like a sportsman making a bid for a record, you will often have to give every ounce of effort to achieve what you have set your heart upon. Dion Fortune wrote: 'If you have a choice of taking up magic or going into the blacksmithing trade, enter the forge for the work is much lighter!' She was right, for it is foolish to think that magic is easy. You *can* learn to wave a magic wand and achieve what you wish, but it takes as much effort on your part as climbing a great mountain or gaining a University degree. Meditate on all aspects of courage and skill, valour and determination. Strangely, this can apply just as much to female magicians as to male, for they may have children to defend, homes to manage alone, and careers in areas usually considered to be male provinces. There have been a number of fully trained priestesses who wield their magical swords with as much right and power as any male adept, for the mage is one who balances the male and female parts equally, and can function in either magical role.

Wednesday is the day of Mercury *(Mercredi* in French, or Woden's day in Saxon). He is the messenger of the gods, the communicator and bringer of news, a great traveler, but also a joker and thief, so beware of this aspect of the Mercurial nature. His colour is either orange, according to Qabalistic symbolism, or light blue; his metal is quicksilver or mercury, but today talismans for travel are made of aluminium. His number is five, and his incense is storax.

On Wednesdays you could make travel plans, design talismans for safety or use in all forms of communication, preferably on the mundane rather than the psychic level. If you are working for some material gain, it is the time to write letters, make telephone calls, and direct your attention to any form of communication that will help with your project. Mercury has a joking aspect, so beware of being misled by a red herring, or have some gain stolen from you by a rival or a misunderstanding. Be certain you know what you are after and exactly what you are doing to achieve it, for misinformation can trip you up now. Mercury's stone is the mystic opal.

Certainly you can meditate and apply your inner senses to discovering new information, but this is a practical day, too. Often news can be received showing that you are on the right lines, or that you have missed a trick somewhere. Be open to change and keep a flexible attitude to anything you learn. Magic *does* work, but the specific manner in which it does so is not easy to predict—even adepts get caught on the hop sometimes! Things can be helped to change and become favourable for you, but do not expect to be able to predict every stage of the transformation. Change is in the hands of the gods, who do not work with either human logic or human restrictions.

Thursday and Friday

Thursday is a time to make use of your knowledge about Jupiter, whose power is that of expansion and growth, especially in the field of material success, business acumen, and luck. You may find that you actually get somewhere on a Thursday if you wish to progress in material matters. Jupiter's colour is a rich royal blue; his number is four, so you could make square talismans from his metal, which is tin. Often brass is used, as tin is now a rare metal. The incense of Jupiter is cedar. This wood is used for cigar boxes as well as garden sheds and it may be possible to get small pieces that can be shaved into tiny splinters to burn on charcoal, though like all the other gums and resins, cedar can be bought from a specialist supplier.

Rites to Jupiter require the most sumptuous setting, with rich robes and fine candles in deep blue, or even royal purple. His gem is amethyst and a talisman for success could be made of tin or brass with four of these jewels set in a square; alternatively, it could be cut from royal blue paper and the sacred names written in gold as a contrast. You will find you receive meditational guidance about material activities during a Jupiter rite and might even feel impelled to make investments to help your money grow, or plant seeds of some sort for the future.

You have the chance to examine your own position in the world and see how you can expand your own empire. Through your magical skills you will be able to take a helpful role, giving wise guidance and inspired instruction to people who may come to you for help. It may well surprise you how your abilities, which seem mystical and other-worldly, have practical, down-to-earth applications in your ordinary life. Any healing skill, especially if you have had the sense to study conventional first aid or emergency treatment in cases of illness or accident, can come into play in the street, at work, and in the home. You will find the self-assurance that develops in the wake of magical skill will carry you through difficult or dangerous times, and your calmness, knowledge, and practical abilities can often turn an emergency into a safe situation. Jupiterian magic can often be applied in this way, just as it can in the running and reorganizing of any business activity. As you become adept at various magical activities, you will find that your 'empire' or circle of influence will spread and more opportunities for you to succeed will arise.

Friday brings the day of Venus, the Goddess of Love. Her colour is green, her metal copper, her stone emerald or green agate; her active principle is love, harmony, partnership, and her number is six. Many people imagine that magic can be effectively used in affairs of the heart, and in some respects they are right; but magic gives no one the authority to interfere in any way in the lives of others. Imagine you were on the receiving end—would you like having your affairs manipulated and your relationships dictated by someone else? If you wish to use magic to gain the love of someone else, you will find your spells work—but on you. You will become someone lovable, your attitudes will change so that you actually attract the sort of company you seek; but you cannot change other people to suit your wants.

Often people ask for talismans for love without realizing what will happen if they try to impel the affections of another person. They end up burdened for years, perhaps, or even several lives, with an unwilling, unhappy, and joyless partnership, united not by love but by knots of karmic debt that can take ages to unravel. To win love you must give it out; you must be someone whom people long to be with. Then you will get as much love as you give out.

You can certainly use the attributes of Venus to help you in your work. She is concerned with all kinds of partnerships, harmonies, and feelings of unity, which can apply to many situations of ordinary life. She teaches inner harmony as well as outer balance, victory over the less well controlled parts of human nature, gentleness, patience, and cooperation with all levels of our beings. She is also Mother Nature and anything to do with the natural world can be worked under her symbols and power. She is strong, for it is written that 'Love makes the world go round.' It is also well known that love will overcome all sorts of odds, not only in fairy tales like Beauty and the Beast and Sleeping Beauty, but in everyday events. Many acts of courage or heroism are due to love of life rather than to some idea of material reward. It is seen in the way people react in a crisis, performing great feats of strength, daring, and courage, not because of a war or struggle, but to rescue a trapped kitten! That is the effect of Venus, overcoming natural fears of fire or water, and her strength is greater than that even of Mars, for it is unselfish.

If you lack inner harmony, put on a green robe or cord, find some item of copper, six green candles, and a rose or benzoin incense and see what a meditation on Venus will do for you. Green used to be thought of as an unlucky colour because it was associated with the fairies; but as green is a magical colour, it can be safely worn by anyone who recognizes its importance. Try to work with and for others, not for selfish ends, and the Goddess of Life and Harmony and Love will bless you, and her power will guide you in the darkest times.

Saturday

On Saturday you come to the end of a week of effort with the planet Saturn. He is the old man of the universe; his power is constrictive, limiting, his colour black, his metal lead, and his jewels jet and onyx. He is a hard taskmaster, ruling with a firm hand, fencing us in to a world of tough reality. He sets edges to any enterprise, but as we grow older we come to a greater understanding of his basic wisdom and stillness. In old age we are his companions and can work within the boundaries he makes for us without wasting energy. His rituals are slow and solemn, conducted in sonorous tones. His incense is the bitter myrrh, the perfume of sacrifice and self-abasement. In a week of magic, it is the time to consolidate all that has been gained, reflect upon advances made, and set limitations on new ventures. He is also stability and can make a firm foundation for any future activity, and his strong fence can keep out unwanted distractions and influences. Saturn rules the ends of life and light, yet he is not a cruel tyrant but a firm grandfather who can see his children's mistakes and tries to guide them on a sensible path, usually to be rewarded by being called a silly old fool. In his age is wisdom and common sense, yet it is hidden in the dark cloak of experience and suffering, which makes it hard for the young and inexperienced to talk the same language. His stern solid nature is easy to dismiss in a hasty life, yet when things start to disintegrate around us, or when our castles in the air are discovered to lack the foundations of reality, it is to the Saturnian powers we must turn for support.

Some talismans made of lead contain a Roman acrostic, a Latin invocation which is sometimes used as a good luck charm. There are many interpretations of SATOR AREPO TENET OPERA ROTAS, but it is certainly a Saturn spell. One translation gives it as 'May the destroying might of the Triple Goddess work until the world has turned full circle.' Not a happy charm! The Triple Goddess has a dark side, sometimes called Hecate or the Morrigan, who has a destructive and dark appearance in her dealings with mankind. She is the Third Fate who cuts the thread of life, spun and measured by her sisters; she, like Saturn, is a limiter and shares the symbolism of the yew tree, the dark of the moon, and black stones, which in her case are used for scrying and receiving wisdom. But then youth is not the time of wisdom and understanding, of experience and knowledge; it is the time for action not thought, for outgoingness not reflection, and so the dark ones, Hecate and Saturn, are feared: Their stability is seen as a hinderance to living, and their calmness and experience as a fence or barrier to what is so important to youth. They will be more important later, for they are the Masters of Time. They will allow youth its moment, for in old age all of us come into their sphere of influence, whether we like it or not; they can then be seen as friends and strong companions, firm supporters and wise counsellors.

Saturn completes the revolution of a week's magical acts, yet you will see that you can continue, starting a new cycle of healing solar work. Probably you will seldom complete a whole week on any given project, but it is one of the best ways to learn the arts of ritual, the arrangement of symbols, the use of colours, numbers, and other correspondences that are given here. Go through this chapter several times, building up a list of the correspondences that are given here for each day, and as you read other books on magic, you will be able to gather material on all manner of things relating to each of these planets or days. Later you can add the information for Uranus, Neptune, and Pluto, the outer planets that were discovered much more recently. All have a magical application, all are important in the horoscope of any individual, and there are a great number of different things attributed to each. In some cases you will find different correspondences given, and it will be up to you to choose which colour or number, etc., seems most appropriate to each planet.

When you have consecrated all your equipment, which you may well continue to add to as time goes on, you will be able to make a talisman for most of the planetary matters, or to help in all sorts of enterprises. You will learn to keep silent about your activities, and not to boast of your successes, nor complain about your failures.

Secrecy adds a great deal of power to magical work, and though it is vital to be completely open and honest with any companions in the work, it is equally important not to brag about your magical interests. If you do show off, turning up to fancy dress parties in your robes, or making charms for people to affect others, or dabbling in the affairs of those who have not asked for help, you will soon wind up reaping the whirlwind you have sown. If you have any psychic abilities, but have not learned the skill of 'switching them off,' you will be prey to all manner of unpleasant experiences, all gleaned from unexplored aspects of your own nature—nothing from outside will 'come and get you': It is all there within you already. Being haunted by your own inner fears, failing at the simplest counter magic, losing the power to help, the ability to meditate or be calm is sufficient to show how you have transgressed the code of magical ethics!

There are no vengeful gods lurking unseen, but there are inner depths within you which can be challenged and unravelled, or which can make their presence known, like a rotting carcass under your nose. If you have seriously tried to get to grips with the factors that make up your human character, and have striven to raise yourself up, nothing can or will harm you. There are no fears you cannot master or overcome by yourself so long as you are really trying to learn and are acting in a reasonable manner. Certainly it will feel very strange the first few times you dress up and perform your rituals. You may feel embarrassed and self-conscious, even if you are alone, and doubly so if you have a companion—who is just as likely to feel the same! You will have to get used to moving about in a long skirt in a confined space and of dealing effectively with all the regalia of ritual; you will need to learn to cope with a strange state of consciousness, yet move and walk, talk and think whilst partly in this world and partly out of it.

You will never cease to learn; you will never come to the end of the applications of your magical skills. Each book you read will open new doors, raise questions which can only be resolved by personal discovery. You will have many strange experiences, and with perseverance you will reach new heights of skill and competence. The only limit on what you can achieve is what you set out to do.

11

THE MANY PATHS OF MAGIC

If you have worked your way through this book or have already learned many of the techniques described here, you may well be wondering how you can apply the knowledge. From the previous chapter you will see what sort of magic can be successfully worked on each day, and there is enough information to set up a ritual for any purpose, to scry or magically meditate, to make a talisman or work for some other objective. Although there are many sorts of rituals, they all follow a similar basic pattern, and though the purpose may be different and the gods and goddesses invoked may vary, or the powers called upon in another way, most rituals are based on the same plan.

To begin with, you will always have to know in advance the aim of the ritual you are about to perform, and though it is possible for some new direction to emerge during the course of the rite, that is another matter. If you are working with others, make sure they know as well, and are in agreement. Write down the purpose in your magical diary, sort out any special regalia, wine, cakes, candles, materials for talismans, scrying balls, or a link with a sick person if it is for healing.

Once you have double checked that everything is ready, and have had a ritual bath or shower, or at least a good wash before any major ritual, put on your robes and sandals slowly. Now is the time to gently shift into your raised magical personality. Say a prayer or a rememberance of the symbolism of the various things you are putting on, recall your magical name or motto—think about this too. Do not rush; it is time to change yourself into the magus you are aiming to become, competent, calm, and powerful—this takes a few moments. Go sedately into your magical room or temple, take your place and look around to assure yourself that everything is ready, and that your companions are where you expect them to be, looking calm and alert, awake and attentive. Using whichever form of self-blessing you prefer, make your first ritual gestures, sealing yourselves, lifting your consciousness to a higher, more concentrated level of magical reality.

Now you must use the elements of Earth, Water, Fire, and Air to bless the place or circle. Light the central candle or lamp, and then with a taper or spill, light the charcoal for the incense. This will usually take a moment to burn through and stop sparking. Take a small spoonful of incense grains and sprinkle these gently on the hot charcoal—a pinch is enough to begin with. In turn, carry the elements around, pronouncing a blessing and consecration on each in turn, asking for protection and enlightenment. In some lodges, the images of the four archangels, Uriel, Gabriel, Michael, and Raphael, or the powers of the elements in some other form, are called up to watch over the working, with appropriate prayers. Once this has been done and you and your companions are back in your places, you will continue to the next phase.

Having consecrated and sealed the place, you then have to change it to the magical temple, sacred grove, or holy place in which your work is set. This may be a form of pathworking, or a piece of description, a single image, or even some music which fits the intention and place which is your setting. This again should be a slow transition, as it allows images and feelings to build up and it can have rather strange effects if you rush on too fast, leaving some of your companions behind. St. Ignatius Loyola called this 'composition of place' and he taught his monks to re-create in their chapels scenes from the life of Jesus so completely that they became first-hand witnesses to it. Now is the time to state the purpose of the ritual out loud and to call upon whichever gods/goddesses, powers, angels, or other influences are to assist in the work. If you are making a talisman, each stage may need to be blessed, and at the end the completed object will have to be consecrated with Earth, Water, Fire, and Air, as described previously. A blessed talisman must be wrapped in a soft cloth (silk is best) to keep its magical charge inside when it is carried around.

You may now like to have a divination session, or a meditation to assess how things are going or receive instructions from the powers with which you are working. This also gives you a chance to remember anything you have forgotten about the work you have done and allows the level of concentration to rise or fall so that you are ready to proceed.

The next phase is the communion or sharing of the magical food and drink. You can use all kinds of things, even have a real feast with several courses, if you wish; but for formal ritual, a shared goblet of red wine and a morsel of bread dipped in salt is sufficient. The three parts of the feast should be blessed in the names of whichever powers or deities you feel to be appropriate. The bread/salt is offered around, either by one person offering it to all present or passed round from hand to hand. This is followed by the consecrated wine (you can use spring water or unfermented fruit juice if you wish, but most groups use real wine). Again, do not rush; make sure each person gets time to eat and drink, and when the last one has finished the bread and wine, and the empty goblet has been turned onto the platter, it is finished. You may also like to pass round a lighted lamp so that all can share the element Fire, and perhaps a scented flower, or carry round the incense burner with a few more grains of incense added. See what feels right for your group.

This is the culmination of the ritual, after which you will need to gently unwind, beginning with prayers to each of the four quarters, for peace, for plenty, and for healing, remembering especially anyone known to you. Lastly, pray for the companionship of all who tread the mystic path and who, though they may be unknown to you, are striving for the same sorts of things.

Reverse the carrying round of the elements, placing each on the altar; if it has been lodged at the edge of the circle, then walk round in the reverse direction yourselves, perhaps saying the self-blessing with its gesture as you do so, so that you gradually unwind your magical nature, coming firmly back to earth and this level of reality. Quietly disrobe, clear up, dispose of the dregs of wine and crumbs, and change out of your magical state.

Do not discuss the ritual with 'outsiders.' Shakespeare wrote: 'Peace, the spell's wound up . . . ,' and he was right. You must allow the power to get on with the job, settle down, and work in its own level of reality. Perhaps you noticed some strange shapes in the smoke of the incense; perhaps the candle flames seemed to flicker or sway in an odd fashion; perhaps one of you forgot a line, or moved in the wrong direction. Well, it is over. Write all the details into your magical diary, and then as far as possible, forget all about the matter. Like a seed, once planted, a magical act will not benefit from being dug up to see how it is getting on. Be patient, and in the next few days leave time to meditate on the objective and then you will receive information, hints, or inspiration. You might also simply discover that whatever it was you performed the ritual for comes to pass.

Magical Festivals

As well as practical rituals, there are many festivals that can be celebrated in a magical way. If the path to which you are drawn is that of witchcraft, you will find that any rites you come across or take part in with a coven will be more religious in form. There are a series of traditional festivals that enact the year of nature, and in which the Goddess and God, portrayed sometimes by the High Priestess and High Priest of a group, act out their meeting, mating, and the bringing forth of the Child of Promise at the Winter Solstice. The festival of Brigid, Bride, or Candlemas, at the beginning of February, is when the Goddess, who bore her son at Yuletide, returns as Goddess of Nature and is feted with snowdrops and other early spring flowers. Next comes the Spring Equinox when the sun enters Aries on about 21 March (check the exact dates and times of solar and lunar feasts in an ephemeris). At this time of equal day and night, there is a celebration of the sown seed, the re-emergence of life in the spring flowers. Day and night are equal, so the God and Goddess should stand together, and this is their time of mating if the new Sun God is to be born at Yuletide.

At the end of April is May Eve, the wedding of the Goddess and God. The Goddess is magically changed into a white hind and the God, as the Hunter, seeks her in the woodland. After the chase they may dance and jump over a bonfire, the Beltane fire, named after the Sun God, Bel or Baal. There may be a wedding feast, and houses are decked with Hawthorn blossoms, unlucky at any other time.

After May Day, with its child May Queens enacting the bridal procession of the pagan Goddess, the Sun continues to climb to his zenith at midsummer and enters Cancer on or about 21 June. Here the God of Summer and of Winter fight for domination. At the beginning of August is Lammas or Loaf-mas, the time when the first corn was reaped and turned into bread. Here the God is the Spirit of the Corn and his sacrifice is enacted as told of in the song 'John Barleycorn.' He is cut down and laid into the arms of the Goddess, his widow and mother. The last sheaf of corn is saved and from it are made the Corn Dollies, or Kern Kings, representing Cernunnos, the antlered solar God as the spirit of nature. This is part wake and part celebration and both aspects ought to be shown in rituals at this time.

September brings the Autumnal Equinox on or about the 23rd, and the old feast now known as Michaelmas. St. Michael, who threw down, but did not kill the 'devil,' is the name given to another solar God. High places and chapels built on mounds are often dedicated to St. Michael or St. George, who slew his dragon. Michael has taken over from Bran the Celtic solar God, represented by both the crow or raven and the Alder tree, whose wood bleeds red like blood yet 'lasts forever under water.' This is a harvest festival in pagan circles, when fruits, nuts, and garlands of late flowers are brought into the circle to be offered to the God and Goddess.

Hallowe'en is the best known of the old feasts. Games of divination, looking in mirrors at midnight, bobbing for apples (the tree of knowledge and immortality), or eating them from strings enacts the battle for life in death. It is a time of ghosts and weird stories, but as a pagan rite it is the time when the dead and the living and the unborn children step outside the circle of time to meet, to talk, and to exchange information. The door of the circle is left open and a place is laid with rich food and wine to be offered to the Goddess when she joins her worshippers, who are her children.

The last festival, at the time of Christmas, is Yuletide. It is in part the Winter Solstice on 21 December, part the feast of Mithras, a Persian Sun God who was born in a cave on about 25 December. The Goddess brings forth the infant Sun God and is offered candles, garlands of holly for the God and ivy for the Lady. Mistletoe, the sacred Golden Bough of the Druids, whose white berries represent the seed of the Sun upon earth, is still not allowed in some churches. This strange 'All Heal' has not yet given up its secrets to herbalists, but it is often used by them. Yule (the word means 'wheel' in Saxon) is the turning point of the year, and the relighting of a great tree trunk from the nub of the last year's log symbolizes the continuity of light and warmth.

On 6 January the decorations are taken down and it is the end of the Twelve Days of Christmas. This, too, is a pagan festival, for it is the day when the Goddess presents her son, now twelve years old, to the people and when he is given his magical sword, shield (platter), arrows or lance (wand), and perhaps also a magical stone. He is paid homage to by all the participants and sent on his way to shine over the world.

Not every coven follows this set of events but usually they have some form of ritual on each of the solar quarters and the cross quarters on or about these dates. Only traditional groups celebrate nine festivals, though most groups also have working rituals on the day of the full moon, or sometimes the nearest Saturday or convenient date. If you wish to study witchcraft, you will see that there are plenty of chances to share feasting and ritual with friends and other witches, or you may prefer to work alone, as did the village witches in most parts of Britain. It is certain that each place had a healer, scryer, and herbal expert, often one old lady or gentleman, or perhaps a family, though there is little evidence that the coven of thirteen witches existed in many places. Most of the evidence about witch groups was wrung from the accused under duress, although torture was never used in England, nor were witches here burned at the stake. Scotland used both torture and burning, but the information thus obtained is far closer to what the accusers thought witches ought to confess than what they actually did. It also assumes that the real wise folk were caught: Most of them would have known psychically about any local witch hunts and kept out of the way. Many of the folk who were imprisoned or hanged were old men and women who had no one to stand up for them and probably lived by begging. Read any accounts of modern or ancient witchcraft with this in mind.

There are a small number of training lodges in Britain at present but they can only take in and teach a tiny percentage of all those who would wish for initiation into a regular, properly set up working lodge. Usually these require a period of study and work with other novices on different aspects of meditation, visualization, pathworking, symbolism, mythology and religion, psychology, and the various traditions of magic. If you feel you would like to join such a group, you will have to read the announcements in various occult journals very carefully to see if there are any vacancies or fresh training courses beginning. There are also postal courses.

Scientific Perspectives

The purpose of this book has been to encourage each individual to make the best possible use of all his or her innate skills, abilities, and strengths, and by trying to grow into the light of knowledge, gain experiences that will help all mankind. You began by learning techniques to expand your understanding of yourself and the world you live in. You will be surprised how the simple-seeming exercises will have effects upon you, perhaps explaining long-held problems or doubts, opening new vistas of knowledge and experience, leading you to deeper understanding. If you are able to continue practising these basic arts, you will develop magical abilities and perceptions far beyond what you might imagine. You will be able to relax in times of stress, your health will improve, and your mind become clear and retentive. You will discover joy in living and the freedom brought about by being able to see many aspects of any situation and being able to exploit what is the best path.

Recent scientific experiments have demonstrated that the two halves of the human brain function in different ways. One half, the left, is concerned with logic (for instance, mathematical thinking) and it is most closely linked to the right side of the body. The right half of the brain is more perceptive, intuitive, aware of subtleties, and it controls the left side of the body. The exercises of the magician go a long way in bringing both halves of the brain into play at once. The use of imagination and creative visualization, which are the most powerful tools of modern occult work, together with the practical, physical skills of movement, making, designing, and assembling talismans, brings all aspects of mentation into work. This helps to bring about a balance between the 'intellectual' type and the 'earthy, emotional' type of person, so that the perfect mage is competent in both modes of thinking.

Although it may seem a far cry from magic, the work of modern sub-atomic particle physicists is surprisingly close to some occult work. In Fritjof Capra's book *The Tao of Physics,* he explains that the movements of the minute particles within the atoms are cosmic dances, such as are described in Hindu mythology. The gods dance and the world is created; we now know that the electrons, protons, and neutrons match this dance, which conforms the bonds of continuity (which the magician manipulates) throughout the universe.

Many of the latest discoveries in science, rather than refuting magic as nonsense, seem to indicate that some of the ancient arts hold keys to processes within man and the universe that had not been fully understood before. In the field of parapsychology, experiments to project consciousness away from the physical body to view scenes and activities miles away follow the traditional ideas about 'astral travel,' and these have been demonstrated in the laboratory. In order to help subjects achieve this, they sit relaxed in a dimly lighted room, perhaps lulled by white noise or soft music, and often a kind of pathworking is given to help them get away from their immediate surroundings. Certainly experiments in hypnosis, altered states of consciousness, and other varied forms of inner awareness and control very closely match the magical model, known in the temples of ancient Egypt and the Druids' groves. These altered states are thought to be valuable keys to understanding the processes in man of pain control, or recovery from illness, injury, or cancer and the like. There are such vast areas of life and living that are still not understood. Yogis have demonstrated for hundreds of years that they can slow their heartbeat, stop breathing for long periods, remain warm whilst sitting naked in the snow, and walk on red hot stones. It is true that these events occur, but as they are magical techniques, they have not been readily available for study outside the secret temple or hidden school. Now we are seeing serious study being given to control of blood pressure through biofeedback, or the easing of migraine pain by altering the flow of blood from the head to the hand. Patients can even learn to slow their heartbeat and relax without drugs.

Music

The effects of sound are being studied, as well as the changes to breathing and blood supply caused by rhythmic chanting, previously only known by the occult teachers. Music is a very powerful medium and it can be used to excellent effect in ritual. It can help if you are shy and do not like speaking or singing. You can devise entire rituals of music instead of words. The most familiar piece of ritual music is that of the 'Planets Suite' by Gustav Holst. Although astrologically the music does not quite fit, each 'planet' does have a very valuable influence on anyone using it for meditation or ritual. Much classical music can be used for effect or to space out the action of ritual prayers, or incantations can be said to a musical background, giving power and timbre to your voice. Each session of meditation or pathworking can be accompanied by some appropriate sounds or soothing instrumental backing. Although classical music has something suitable for all moods and all stages of any ritual and can be selected to represent invocations of the elements and so on, there are many modern composers whose works are also fitting. Mike Oldfield's various synthesiser compositions can be ideal if you like that sort of music; and Steve Halpern, who writes music specially designed for meditation and mood softening, has a wide selection of tapes now available.

It is another vast field of research and experiment, and like all aspects of occult work, the more effort you put into it the better the results will be. If you have an important ritual pending, it is an opportunity to make sure that all the equipment, regalia, and background music are in complete harmony with your intentions. Again, do not rush into anything. As has been said all through this work, you are entering a huge field of study which has no clearly defined edges. You can practise ritual, divination, astrological interpretation, study the Qabalah or mythology for the rest of your life without coming to anything like limits of the subject.

Perhaps you will have had the opportunity to sample some of the most basic magical skills and are already looking forward to an age when occult matters have their true place beside what is usually called science and religion. Perhaps you have already been able to open some windows on your world, seen new horizons, gained new insights. Perhaps you have already begun to come to terms with who you are, and who you might become if you apply yourself to creating a better, clearer, stronger, more efficient self, aided always by the inner you. Any change is probably only a beginning. This may not seem so romantic and glamorous as you had thought magic might be; but magic is predominantly a practical art. There is a place for glamour and show, within the lodge—worshipping, calling aid from the higher powers, giving thanks and receiving blessings; and you may go in for the most elaborate regalia and the most costly settings you can devise. In the world, however, you will need discretion, capability, and the skill to cope with *human* situations.

This is just a beginning. Its end may be many lives hence, when man is using his skills to know, to learn, to heal and to intuit on distant planets. We cannot see where man's destiny will lead him, any more than the medieval alchemists (whose psychological texts are only now being fully understood). But one thing is certain: The arts of magic are not those of a forgotten age, outgrown and fit only to be cast aside like an old coat. They are the skills of the mind, and that is a region on this well-charted planet that is scarcely known at all. With imagination, with creative ability, and with common sense we can take magic from the hidden cupboards into all aspects of human experience. We may have not yet grown into Aquarian people, but we do have the keys to Aquarian Magic, as we have had them through all past ages. All we need now is the skill, the daring and the patience in which to use them.

CONCLUSION

If you have simply read through this book, you might wonder how it could be called a book of magic; but if you have already tried some of the exercises, or have learned some of these ancient arts from another book, you will have been able to experience some of the fascination of the enthralling practices, the strange arts that suddenly begin to *work*—to produce results and unfold information previously hidden from you.

This is not the end, though, by any means. To become skilled in the magical arts may take many years, for there is such a vast field to cover. It is for this reason that it is suggested that you read a great deal more, continue with the basic exercises until they are second nature, and, if at all possible, find a friend or two who can share your work. Once you have mastered the first steps in magic, it is up to you to choose a system, perhaps apply for membership to a group, or join a training course. You will need to read books on a broad spectrum of subjects—psychology, magic, comparative religion, the Qabalah, ancient history, mythology, poetry, ritual, witchcraft, country spells, as well as practical arts such as costume making, embroidery, woodcarving, painting, brewing of sacred wines, and baking special cakes for your ceremonies. You will need to master the lists of correspondences, discover gums and scents that apply to all the planets and for any other form of magic. You may wish to study healing arts, grow herbs, and study music and dance to enliven your rituals. As you go on, there is no limit to the situations into which your wider magical knowledge may lead you—life will be full of surprises, it will be healthy, joyful, and enthralling, filled with wonder and child-like delight.

FURTHER READING

This is only a selected list of some of the more relevant books covering the material in this book.

Ashcroft-Nowicki, Dolores, *Building an Occult Temple* (Pallas Aquariana).

———, *First Steps in Ritual* (Aquarian Press).

Brennan, J. H., Reincarnation: Five Keys to Past Lives (Aquarian Press).

Bowness, Charles, *The Practice of Meditation* (Aquarian Press).

Butler, W. E., *Apprenticed to Magic* (Aquarian Press).

David Conway, *Magic: An Occult Primer* (Mayflower).

Fortune, Dion, *The Mystical Qabalah, The Training and Work of an Initiate* (Aquarian Press).

Graves, Tom, *Dowsing* (Turnstone Press).

Green, Marian, *Magic in Principle and Practice* (Quest).

———, *The Paths of Magic* (Quest).

Inglis, Brian, *Natural Medicine* (Fontana).

Knight, Gareth, *A History of White Magic* (Aquarian Press).

———, *Occult Exercises and Practices* (Aquarian Press).

Regardie, Israel, *Foundations of Practical Magic* (includes the essay 'The Art of True Healing') (Aquarian Press).

Valiente, Doreen, *Witchcraft for Tomorrow* (Hale).

Wilson, Colin, *Mysteries* (Mayflower).

———, *The Occult* (Mayflower).

INDEX

Acupuncture, 41
Age of Aquarius, the, xv, 21,
    92–93
  Pisces, the, xv, 21
Algarve, 35
Arthur, King, 53
Autumnal Equinox, 117

Bach, Dr. Edward, 43
Bach Flower Remedies, 42, 68
Barrie, J. M., 53
Brigid, festival of, 116

Capra, Fritjof, 120
Chalice, 84
Chiropractors, 41
Christian Mass, 73
Consecration ritual, 88
Crystal gazing, 70, 103

Divination, 61
Dowsing, 64–66

Earth Mother, 51, 91
Einstein, Albert, 13

Fortune, Dion, 10, 52, 104
Four Elements, the, 79–80, 89,
    97, 114

Gnostic Mass, 56

Hallowe'en, 117
Holy Grail, 7, 54
Homoeopathy, 40, 68

I Ching, 10, 11, 52, 61
Incense, 82–83, 98, 102, 104–
    106, 108, 115
Initiation, 92–100

Jung, C. G., 51

Karma, 58

Lammas, 117
Land of Nod, 36
Ley lines, 67

Macrobiotic cookery, 9
Magical diary, 11, 84, 92, 101,
    113, 116
May Eve, 116
Merlin, 53
*Modern Man in Search of a
    Soul,* 51

Naturopaths, 42

Old Religion, the, 50, 54, 73
Osteopaths, 53

Pendulum, the, 66–70
Pentacle, the, 83–84
Peter Pan, 53

Qabalah, the, 31

Radionics, 42, 67–68
Rapid Eye Movement, 13
Reflexology, 68
Reincarnation, 57–58

Rolls Royce, 27
Rune stones, 61

Salmagundi, 47
Sea Priestess, The, 52
Spring Equinox, 116
Sword, ritual, 84–85

T'ai Chi, 9
Tao of Physics, The, 120
Tarot cards, 11, 23, 61–64, 67,
    79–80, 85
Theory of Relativity, 13
Tree of Life, the, 31

Virgin Mary, the, 50

Wand, 85, 104

Yuletide, 118

Zen, 9

PART II

EXPERIMENTS IN AQUARIAN MAGIC

INTRODUCTION

Magic still holds its ancient enchantment. Although we find ourselves living in a technological civilization at the end of the twentieth century, the fascination for things hidden, occult knowledge,
and the workings of esoteric societies still draws many of us to the
doorway to the Mysteries.

This book is an attempt to explain some of the many arts whose
roots are lost in the distant past, yet whose fruits and flowers may
still be gathered in this modern age. We now have the language of
psychology to give us contemporary terms for what our ancestors
spoke of as 'supernatural.' We have electronic equipment which
can measure, assess, and store information which magicians in the
past could only know by intuition, and retain in memory. We talk
about 'altered states of consciousness' whilst the priests of the past
knew of visions and oracular messages. We discover answers in
books, and stored on tape and computer discs. Long ago, when
it was believed that writing down secret knowledge profaned it,
the magicians relied on their own memories, on nature, and the
tides of the world to remind them of their sources of wisdom and
inspiration.

Even now, to walk the paths of magic involves taking a journey
into an unseen and largely unmapped domain. Much of it is within
the mind and consciousness of every individual practitioner. It is
possible to be guided by signposts, be directed by those who have
made similar journeys, but really every assay into the realms of the
occult is an adventure, or as expressed in the title of this book, an
experiment. Like laboratory experiments, it is necessary to gather
equipment, keep a log-book or journal, plan each stage of the work,
and dress in clothes suitable for the job in hand. You will need to
cleanse yourself, the physical space for these experiments, and the
'psychic' area, as well. Just as the bacteriologist has to be very careful about contamination affecting his work, so must the magician
leave outside all disruptive feelings; he must avoid disturbances
and achieve a complete focus of attention on the object of his ritual

or meditation. In both cases the more familiar you become with the techniques of the experiments the more reliable the results will be.

Magic is not for the faint-hearted, nor is it a subject which can be tackled entirely from your armchair. Just as with any other subject, you will only succeed in working your magical will if you dedicate yourself wholeheartedly to the process. You cannot dabble and expect to get safe or satisfactory results from desultory acts. You must be prepared to commit your time, your energy, and your resources (not necessarily money) to the study, practice, and mastery of a wide variety of skills. You will need to examine closely your beliefs in your own abilities, in the concept of God or the Gods and Goddesses of modern pagan religions. You will need to persist, to work with patience and perseverance even if nothing seems to be happening.

As you will realize, magic does not necessarily work to satisfy greed, nor to give you power, nor to solve all the little difficulties encountered in the modern world. You won't become rich overnight, nor will all your feelings of insecurity or inferiority vanish in a puff of incense smoke! To obtain results you will have to WORK VERY HARD, commit yourself to continuous effort, perhaps for months or years, and always strive to become a better, more effective human being.

The ultimate aim of all magical work is SERVICE. We may use the ancient arts to heal, to disclose aspects of the future, to become wiser, not purely for our own benefit, but because that is part of the purpose of our existence on Earth. Any traditional school of magic will make this very plain to students, and so will reputable books on the subject. You must be prepared to have your life shaped by the kind of magic you intend to use. If you join a coven and devote your work to knowing the Goddess and the God as they manifest through the festivals of the year, or you work Natural Magic (healing with herbs, divining with twigs, cherishing the Earth), you will follow a different path to those who seek knowledge of the inner Temples and the rites of High Magic. In either case (or in any other you may discover on your journey through the Mysteries), you will be directed so that the

Great Work may be accomplished. You may meet people seemingly by coincidence; you may read books by chance, or from your own inner resources discover the precise key which fits the door to your next stage of unfoldment. Things will certainly happen to you if you dare to take up the challenge of Aquarian Magic—they always have! But that is part of the adventure of magic. Remember these techniques ARE EXPERIMENTS—*you are* the guinea pig, and your results may not be the same as those of any other practitioner. TAKE CARE, ACT SENSIBLY, and WORK PATIENTLY through these different experiments in Aquarian Magic.

In *Magic for the Aquarian Age,* some of the most important techniques were spelled out, whilst other areas were passed over in a more superficial manner. In this book, less attention will be given to detailing topics. Here sufficient information is given for students to make their own tests and trials of a wide variety of different subjects. If you find ideas here which you have never seen dealt with in the context of magic, or if the path which led you towards the occult way has come via some other field of knowledge not covered here, this book will help to open new doors to understanding and interest.

There are many aspects of modern occult work which some magicians or witches or other practitioners may not yet have attempted, but now at the beginning of the Age of Aquarius, their knowledge should be expanded to cover a wider field than ever before.

One of the mainstays of effective magic is balance. The magician needs to balance the powers of change invoked by his rituals with his human skills and strengths. He or she needs to balance the inner forces with their outer understanding: the power of sun with the power of moon, the energy for growth with that for decay, justice with mercy, and, equally important, male with female. Many people have stepped upon the path of the Mysteries because it seemed to lead away from the imperfect balance of patriarchy. They became pagans and worshipped the power of the Earth Mother and the Moon Goddess. The Aquarian magician, whether male or female, will need to explore both aspects within his/her inner nature and outer physical form and bring them into perfect harmony. Returning to the arms of the Mother is no better an idea than forever seeking the protection of the Father. We are all children of the Universe, just as we all have physical mothers and fathers. The Aquarian mage will seek the middle way, acknowledging Mother and Father, God and Goddess, Sun and Moon, not only without, but within his/her inner being too.

The experiments set out here are safe for anyone with a degree of common sense to try. Follow the instructions carefully, just as you would those on a packet of cake mix or for a new electronic gadget. If you feel you are getting out of your depth, or losing control, place your hand upon the floor, and 'earth' the power. If you design a pentacle and place it before you whilst you are working, it will have the same effect. Work at a steady pace through the different experiments, allowing time for each to work before going on to the next. Keep detailed notes, recording time, place, people, and intention clearly—only then can you look back to assess your results. Enjoy this study, treat it seriously, make an effort to do the best you can in everything you attempt, and discover the excitement of achieving magical success.

12

OPENING THE DOORS
TO YOUR INNER MIND

Successful magic is the result of control on the part of the magician. If you set out casually to try some technique, forget some of the vital equipment, hear the telephone ringing in the middle, and have no definite plan or purpose, you are hardly likely to be successful, whether you are trying magic or biochemistry. If you are new to the subject, decide on an easily achievable goal for your first attempts at occult work. To hasten slowly in these ancient arts is never a waste of time. Make things as easy for yourself as you can. Cut down distractions from the outside, such as noise, interruptions, or anything else which might prevent you from relaxing or carrying out your intentions.

Meditation

The first technique with which you ought to become very familiar is meditation. It permits you to 'switch off the world' and opens up the door to your memory, subconsciousness, and what Dr. Jung defined as the 'collective unconscious.' It doesn't matter if you don't fully understand these terms at present, as long as you are willing to take the view that there are areas of your personal memory, for example, which you cannot get at immediately. Can you recall the presents you were given for your sixth birthday? No? Well, somewhere in the depths of your memory that information is stored. Jung was convinced that as well as our personal memories we are able to delve into the memories of other people, either individuals or even whole countries. It is where myths and ancient legends, shared by widely separated people, seem to have their roots. Anyone can learn to enter a relaxed state when the gates between the normal, waking, conscious mind and the inner self, collective unconscious, personal subconscious, or Akashic Records (to use an occult term) may be gently caused to open. It requires a little patience, perseverance, and a relaxed 'let's give it a try' attitude. You cannot force open these gates by will or by gritting your teeth, but by cunning and delicate pressure!

Find a time and place where you won't be disturbed for at least half an hour. You will need an upright chair and a notebook and pen for keeping a record (unless you already have a large 'magical' diary in which you enter dreams, books you have read, and any other magical work you are trying). Sit upright with your feet flat on the floor or on a thick book, and your hands resting comfortably on your lap. Breathe out fully, and then counting at your own speed, breathe in for a count of four. Hold your breath for four, breathe out for four, hold your breath out for another count of four, and then repeat the entire cycle six times. You may find this pattern difficult, in which case you can try 4-2-4-2, or even 8-4-8-4. You can count quickly or slowly, or if you can feel it without strain or ceasing to sit in a relaxed position, use your own pulse beat, felt in your wrist or neck. Focus your whole attention on counting and breathing comfortably. Gradually you will find this helps you to relax and bring your attention to the subject of the meditation. This may be a word, a name, a phrase from a book or poem, or a concept like 'peace in the world.'

Meditation is a knack, like balancing on a bicycle or swimming. Once you can do it, practice brings you greater rewards and longer periods of concentration. Don't try TOO HARD. Relax, and suddenly you will find words, images, still pictures, or actions flitting past your point of awareness. Try to watch without attempting to grab hold of this material. Gradually you will find the film show slows down, or the images or non-visual concepts remain in your mind long enough for you to study them. Like remembering dreams, you may need to tell yourself what is happening to fix it in longer term memory.

Recent brainwave studies have shown that meditation tends to bring the patterns of brainwaves in each hemisphere of the brain into harmony. Many of the tasks of modern living, like language, mathematical logic, and the written word seem to be dealt with in the left hemisphere, whilst imagination, pictures, spacial judgements, and less 'logical' matters occur mainly in the right half. Any technique which brings about a better degree of balance between both halves, and allows more faculties to be used on any activity, will help to balance the whole individual. Other studies have shown that intuition may be a cross-brain form of communication. (Some arts are performed with the left hand by right-handed magicians, because information such as that obtained with a dowsing pendulum can be processed more subtly by the right half of the brain.) When you begin to meditate, you may almost feel the links within your brain being formed, or channels of information reopening—it's a weird sensation!

You can choose pictures, symbols, words, or sentences taken from a book as subjects for meditation, but don't give up if nothing much happens the first few times. Sometimes it will take three or more sessions of about ten minutes each before you get the flow of information to start. It does get easier with regular practice. If you feel very tense or embarrassed at first, you can jog on the spot or do any sort of stretching and bending exercises for a few minutes. Try to gently extend your spine, chest, and shoulders, for these can limit your ease of breathing, and many tense people find areas of stiffness in the neck, shoulders, and upper back. Dancing to lively music where you move your whole body is good too, and the rhythms can help you get away from the stresses of everyday life. Meditation early in the morning is generally better than sessions late at night, but if you have time during the day, a quarter of an hour of relaxation and study can be extremely beneficial. Whatever you do, don't merely slump into bed and expect to receive revelations as you nod off. All these experiments need to be performed under proper controlled conditions—even those as basic as this! Your results will only become reliable if you persist with regular experiments.

Visualization

Another key method used by all magicians and witches is the art of creative visualization. Whereas meditation makes you the receiver of the 'programme,' as it were, visualization puts you into the film-maker's chair. With your imagination, the most valuable tool of any *magician,* you can shape the future. You can find lost objects by seeing, in your inner mind, their location; or heal, by creating a picture of the sick person in full and happy health. You can build up an entire world, as do many writers of science fiction or paint-ers of inspired pictures. You may create a magical Temple, a sacred sanctuary, or even discover a guide to lead you through the doors of inner reality.

Like meditation, you need to relax, to calm your body and direct your attention by breathing in a regular, steady pattern for a few minutes. With your eyes closed, place the image of a familiar object in view. Some people can't 'see' this object, but you should be able to sense it, or imagine what it looks like by describing it in words. For example, say you choose a blue vase—either you see a 3-D solid image of the pot, or you see a vague, bluish item, chang-ing shape and 'real-ness,' or you get words like 'round,' 'powder-blue,' 'china,' 'flowerpot,' 'shiny,' 'hard,' 'symmetrical,' and so on. You may feel the coolness of the china, or sense its solidity and stability. Different people get impressions in a variety of ways, but seeing a really solid picture is most helpful. Try objects which you know well, from ornaments to whole rooms, and DO CHECK YOUR OBSERVATIONS. When you begin to look into the future, details could be very important—so could those from the past.

If you visit ancient sites, or sacred places, try to focus these images for later recall. Take photographs or slides, if you can, to remind you of the real monument, the texture of building materi-als, the local plants and trees, the weather or temperature of the place and the entire ambience. Study illustrated books or films of places like the Temples of Ancient Egypt or Greece, sacred groves and stone circles or earthworks. Absorb all you can about the atmosphere and the patterns they make against the sky. If you are drawn to a particular place or period of history, soak up all the data you can because, if later on you wish to create your own modern version of the place as a Temple or personal shrine, you will have the information already in your memory.

Once you get into the swing of using your imagination to create new scenes, you might like to experiment with some of the more specifically magical techniques. The first is a circle of protection. There are lots of books on elaborate ways of performing the Lesser Banishing Ritual of the Pentagram and so on, but basically you only need to see yourself within a circle of bluish-white light to achieve the same effect nowadays. Sit on your chair and place, in your mind's eye, a ball of glowing fire about three feet (one metre) from your feet; see it spinning and glowing strongly. As it whirls within itself it begins to rise off the ground. It swings outwards to the right trailing a comet-like tail of vivid light. Slowly you will find it makes a complete circle, rising above your head, then returning to the ground. You will now find that you can draw the entire circle towards you so that it goes below your feet and above your head. Once you get it there, you can get it to turn over as if it was pivoted at about your hip level. It will swing round like a hoop, enclosing you in a sphere of brilliant, protective light. You can try the same experiment whilst standing up but remember, if you are relaxed, not to fall over when the light starts to swing end over end! It may take a few sessions of practice to get the clear feeling or vision of the circle being formed and then turning. When it has completed the circle the bright line will vanish, but a dimmer glow around you will remain. If you do this at least once each day, gradually it will strengthen your own aura.

The aim of such an exercise is to disinfect the area around you when you are meditating, or later performing magical work. Stray thoughts, worries, or leftover problems will be kept at bay by this technique, so that what you perceive will be a clear vision, not scraps distorted by mundane matters. Just as the surgeon or chemist sterilizes his equipment and laboratory, so do magicians purify their immediate surroundings. You will be more aware after your sessions of meditation or visualization and so more sensitive to the feelings of others, or to the atmosphere of your home, etc. This will help you get over the 'culture shock' of new, wider perceptions, which could otherwise be a bit unsettling. Remember to reverse the process at the end of a session to 'switch it off.'

Some simple tests of your ability to visualize properly can be tried out, when you have a few days with plenty of time to spare. Each needs to be repeated several times. First, imagine a person you know well standing before you. Look at the image. Is it correct, does it capture their personality? Can you change the colour of their hair, their eyes? Make them taller or fatter? If you can, your imagination is playing tricks—because you have an image of a *real* person in front of you! You will need to bear this in mind if you start to explore your past lives, for example, because if you can 'bend' real people like that, what can you do about your supposed past?

Some Experiments in Creative Visualization

Sit down, perform your breathing patterns until you feel calm, then close your eyes. Imagine in front of you there is a large book. See its cover, examine the binding, the size, the thickness of it. Study every detail, and see if you can read its title. Reach out, in your mind, and feel it, smell it, caress the edges of the pages, the firmness of the spine, the hardness of the corners. Apply every one of your senses to this great book. (You may find this is a sufficient experiment on its own at first, as it is a difficult skill for some people.)

In the next few sessions, open the book, study the printing or writing within. What can you read? Even if you only get glimpses, or if because you can't actually 'see' you sense the pages, try to imagine what could be written there. In any case, please note in your diary what you sensed each time. If nothing seems to work, try a different experiment, but do come back to this, for it could be the book of your life—or the future history of the world, made ready for you to read!

In another experiment (again to be carried out over a period of about a week, with one attempt each day), try to create the picture of a seed. See it in your hand, tiny but full of potential. In your mind plant it and over the next few days discover how it grows, what its leaves are like, the colour and shape of its flowers, their scent. Gradually allow it to develop, spreading branches, blossoming, and growing taller. Watch it being pollinated, and see the fruits begin to form and ripen. Feel them, pick one and taste it. Describe every stage of the plant's development in your notes. Compare it with your own life—where are you? Just a sprig? In blossom or ready to cast off your leaves or your ripened fruit? Think about it.

Another week of creative visualization can be concerned with a fire. See, in your mind's eye, a tiny spark struck from flint and iron, set alight a tuft of tinder. Let that minute flamelet attack a twig, and gradually take hold on some dry sticks. Watch it burn through several sessions. Mentally pile on some green wood and watch the smoke, smell the steam and woodsmoke, feel the heat of the flames, hear the crackling twigs. See it send sparks and smoke upwards from its glowing base. Discover within the dying embers a cave of wonder and imagination. Find the mystery at the centre of the 'need' fire, the oracular hearth. Keep accurate notes of what you discover and perceive.

An exercise in which you awaken your ability to create within your mind's eye is the way you can offer service to others. I expect that if you think back through your life you will recall someone to whom you owe a debt; maybe it is money, maybe some good turn you never paid back. To exercise this new faculty, try to imagine a situation where you repay your debt to your friend. Again, don't rush. Set it up as a problem and seek a real solution. Obviously your friend may be someone with whom you have lost touch, or may even date back to your school days, so that an actual repayment of the debt is not possible. Set up a visualized situation in which a way is found to help or bring luck to that person. Imagine him or her getting an unexpected gift, which somehow repays what you owe. If you can begin this particular experiment in a waxing moon, it will make it more effective. Focus on the debt being repaid—then after about seven attempts, forget about it. You will eventually get to know what happened.

If you are owed a debt by someone else, or need a small favour or bit of luck, AFTER YOU HAVE ASTRALLY PAID YOUR DEBT, you may have a go at psychic debt-collecting. If a particular person owes you something, you don't necessarily have to collect from them. Ideally, as this work is using the magical forces of the universe (which can redistribute the finances, etc., more fairly than mere humans would do), allow these forces to decide how your debt is to be repaid. Simply imagine the cash clearly, in crisp new notes, or in whatever form it is needed, landing on your doormat. Please note—angels, in the twentieth century, do not turn up with gold bricks at the whim of amateur magicians. Focus on the required thing arriving in an ordinary way for about seven sessions. Strangely, this can work quite well in a waning moon. It is usually more effective if you have a real need for something other than actual cash. A present, a holiday, some clothes, and so on can all turn up as a result of this technique—but remember NEED not GREED will get the best results.

Energy Raising Methods

Sometimes meditation can leave you feeling a bit sleepy, or you may feel too tired to cope with something as relaxing as your regular visualization exercises. If you are physically tired and have things to do, this method will work well too. In fact, if you go outside and lean on a big tree, you can get even faster and more active responses. To try this with a real tree, remove your shoes and stand with your back against the trunk of a large, healthy-looking tree. Lean back and close your eyes. You will begin best by imagining the life force from the earth being slowly drawn in through the roots of the tree, which spread out as far below you as do the branches above. You may visualize this as a dark greenish current, flowing steadily, slowly but extremely powerfully upwards, taking with it the essence of the Earth, the blood of Mother Nature. Just as it is drawn up within the trunk behind you, you will begin to sense a similar cool, strong flow rising upwards through your feet, gradually filling you with calmness and helping your spine to straighten and feel relaxed and stronger. If you can clasp your hands to the tree behind you or above your head, you will allow the flow of life force to go through you and return to the tree. Take your time over this.

When you have the Earth-force working steadily upwards through you, you can begin to focus your attention on the down pouring Sky or Sun power. Whereas the Earth's energy is slow and steady and dark, the Sky power is bright, sparkling, and darting. If you can imagine something like the sparks given off by a firework, silvery-gold fizzing down from the sky, entering every leaf and twig and sizzling downwards into your body, that is a way to experience it. Imagine a rain of light pattering upon the canopy of leaves above your head, and this sparkling energy gradually seeping down into your fingers and arms, your head and body, right down into your feet. It is the healing power of life and light, and is quite different from the steady, seeping Earth power. Feel the warmth of sunlight, the gentle play of a breeze, the effect of a spring shower on a thirsty tree, refreshing the leaves, and running into your veins to awaken sluggish thoughts, weary bones, and stiff muscles. Allow your body to relax and revel for a while in the sprinkling downflow of Sky energy.

After a while, when you have fully appreciated the upthrusting Earth force, and the sparkling energy of the Sun and Sky separately, perform the harder task of feeling both at once. This may take a little practice. As the two energies are so different, you ought to be able to sense them together. It is hard to explain the sensation, as everyone may feel a different version of it, but it is an extremely pleasant, refreshing, and calming experience, and well worth doing a number of times. You may find that each variety of tree has its own way of transmuting the Earth and Sky forces. Oaks are slow-growing, immensely strong trees whilst beeches are more delicate. Birches seem to dance beneath the sky; willows may feel sad, though they are healing trees. Yews offer the dark wisdom of the Lady of the Waning Moon, and ashes the direct might of a King on his throne. The rowan will protect you from harm, and if you experiment with the trunk of an apple tree, you may find you can enter the world of the Unseen, for it is the tree of the Silver Branch, which is the key to the Celtic otherworld. Although this may seem like natural magic rather than a ritual method, it is well worth trying out with an actual tree. Once you have perceived these energy flows in the wild, you will be able to bring the same exercise into the Temple, and receive the same sort of effects.

Indoors, stand with bare feet and comfortable clothing, facing east (or which ever direction you have decided is ritually east), and begin to sense and see the up-welling dark Earth power. Concentrate on this for at least a minute, until you feel calm, strong, and balanced. Then begin to feel the descent of the sparkling bright Sun power, invigorating and energizing, helping you to switch into a higher gear for magical work, be it merely a meditation, or an elaborate ceremony.

If you wish to turn this into the first part of a ritual, you may say the following words (or make up some to suit your beliefs or ideas, adding God or Goddess names, angels, or whatever seems most appropriate).

From beneath me arises the energy of the Earth, my home and my foundation,

From above me pours down the Power of the Light of the Sun and the enchanting Moon,

To my Right hand flows the strength to control and direct, the power of magic,

To my Left hand comes the skill to divine and to heal, the source of blessing.

Before me arises the perfected one I strive to become, my magical true self.

Behind me falls the one I was, and with it, all my discarded failures.

Around me circle the eternal stars, lamps of wisdom in the deeps of space.

Within me grows the flame of life, the light of experience and understanding.

This is a very powerful invocation which should be said very slowly, allowing the full meaning of the words to become apparent to you. Imagine the various forces flowing to you. See clearly or imagine your perfected self, your balanced magical personality standing in front of you. Sense all your faults and failures being gradually cast off, like a snake shedding its skin, curling and crumpling down into ashes behind you. Try hard to overcome any faults you have, deliberately setting them behind you.

You may observe that this prayer or invocation has similarities to those found in other books you may have read. This is a new version for students working towards the new age, but you will find it as powerful and effective as that used in the past. Done with intent, you will find it will completely clear the atmosphere for ritual, especially if you don't have a room which can be set aside purely for occult work. This invocation should be repeated at the conclusion of any work, and then you should firmly stamp your right foot twice, to complete the ceremony or meditation, and so on.

If you have difficulty sleeping, or are worried or disturbed, you can imagine the circle which forms a ball around you, as described above, but see it as a glowing blue sphere. It will become an egg shape if you are standing up, and after a few moments it will shrink and become invisible but will act as a shield from distractions so that you can sleep, or perhaps feel safer in an unfamiliar atmosphere. Sometimes if you are traveling, or among strangers, or in some other sort of crowd whose pressure is uncomfortable, you can use it. This should only be a temporary form of protection, for the competent magician will be able to cope with alien atmospheres or a crowd of strange auras without becoming upset.

Although these basic exercises may be familiar to you from other books you have read, unless you have genuinely tried to master them, then none of the later experiments in this book will work so well for you. To be unable to switch off the world and enter a relaxed and receptive meditative state, or to be unable to picture clearly in your mind's eye or imagine and sense in some other way the surroundings for a ritual, a lost item, or the recovery of a sick friend, then you will have a difficult task getting your magic to work. If it takes you months to perfect these methods not a moment of that time will have been wasted.

13

JOURNEYS TO VISION

The Aquarian magician may be either a man or a woman, but there are many esoteric skills and arts which are much easier if you have a partner to help you. A lot has been written about 'soul-mates,' 'twin-spirits,' or 'magical partners' but much of it has misunderstood the true magical partnership. In the distant past, the schools of magic trained young men and women each to fulfil particular esoteric roles. In the last century there were quite a few magical lodges where the select few contacted angelic forces, worked powerful rituals, and progressed through a number of degrees, just as many of them still do. Like the patterns of everyday life, those which direct the magical work for the new age are also changing. Instead of working in huge factories, each being a little cog in a large wheel, more and more people are working alone, in small concerns, or for larger enterprises, but instead of joining up in a vast building, they are linked via telephone or computer lines to their own terminal. Read Alvin Toffler's *The Third Wave* for a detailed explanation of the changes that are affecting the world of work. A similar current is washing through the occult world too.

The Aquarian Magician

The magician of the Aquarian Age will be a balanced, competent individual who probably works with just one partner, or in a small group of less than ten people. He or she will be less concerned with passing through many degrees than with achieving a better understanding of the ways in which it is possible to serve the forces of magic, and the world in general. The underlying reason for magical work has always been service, but it has often been overlooked by self-centred individuals whose striving for personal power and position has formed the theme for many occult novels. Some people still yearn for the ability to dominate, to control, and to direct the wills of less secure individuals, but that is only a short-sighted and limited use of the real forces. The competent modern adept will have sought to perfect his own understanding of life, have sorted out his material situation and have gained a deep knowledge of his inner abilities. Any skills he needs will have been practised and refined. Any weaknesses in his character or situation will have been examined carefully, not hidden in the depths of his psyche to bother him later on. The way to recognize an adept is not by the collection of ankhs and pentagrams around his neck, nor the flowing black cloak he wears to esoteric fairs, but by the effective way he copes with crises, the control he has when provoked, the span of his knowledge, and his sympathy towards other people. If you can't cope with the ordinary world, you can be certain that you won't manage the inner worlds!

Any exercise or experiment which helps you to understand yourself, which bridges the gap between inner awareness and the 'real' world, such as meditation on your name, horoscope, or ambitions, will all help you to be able to assess the needs of others, and so help them. Certainly, sitting alone, or with a friend, listening to quiet music and trying to understand where you want to go in life doesn't sound half as exciting as intoning sonorous words in a forgotten tongue, in an elaborate Temple thick with incense smoke, whilst wearing fabulous robes—but it is a lot safer, and is likely, in the long run, to be more effective! Later on, when you have an idea of where you want to go, can you begin to collect all the paraphernalia, make the robes and regalia, construct, dedicate, and make use of the Temple. To begin with you will need to open gently a few locked doors inside your mind, and explore some of the nooks and crannies of you own experiences before doing anything more exotic.

Magic tends to produce quite a number of 'Which comes first?' syndromes. If you want to meditate, you may have been told that you need to consecrate the room first, and to consecrate a place, you will need certain equipment, which also needs to be cleansed and dedicated before use, and maybe you don't have the finances to purchase the things needed for this elaborate process. If you use the simple invocation in the last chapter, seeing or imagining clearly each part, this gets over the 'bless-the-items-to dedicate-the-objects-to-consecrate-the-room-with' problem! You will be using the ultimate instrument of Aquarian Magic; that is, the trained human mind. Later on you can get on with the consecrations and rituals when you can imagine the ideal setting, and have sufficient confidence and experience to make them work.

Meditate on your own name, on the body you have (and look for ways of making this better, healthier, and more skilled—no one else can do this for you!), and on your aims in life, both magical and mundane. If you can construct an image of how you would like to be, and then compare it with what you are, noting the differences, you can gradually begin to change for the better. Without a concept of the ideal, you will have no form to use as a pattern. Only you can decide what your own criteria are, based on previous experiences, situations, and expectations. Examine the people around you for someone who can share, equally, your attempts to master magic and gain wisdom and power. Ideally the mage of the Aquarian Age will be one of a pair or small group, of men and women, all striving to become whole.

Choosing a Partner

It is difficult trying to understand what sort of partnership this may be, especially if forming relationships is not one of your best skills. You will need to find a companion you can trust, and who will trust you. He or she will need to be a person with whom you get on well, and who can be relied on, just as you must also be totally reliable. You will need to become firm friends, but it doesn't imply you need to go to bed together, nor that you must live in each others' pockets. You will have to be patient and tolerant, and neither should dominate the partnership. Each will excel at certain things, whilst the other is only fairly good—each will need to discover and refine any inbuilt talents, be they for healing, for ritual, for organization, or for specifying what sort of work you will do together. You will have to find ways of operating, in the words of the witch's rule, 'In perfect love and perfect trust.' This is no easy undertaking, because each of you will have to give and take, to act unselfishly and with the common good always above your own needs. Don't rush into a partnership with the first half-interested individual you encounter. If you start to train your inner awareness, it will help you find and recognize a companion on the path far more reliably than searching the small ads in the papers!

Pathworking

If you do find someone who is willing to work with you, then you can experiment with the ancient art of pathworking. This is the magical application of story telling, yet another aspect of creative visualization, and an important key to effective magic. You can manage alone, recording the words on a cassette tape, or by learning the stages and telling yourself, but it is much easier if you are with a friend or in a small group. You should take it in turn to read the narrative, or make up the details of the story or description, so that you each gain the confidence of speaking in a magical context, and of being able to imagine and invent the situation of a occult operation.

Originally the paths were those of the Qabalah's Tree of Life, and the images were specifically related to the colours, the angelic forces and the mystical symbols which were associated with each path which joins the spheres on the Tree. An excellent modern work is *The Shining Paths* by Dolores Ashcroft-Nowicki (Aquarian Press). Today, a wide variety of magical paths may be walked in the imagination, from the examination of a specific symbol to lengthy journeys through time and space. This is a very effective way of reaching the relaxed yet perceptive state required for magical work. You may find a selection of contemporary books which detail ways of traveling into the recesses of the mind by way of a trip to the seaside, by becoming an actor in a medieval legend, or by entering your own, ordinary familiar workplace or home, and interacting with your family, your boss, and your colleagues in a new way. Paths to the contemporary world can be just as important and effective as those which lead to the land of legend and the matter of myths! You will need about half an hour when you won't be disturbed, and either a companion or a tape recorder to tell the story. If you wish to relax first, do a bit of bending and stretching and perform the invocation which will help clear the atmosphere and make the work easier. You can light a candle and some incense, close the curtains and change into a magical robe as well, if you feel this will help you. If none of these things is important to you, simply ensure you won't have to answer the phone or the door, etc. Sit upright in your meditation chair and breathe slowly for a while and then start the tape, or ask your story-teller to begin. Your partner might say something like the following:

You are standing on a path at the foot of a rocky hill. It is late afternoon on a warm summer's eve. You are alone. You can sense the rough track beneath your feet, hear the wind rustling the grass and bushes near the path, and feel the afterglow warmth of the setting sun. It is very quiet. Soon you begin to climb the path, following its twists and turns, climbing upwards all the time. You notice the colour of the rocks, and the small flowering plants that cling to crevices. You touch the stone as the path gets steeper, seeking handholds, feeling it rough and warm beneath your hands. Up and up you go, scrambling up a narrow crack where the tread of other climbers has worn a clear set of footholds. After a really steep bit, you find yourself on a small plateau, and as you begin to get your breath back you hear the sound of running water. At the back of the plateau is an abrupt cliff, and a tiny runnel of pure water flows from it, into a natural smooth basin, carved out by time from the bare stone. Here you pause, washing your hot face and hands, drinking the chilly, fresh water. You feel refreshed and filled with a kind of blessing.

Looking about you, you notice that the sun is about to set, and scarlet streamers of cloud seem to be on fire on the western horizon. It is like watching a great bonfire gradually cooling, with dark grey-blue smokey clouds rising out of the red-orange lit sky. Above the darker clouds the sky is still daylight pale, yet here and there the bright points of stars and planets glitter above you. For a long time you stand, just watching the fiery colours fade, the piled clouds darken and turn grey, the sky change from blue through greenish-grey to indigo as the last rays of the sun fade below the horizon. It is very still, but you gradually notice a cool wind has sprung up, it puffs a sharp and chilling breeze on your face, and you turn your back to stop bits of grass blowing into your eyes. It gets stronger and almost pushes you towards the steep track where you came to the plateau. You find yourself gently shoved over the edge, down the smooth rocks, finding each hand and foot hold firm where you need it. Gradually the path becomes less difficult, levelling out as you reach the bottom of the hill. In the twilight you can still make out the plants and the white flowers which seem almost to glow in the fading eventide. Once you are certain you can go down no further you will find the image of the hillside fading. Slowly you sink back into your ordinary room and when you are ready, your eyes open and you feel you have returned from a refreshing and relaxing journey.

Your companion should allow you plenty of time to breathe deeply a few times, and get up and stretch. You should write down the images, the impressions, and feelings you received during your journey, as these tend to vanish like dreams do, unless recorded or thought through quickly.

This is a very simple experiment. You will both need to try out ways of reading the text, to get the speed and atmosphere right for you. If you wish to add recorded music or even sound effects like the sea, or the wind, or just use quiet background music to cut out the distraction of traffic or other disturbing noises, it will all help. This first path was just a trip through the elements, and if you examine your experience, you ought to be able to detect which was most real—the rock and path; the trickling spring; the fiery sunset and its warmth on your skin, or the cool breeze. Think back and reread your notes to discover which was the most potent, not just as a scene but as an experience. When your companion has also made this journey or a similar one, you can discover which sort of narrative is most helpful.

A pathworking is a way of exploring ancient sites, the Temples of Egypt, or the Tombs of Mycenae, by visiting them when they were new. We will come back to other applications of the art at a later stage. For now it is necessary to practise the technique of traveling, and of reading or making up a story or journey as you go along.

You will need to change gradually from the ordinary world into the visionary place and then return equally slowly and carefully. This is a very effective relaxation technique, and it doesn't help to have the telephone ring in the middle, or someone come to the door. It won't do you much harm, having to leap up suddenly, but it makes it much harder to relax and tune in to the other scene the next time. Do your best to get rid of anything which might interfere, and ask your companion to deal with the unexpected.

This exercise is a good way of creating a calm feeling which will help you if you are using any form of divination. You can imagine yourselves going to the place of wisdom and understanding so that when you look at the Tarot cards, or throw the hexagrams of the *I Ching* you will see their message more clearly. If you have plenty of time to experiment, you can see each card of the Tarot trumps, for example, as the symbol on a door through which you pass to the world shown thereon.

Combining Divination and Pathworking

To combine the techniques of divination with pathworking you could make a set of symbol cards showing a straight path, a crooked one, a field, a mountain, a valley, a well or spring, a sunset, a bonfire, clouds, a street, a cave, a forest, a glade, a chapel, an ancient monument, a castle, a garden, a stone circle, a gate, a coffer, some treasure, a magical object which is personal to you, and so on. You could cut out pictures from magazines if you can't draw (you would be surprised how many relevant images can be found in advertisements, holiday brochures, and travel catalogues). Shuffle these pictures face down and then select about seven of them. Turn them over and then work out a narrative which takes you from your own home along a familiar road and out through a gate in a wall, or through the entrance to a building which you have never entered—you don't know for certain that it isn't the entrance to fairyland!

You can collect colours, images, and relevant symbols, and on a large diagram of the Tree of Life, or a magical journey, place the pieces to make a sensible transition from the base which is your home, or Malkuth on the Tree, upwards on the journey. You can even devise a game, in which you have to collect items, colours, symbols, or friends, rather in the way some of the computer or 'Dungeons and Dragons' games suggest, so that you can progress. Although this may seem a light-hearted way to approach something as serious as magical training, it is nevertheless a good way of becoming used to the images and patterns associated with whichever tradition you have chosen to study. You will allow this important material to sink into your memory and subconscious mind where it can work with your intuition, which you will also be training during such games, to produce clear and wide-ranging answers to divinations and meditations. You cannot expect to get out information or understanding if the raw material for it doesn't exist first, any more than you can learn to speak the words of another language without some sort of training. Put in plenty of data, and your inner self and mind's eye can produce intricate and relevant answers and explanations. Experiment with simple methods until you can easily recall a range of 'correspondences'; symbols, colours, planetary information, and God/Goddess names, etc., associated with any topic that comes into your head. It is the framework of many later magical operations, like making talismans, designing a personal sigil, visualizing the Temple of your dreams, and so on.

With your magical companion, do practise reading the answers to simple questions from your divining arts, wandering along the inner pathways, and becoming used to the gentle transition to the meditation state with a friend in attendance. Play games with symbols, learn the basic skill of astrology and the images of the Tarot, always allowing your own intuition, rather than someone else's interpretation, to guide you.

You can design paths to strengthen your own or your companion's balance between the elements. Invent paths about the Earth, with fields, trees, caves, farmland, and rocks if you feel 'out of this world' or if your charts show a lack of earth signs or planets in earth signs. Imagine every leaf on a tree, the development from a seed to a fruiting plant, and so on. This is a slow session, gradual and powerful.

If your emotions give you trouble, work with Water, visualizing a spring welling from the hard rock, flowing gently into still lakes or imagine the pounding waves of the tide-surging ocean. Become part of that water, as gentle rain or storm-tossed waves; a trickling streamlet laughing over the waterfalls, or a slow-flowing broad river mouth, finding unity in the great sea. See cups and cauldrons, the banks of rivers and the cliffs by the beach and notice how they shape and control the water, changing and limiting it. Become a cup yourself, even the Holy Grail, when all your feelings are natural, when they find their own level and are not repressed, and you can respond honestly to all those around you.

When you feel weary and lacking in vitality, or your horoscope shows a deficit of Fire, then you will need to try the images of volcanoes, lightning, bonfires, furnaces, flames, and lantern light. Feel the heat, smell burning incenses, and see flowers glowing in bright sunlight. You should find this will raise your energy level, especially if you imagine the vitality and healing power of the sun, the darting light of flames and lightning flashing through you to awaken and add zest to your life.

If your mind is troubled and seems forever to be flitting from one subject to another so that you can't concentrate, look at the clouds. Watch from a high window, or lie down on your back in a garden, see how slowly clouds form and reform, change and merge, split and vanish. You can actually push them apart if you try, with a single large cloud. See a gap forming in the centre of a long cloud, and you will find it will begin to happen. Once the cloud has divided, you can cut up one half as it drifts lazily across the azure sky. It will take quite a few minutes of concentration to get this to happen, but it is a way of improving your attention span, and directing it towards Air, which is the mind element. For visualizations work with the effect the wind has on trees or fields of wheat. See mountain peaks, journeys by plane, birds winging free and safely through the sky; imagine flying with them on a homeward flight, above the houses of cities or the forests of the country. Become a kite safely anchored to earth, or a cloud shedding rain upon the waiting fields, a wind whistling through a rock, or a gentle breeze caressing the face of someone you love.

How to Awaken Your Senses

You can awaken your own senses by simple experiments. Close your eyes and examine the textures of things around you; the carpet, the edges of pages of a book, a wooden spoon, or the petals of a flower. Touch them as gently as you can, not only with your fingertips, but with your cheek, your bare toes, your elbow. When you next eat a salad or a crisp apple, shut your eyes and savour every texture and sensation, not just the taste but the very feel of each bite. Play games with your companion, allowing him or her to feed you samples of things to recognize by taste or texture, letting you smell things without seeing them, or feel objects or materials hidden in a plastic sack or cardboard box. Find similar objects for your partner to examine with different senses to those normally used. It all helps you become aware of small clues, which can often be all you get during magical activities.

When you are divining, you may only get a hint which flashes across your awareness very swiftly; or catch a glimpse of an image in a crystal; or smell a whiff of something during a ceremony; or feel a texture whilst traveling some distant path, and from that you will need to be able to detect a great deal. If you have a few moments to spare each day, do practise feeling, hearing, sensing, smelling, and so on. I am sure you will remember instances when a trace of some long-forgotten scent awoke strong recollections of school, or your childhood, or a place you used to live in. The same can happen when you are delving through past lives or distant places.

Another valuable but frequently overlooked source of valuable material is literature. We have become so used to the written word that we forget it can provide valuable material to practise expanding our awareness with. Take any well written thriller, science fiction book, or adventure novel and try to live through the character's experiences. You may well find the places described come swiftly before your inner eye, the excitement speeds up your heartbeat, the scenes encountered blot out your real surroundings. If you don't like fiction, there are plenty of excellent books on mountaineering, jungle explorations, adventures with unknown people, encounters with wild animals and so on, and even biographies of not very well-known people can produce episodes so vivid and exciting that you can share these experiences. They will never be the same as your own experiential material, but they do strengthen and test your abilities to enter into a rapt state when reality can be changed, and that after all, is a valuable asset in the magician's armory of practical skills. Radio plays can expand your ability to 'see' in the mind's eye; descriptions in books can expand your awareness; using your fingers, your cheek, your nostrils, or your tongue you can enter new worlds of sensation and experience. Though these ideas may be a long way from your original idea of magic, this is simply because the world we are living in is changing rapidly, and senses like memory, taste, and touch are being blunted by living in a world which does not need them for survival. In days before the majority of people could read, everyone had to remember the names of things like trees, plants, animals, and useful materials, whereas we look up the name of an unfamiliar plant, or the varieties of fungi which are safe to eat. Our world is cushioned and soft, not like the roughness encountered in the clothing, building materials, and everyday items used by our ancestors even a hundred years ago. We recognize food from the packet or tin, or the writing on the wrapping, not by the scent or taste—with some things only the written information gives any clue as to what the foodstuff is!

You can write a short path to lead you to a pleasant place for your meditation—into a summer garden, to the side of a still lake, or a forest glade. Enter gently into this sanctuary away from the bustle of the everyday world and you will be surprised how much easier it is to unravel the subject of your meditation. In the clear air of the magical landscape images flow, ideas unroll, and the most complex topic is sifted into more easily understood patterns.

When you have made more progress in the magical arts, this same technique can be used in many ways, one of which is the creation of a Temple of Wisdom, exactly tailored to your ideals and needs. Gradually its form will be shown to you and your companions. If you explore, discuss, and shape it between you, it will become very 'real' within the magical context, and when you are ready to perform ceremonies, or enter into the deeper studies and thanksgivings, or ritual workings you will have a home to go to which you can replicate in this ordinary world.

Scrying

Another basic experiment which you can try at this point is a version of scrying, the old name for crystal gazing. A sphere of polished rock crystal is a very expensive and rare item and it is not the easiest scrying glass for a beginner to learn with either. You can make a 'black mirror' quite simply, and the dark glass will tend to evoke clearer images for novices. Get a small round picture frame with its glass, either a piece of black velvet or a pot of matte black paint, and some silver paint, too. Take the glass out of the frame and paint one side with at least three coats of matt black paint, or place a circle of velvet cut to fit the frame under the glass. Meanwhile paint the frame itself silver—this is to link it with the 'psychic' energies of the Moon. When the paint is completely dry, make sure the unpainted side of the glass is outwards. Meditate, focus with a path to a place where a door to vision can be encountered, or simply light a candle and relax with a few cycles of the breathing pattern. Hold the black mirror where you can look into it without there being too many patches of light reflected in it. It should seem to be a deep pool of dark water. Allow your vision to go below the surface, and casually observe what you can see with your eyes focused within. Try to watch without tension and without worrying what you might see. Only by getting the balance of attention right will you see anything at all.

It is usual to find that the glass seems to cloud over, becoming dull as if mist had swirled across it. Usually you are so surprised by this that you lose the sensation. When this has become steady again you may find a sort of clearing within the smoky outline begins to form, and you seem to be absorbed into the dark centre. Here proper pictures, moving or still, black and white or coloured, scenes or symbols, numbers, words, shapes, people, or action will be perceived. Different people will see a different version of this material. Some of it may be from the future, the past, or some other place. It can be like television, with short flashes of information or lengthy activities and events. You can feel as if you are a part of this, or merely an observer, unable to influence or participate. To get regular, clear images which make sense will take A LOT OF PRACTICE. You will need to make continued attempts for a long time before you have the skill to perceive consistently the future, events remote from you, or other material in which you are interested.

The curved glass from an old-fashioned alarm clock set into a round rim and backed with layers of black paint makes another good scrying glass, or even a thick disc of plate glass or perspex set into a frame of dull-coloured velvet or felt. Some people can manage with an ordinary glass mirror, a chunk of obsidian, black glass used on shop fronts, or any other reflective material. Experiment! That is what it is about.

Try different ways of getting switched into the receptive mode; use a variety of scrying glasses. Help your companion learn by asking what they can see. Record or write down any images and information for later reference. Don't give up if results aren't seen immediately. Be patient because you are using a new skill and it is bound to take a while to master it. Suddenly, when you least expect it, the pictures will be there—and that is only the start of this useful ability.

14

THE NATURE OF HEALING

Being well and in good health is a natural state, and it is only when something goes wrong that illnesses can afflict us. This simple statement may surprise some people who have never thought about the matter. It is only when our well-being falters and the thoughts of hospital, medicines, operations, and so on loom on the horizon that we begin to worry about our health. To a magician good health is an important aspect of his or her character. As healing has many magical associations, and many witches and other occultists offer advice or treatment, it is very serious if they look like walking adverts for 'Your Life in Their Hands'! Your health is something to which you should pay serious attention because if you are going to offer help to other people they will judge your success by your own state of health.

Although Nature can drop trees on people, strike them with lightning, or drown them at sea, most of the plagues, epidemics, and serious illnesses which afflict mankind are assisted by our lifestyle or our lack of hygiene or simple common sense. Today there is plenty of sound evidence that certain habits can prove fatal; that junk food and unnecessary anxieties leading to reliance on artificial medication can lessen a patient's life span, and certainly diminish the amount of enjoyment and pleasure he may get from life.

Today many people suffer from stress of one sort or another and lay at its door many of their problems. If you think back, our ancestors in the Stone Age must have been just as anxious, looking for shelter, attempting to hunt for food, or simply maintaining a spark of fire on their journeyings so that the clan would not freeze to death in the winter. Their worries were of a life or death variety, and the stresses of inter-tribal relationships such as concern about the safety of some new food item, uncertainties about the prospects of future shelter, and the loss of a knowledgeable member of the clan must have been deeply sensed.

What has become very clear in the last decade or so is our search for alternatives to a number of conventional parts of our lives—in religion, in education, in spare-time activities, and in healing. At this time, when the unifying strength of the Age of Pisces is giving way to the more independent, individualistic current which will typify the Age of Aquarius, people are making choices for the first time in their lives. Before, they had often felt they were in the hand of 'authority' or 'the State,' and had to accept this pattern for their birth, education, job, medical treatment, and entertainment. Now this rigid structure is giving way, under pressures beyond its own making. Within the cracks, new ways are beginning to put down roots and flourish, just as the weeds do in a derelict building. Many of these alternatives provide genuine chances for a new self-awareness, real and permanent healing, and religious experiences previously undiscovered.

The first task of any magician is to come to terms with who and what he is. If you know you have bad habits, eat an unhealthy diet, keep going on gallons of tea, black coffee, or by taking pills of some description, then you must consider this before launching yourself into a career as an 'all-knowing healer.' If you are coughing your lungs out over a cigarette whilst trying to advise some other person about his problems, or need to rely on chemicals to give you the strength to sit down and meditate, you will have to apply first the adage 'Physician, heal thyself.'

It is not necessary to reject any system of healing. Antibiotics can save lives, as can surgery, but many conditions which cause long-term suffering and unhappiness may be treated by some of the alternative therapies, which also include magical methods. One aspect of the Aquarian Plan is that we must find ways of living in closer harmony with the Earth beneath our feet, and with Nature, the Goddess, or life-giving power which shapes our mundane destinies. Nature can provide a wide variety of cures, from herbs and 'simples' to teaching us how to manipulate the life-forces in the Universe to bring healing, peace, and joy to those who suffer.

The Healing Power of Nature

How much of Nature gets into your life? Do you live in the country, grow your own fruit and vegetables? Do you walk through unpolluted fields, drink from sparkling clear springs, breathe deeply air which is sea fresh and filled with vitality? You lucky thing! Most people live in towns and cities; struggle along congested streets where trees attempt to survive the atmosphere and the council tree surgeons; take exercise in indoor swimming pools of chlorinated water, or jog through dusty parks. Most of them survive to a ripe old age, and enjoy many aspects of their urban existence too! Nature is not absent from built-up areas, her healing powers are still available to the town people, but they have to make a greater effort, and seek quiet places where trees and plants grow unmutilated, and where the light of the sun and moon may be seen without the lattice-work of high buildings, man-made structures, and orange street lighting.

Nature is willing to share her healing power with us, if we can take a few steps in her direction, learn her ways, and apply this knowledge, so well-known to our rural ancestors, in ways which fit our technological lifestyles. Everyone can tell the difference between day and night; you can generally decide if it is summer or winter; and if you look at the night sky long enough, you might be able to recognize the phase of the moon and decide if she is waxing or waning—that is the beginning of using the tides of Nature to bring harmony and health to your own life. Every aspect of the solar year, or the lunar phase, or the tides of the sea has a force which can be used beneficially. Just as it is possible to observe a seed put forth a shoot, grow into a tall plant, flower, fruit, set seeds, and then decay, we can learn to discover this same pattern in our own affairs and situations. Every enterprise tends to go through a sequence of changes, be it the course of a disease, settling into a new house, or finding and fitting into a different occupation. In some cases, the seed to fruit cycle is very short; in other instances it can take years or even decades. When you start to apply magic to situations, you should first discover which point in the cycle circumstances have reached, for each needs the application of the correct remedy. Sometimes it is necessary to build up strength, collect material objects, or accrue information; at other phases it is important to throw off links, to eradicate factors, or drive out disease. If you act in haste, or apply the wrong force at a critical moment in cosmic time, you can waste your efforts or even make things worse.

The Sun

The power of the Sun is concerned with life—we wouldn't exist on Earth at all if it were not for the precise interaction of sun and earth, heat and radiation, gravity and distance which ensures the dynamic balance of our solar system to provide conditions suitable for evolution here. This is a delicate balance, and not immutable. The light of the sun provides us with a genuine healing ray, yet too much sunshine can be harmful to the skin. Sunlight helps us make vitamin D, necessary to health, and generally makes us feel brighter, happier, and well. The Sun has been worshipped either as a God (and in some places as a Goddess), or as the symbol of a God visible to us on earth.

To use the Sun directly as a healing force requires little in the way of equipment or preparation. If you are unwell yourself, then merely sitting relaxed in a sheltered spot, and imagining the light from the sky shining through you in brilliant white-gold rays, driving out the darkness of disease, bringing relief from pain or stiffness, can be sufficient to get your own inner healing processes going. If you have a sick friend, tell them to do the same, allowing them to sit calmly in a sunny place as you explain how the vitalizing beams of light can help to set off the healing process, and drive out infection. This technique uses relaxation (which is very important in nearly all healing), and the imagination with which something symbolic of the illness can be overcome and driven out.

Clinics treating cancer patients are now recommending a diet of natural fruits and raw vegetables, without salt or other additives; they teach relaxation exercises and the application of the will to get better, applied through the creative visualization of the cancer cells being eaten or destroyed by the patient's own auto-immune systems. This method of natural healing has had many successes when applied seriously to even very severe cancer conditions. As a rider to this, if you eat a large proportion of raw fruits and vegetables in your diet, add no salt or other chemicals (although herbs and spices are recommended for flavoring), and try not to be overweight, you will lessen your chances of being afflicted with cancer and many other complaints. Add a little exercise such as walking, dancing, swimming, riding, cycling, or aerobic movements and devote at least one period of time every day to meditation, deep relaxation (not nodding off in front of the television!), creative visualization, or any other similar activity, and you ought to be able to live a very healthy life!

The Moon

The Moon, too, has important applications in health. She is more directly concerned with your psychic life; she influences the pattern of dreams. In women, although their cycles may not exactly fit the moon's phases, she will to some extent affect their menstrual cycle, fertility, and sexuality. Recent research by Dr. Jonas of Czechoslovakia shows how the moon's phases combined with information on any woman's fertility cycle can provide a safe, effective, and drug-free method of contraception; or for those who wish to conceive a child, can determine the best day to make love with this in mind, and even choose the sex of the baby!

Everyone can watch their dream pattern change with the moon phases, often peaking with vivid, colourful, and interesting dreams occurring within a few days of the full moon. During the waxing moon it is a good idea to work magical acts which are growing, increasing, and working in the outer world. The waxing moon can be used in healing rituals as a symbol that as her light grows brighter the life-spirit in the patient is increased and his body is better able to fight off infection or pain. With the waning moon, the disease is felt to be waning too, decreasing in intensity and lessening its grip on the sick person. You can encourage the patient to watch the moon through a window, if possible, or in their imagination if they can't see the sky, and as the curved light of the moon changes, to feel its influence on their health. The moon is in some ways a more important symbol, for her light can be seen both by day and by night, and the moon's shape may be seen in the dark sky, as well as during daylight whereas the sun only appears in a light sky! This may seem obvious, but light is a magical symbol of great significance, and the visible light of sun or moon or stars brings tangible forces which cannot be seen with the ordinary vision, but can be perceived in the imagination, or during meditations or rituals.

Healthy Living

You must become aware of the season of the Earth as well, because it is no help at all realizing you need a particular herb when the date on the calendar is December in the Northern hemisphere! Certainly herbs can be gathered at their most potent season and dried for later use, but many are far more effective whilst their life-force is still in them—the same applies to eating fresh produce. If it is still alive when you eat it, you will be taking in the 'virtue' of that piece of food or herb, which will probably be beneficial to you. Cut out the chemicals you take in by carefully reading ingredients lists on packages. Even salt can change your blood chemistry, causing water retention which may put a strain on your kidneys. Of course, if you are living in a very hot climate and are sweating a lot, that is a different matter, but ordinary folk in a reasonable climate ought to bear these facts in mind when reaching for the salt cellar. Most people add salt to food without tasting it—so it is a habit rather than a taste preference which causes this action!

Much the same applies to sugar—we don't really need to eat the vast quantities we consume each year. Like salt, sugar is an additive to many ordinary foods; tinned peas, sauces, and soft drinks often contain several spoonfuls of sugar in an ordinary portion, and if you want to balance your weight to your size, bear this in mind. Once you start reading the labels on tins and packets it is quite a revelation. If you do have a sweet tooth then using saccharin or other sugar substitutes may not benefit your health in the long term. It is better to use the real thing in small quantities rather than take in chemicals which may again change your blood chemistry over a long period.

It might seem that all this information about food and diet, exercise and chemicals is a far cry from magic, but YOU are the key to the abilities you have. If you are addicted to sugar, salt, or heroin you are not fully in control of your own destiny. To try to effect the patterns of the work of the world through magic when you aren't able to determine your own destiny becomes a pointless exercise. Most books deal only with magical arts, psychic skills, and occult activities whilst ignoring the physical and emotional state of the magician who is trying to make these techniques work. Now we are becoming aware of the wholeness of all material reality, and maybe the invisible worlds of the inner, as well. If you change one tiny aspect of your life, in theory you are actually altering the entire universe! This is an awesome prospect for the novice magician to come to terms with, so it is important to begin making changes in something which is pretty well under your own control—YOU.

Healing Others

Once you have dealt with your own ills, allergies, addictions, and anxieties through honest examination and, wherever possible, the elimination of the causes, you can attempt to offer healing to those around you. Perhaps if you have already found a magical companion, you can start with them, or maybe they can practise healing skills on you. Anxieties may be dealt with by meditation. If something upsets you, examine it whilst sitting in quiet contemplation. You ought to be able to trust your partner not to discuss your feelings or doubts with the world in general, and you ought to be trustworthy too! Consider problems from all angles, take advice, and gradually a solution will emerge. This may not be an instant cure, but once it is found the results can be amazing and the whole of your life can take a turn for the better.

To work any kind of healing requires trust on the part of the sick person and responsibility on the part of the healer. If you start meddling with the lives of other folk unasked, you may find you are acquiring some of their karma. Even conventional doctors will not merely cure symptoms—for example, if someone turns up with a pain in the stomach, the doctor won't just give them pain-killers and send them away; he will test them for infection and consider the possibility that the pain is a symptom of appendicitis, or some other serious internal condition. The magician must bear this in mind. By trying to alleviate the pain in a friend or relation, be it physical, emotional, or psychological, it may cause them far more suffering, and the magician may also find himself burdened with their problems too. If a person asks for healing or help, then you should consider the matter very carefully before immediately plunging into a two-hour healing ritual. It is possible that the condition which needs attention is a lesson the individual has to learn, that some part of their nature needs looking at, and some aspect of their life requires sorting out. By all means help and, if possible, examine the situation to find a logical and lasting solution to these ills, but don't take on the burden of your friend relying on you, unless you are ready for it. Often a simple meditation can show you the crux of the matter, or maybe you can help your friend relax and see what underlies his current state, so he can heal himself. In the long term nearly all healing comes from within, even if drugs, herbs, massage, or surgery are needed to start off the healing process.

Suffering is not a requirement in learning, as it used to be thought. Religions don't need to teach its value in their creeds—we have enough to do coping with life's real situations without having the added penalty of suffering laid upon us. Certainly the child with the burned finger learns to be wary of fire, but the mother ground down with the responsibility of several children, ill health, lack of money, and poor accommodation doesn't need to be told 'Suffering is good for you'! The most important lesson pain can teach anyone is that of avoidance. There is no reason to seek pain in order to gain spiritual insights—meditation in a comfortable chair can bring far more interesting revelations than being flogged with a knotted scourge. To open the doors to inner awareness a gentle approach is needed, not cruelty. A healthy and relaxed body and mind can provide far wider awareness of the inner side of life, and a greater understanding of the mundane world. Fasting, binding, pain, and deprivation will not open the vistas of enlightenment in a controlled manner, though they might wring out a few tortured insights into the frailty of the flesh and the difficulty of obtaining eternal wisdom. Whatever methods you choose, do try to make them easy on yourself.

Methods of Healing

Once you have attempted to get yourself in tune with Nature, and so have begun to feel healthy, you can decide what methods of healing you would like to apply. Certainly you can rely entirely on meditation to find the cause, and ritual to supply the cures, but the knowledge of some of the alternative methods of therapy by you and your partner will help in lots of cases. Several of the alternative techniques are based on magical rather than rational theories of healing, particularly radionics, homoeopathy and the Bach Flower Remedies, which work so effectively on anxieties, fears, and inner tensions. There are also a number of interesting methods which use massage, pressure, or muscle testing which can be learned, in some cases from a book, or during a short course given by a trained expert. Do have a look at the introductory books on acupressure, which uses the points of 'meridians,' which are lines of energy flow within the body, discovered long ago in China and Japan. In illness, some of these invisible channels are blocked, thus cutting off the Ch'i or life-force from certain organs or systems. By massaging, applying heat, or, after proper training, inserting fine sterile gold, silver, or stainless steel needles in specific locations, the flow of energy can be released and so a cure can take place. This technique works well for painful conditions, and acupuncture anaesthetics are used for even major surgery as they don't have the side effects some gas or anaesthetic drugs can have. Many of the massage points for treating headaches, anxiety, stomach upsets, and other minor ills are on the hands or feet, and can soon be learned. Try these out on yourself and discover the effect before working on other people, or allow your companion to try to cure your migraine or bruised ankle.

Herbal Medicine

Herbal medicine has become popular again after many years of neglect. There are plenty of simple herb teas which can be drunk purely for pleasure and relaxation, or to relieve tension, sleeplessness, 'women's troubles,' or fever. You will probable find new uses for the parsley, sage, and mint in the garden, apart from stuffing the Sunday joint, for these can help a wide variety of minor ills, and new herbs can easily be grown, even in sunny window boxes, or on roofs or patios. Feverfew leaves eaten in honey sandwiches can ease migraines, and this daisy-flowered herb with its peppery scent is common, growing wild in some places. Comfrey, dandelions, thyme, and camomile are useful, and any good book on herbs will have clear pictures or photographs of these plants so that you can learn to recognize them in the countryside. Many garden centres now stock a wide range of these valuable plants or you can buy packets of seeds. If you have any spare seeds, plant these on waste land, or in overrun gardens so that they are available for others who might need them. Again, share your knowledge with your partner, make teas and bath mixes for each other to try. Learn the applications of all the common plants, trees, and herbs in your area.

Homoeopathy

A more complicated application of natural substances (not only derived from plants, but minerals, tree bark, and even seeming poisons) is homoeopathy. This is a fairly new method of healing researched by Hahnemann in the last century. He found that some substances applied in minute doses sparked off a cure in sick people, but would show their effect on healthy folk by giving them the symptoms of the illness. Like appeared to affect and then cure like. In ancient times there was thought to be a link between a disease which produced spots and a spotted plant used to cure it, and although homoeopathy isn't quite this obvious, it can often genuinely cure long-standing allergies, pains, and complaints, even when other treatments have not done so. To arrive at a medicine, the homoeopath needs a great deal of strange-seeming information from the patient because the treatment is applied to him as a whole and individual person, rather that as a case of shingles, arthritis, or gastric ulcers. It takes a lengthy training and very careful study to be able to apply the many hundreds of homoeopathic drugs, which are given in extremely diluted form to act as catalysts, which lead to a gradual and permanent cure. Often the illness seems to get worse when the drugs are first given, but this is a sure sign that the correct therapy has been found, for it recognizes that the body is fighting the disease, and that the symptoms prove this is occurring.

Bach Flower Remedies

Herbs and homoeopathy both work well when properly applied on physical illnesses, but the Bach Flower Remedies act on psychological ills. These very slow and gentle medicines are made from thirty-eight different flowers or trees and when taken over a period of time can assist in the recovery from fears, tensions, and phobias which other treatments don't touch. Often these states can lead to muscular problems, allergies, or depression which prevents the person being able to cope with life, or overcome ordinary problems. They can even be applied to things like home sickness, or 'psychic' attack if someone is afraid that another person has an unwanted influence over them. Many herbalists stock these remedies, or they can be obtained quite inexpensively, direct from the Dr. Edward Bach Centre, Mount Vernon, Sotwell, Wallingford, Oxon OX10 OPZ, England. Send a stamped addressed envelope for a list of the thirty-eight remedies and their specific applications. There are a number of books available too, explaining this effective form of therapy, which every magician should be aware of if he offers treatment.

Dowsing

Another skill every magician and his partner should acquire is that of dowsing with a pendulum. Get a small, symmetrical weight and a piece of thin twine or cord and teach yourself to allow it to react positively or negatively to questions you ask yourself. Hold this simple instrument lightly and ask a basic question, like 'Is it Wednesday?' You will soon find the bob swings slightly, either in a straight line, or a circle. Command your inner self, which is causing the muscles in your hand and wrist to move, to work harder. Soon you will get clear and decisive movements and can ask a question which has the opposite answer. Again your bob will swing in a different manner. Although some books imply there is a definite swing for 'Yes' and 'No', it does vary from individual to individual. Also, you may find if you ask questions about another person, or someone of the opposite sex, the swing answers reverse their code. Keep on practising with your companion until you can get firm, accurate, and consistent results from this experiment, which although is being dealt with here in the healing section, has many other magical applications. Keep on trying until you are sure you can understand the code your own pendulum is using under different circumstances and then you can test it on healing situations.

You can experiment with lists of herbs, massage areas, Bach Remedies, or forms of treatment with which you have become competent so that you can dowse along the list, picking out things to try in a particular case. You may need a sample from the sick person; a clipping of hair or nails, or a drop of saliva on a clean tissue will be sufficient to link you together whilst you investigate. If they are present you can ask questions whilst swinging the bob over their hands or you might feel more confident if they just supply the sample and allow you to work on their problem when you are feeling in the right mood.

Giving Advice

Quite often advice on diet, exercise, relaxation, new interests, or dedication to getting fit can be sufficient to put someone on the paths to health, or the application of one of the massage techniques, like acupressure, foot massage, Touch for Health (sometimes called Applied Kinesiology), which relies on the tone of certain muscles to determine the state of the body and inner self as shown in the acupuncture meridians. You may suggest certain herbs to drink, to bathe in, or to add to almond oil to make a rub which can be applied to stiff areas, or for a general soothing massage, which will be relaxing and calming.

Read widely, as there are plenty of excellent 'do it yourself' therapy manuals written within the last few years by successful practitioners. Experiment with a selection of different techniques, both physical and psychological, so that you and your companion have a repertoire to offer anyone who seeks help. In the section on rituals, there are some which can be applied to magical healing, but often simple, sensible advice can put someone on the road to health. Anything which leads them to align their life with Nature, choosing natural foods, exercises, and therapies, will not only assist them to get more out of life, but because they are a part of the whole cosmos, which is out of balance, their healing also heals the universe—that is why all magicians must bear their activities in mind and take full responsibility for their actions when healing or giving advice which may affect the life or future of any other person.

The Fountain of Light Exercise

One technique which is well worth experimenting with as an adjunct to healing is the 'Fountain of Light' exercise. In this, by imagining a set of colours up your body with the brightest, purest light above your head, from which you can draw a healing force, you can become filled with this health-giving power. Practise alone at first, or with your partner, until it feels natural and effective. Stand comfortably upright and close your eyes. Imagine that you are standing on a dark, black, curved surface. It is so intensely black that you could almost imagine it is the night sky, spangled with brilliant stars. Moving up your body from your feet the colour changes to a dark, peaty brown, fading gradually as you move up your legs to a russet brown. At the top of your legs the colour is crimson red, in the sexual region. Above that is a band of orange across your stomach fading into a yellow band in the region of your solar plexus. Above the yellow the colour changes to a rich leaf green over the heart region. At the top of your chest and throat the colour changes through turquoise to a brilliant blue at the Adam's apple. From the bright blue the colour changes to deep indigo on the level of your third eye, in the centre of your forehead, and finally there is a change to brilliant violet at the top of your head. Allow these colours to become vivid and definite, and even if you are colour blind, or have difficulty in visualizing, try to discover a gradation of tone, from very dark at the feet to a brilliant white light above the top of your head which you can imagine and use.

See the most vivid and shining whiteness as a great ball above your head and then imagine or perhaps even feel you can draw this force downwards through each colour band. As the light flows down through you, sense it opening up a centre of healing and a balancing force, like a rose unfolding. The one at the crown of your head is the link with your 'Higher Self' through which you may work this sort of magic. At the forehead is a blossom of intense indigo which represents your psychic faculty. At the throat, as the brilliance flows downwards through your body, there flowers the blue rose of communication and speech. Below that there is a strange green flower at the heart centre, through which the power of love and compassion may flow out to others around you. Below that is the main healing centre of the solar plexus, through which the magical life force of the universe may be directed, in rays of sun-golden light, to those in need.

Below that, across your abdomen is an area of digestion and the orange-coloured flower which helps you cope with the mundane aspects of healing the sick, or will assist in digestive troubles.

Below that is the crimson blossom filled with the brilliance of white light which enlivens your most basic urges of sex and true unity. This can be used to heal and balance your own life but it cannot pass out through its scarlet blossom a healing power to others until you have fully mastered the technique of opening and controlling this centre of energy. It is best not to try if you are a beginner as it can get you out of your depth if you are not truly balanced. Below that is a darker region of stability and strength. It is the strong stem on which the blossoms of sacred light grow, and it is rooted in the dark depths of the earth. This is the mysterious firmament which is why it may be envisioned as sprinkled with stars.

When you are healing someone who may be sitting with you, first see the colours—black, dark brown, russet, crimson, orange, yellow, green, blue, indigo, violet—and then draw down the white brilliance. When you have managed to sense this down as far as the heart/green centre, pull it down to the solar plexus/yellow centre and open it as a great rose. Allow the same colour to flow through your arms and out through your hands. You do not need to touch the person at all but hold your hands close to them so that the fiery white/golden yellow light may flow over them. You will be guided intuitively how to go about this and will know instinctively when to stop.

At the end of the treatment, imagine the white light changing to silvery rain, or a great sparkling waterfall which will flow over you, refreshing and cleansing you all over. Let this continue until you are certain all parts of your 'patient's' illness or symptoms have been washed away. Then imagine all the flowers closing one after another, still retaining a spark of the brilliance within the heart of the closed flower. Start at your head, watching the petals firmly close over the glimmer of brilliance, which will bring you health and balance in between times, then close the rest in turn, in descending order. At the end you ought to feel good and not weary, for the energy of healing has been drawn from the great source of brilliant healing light and not from some resource of your own. Don't rush this experiment as it is very important, both to heal your own complaints and to assist other people. Get your partner to work on you so that you can experience the sensation of the healing force. It works on muscle pains, headaches, fevers, and, if you are seriously ill and needing surgery, it can speed up the healing process of tissue or bones.

Psychic Activity

One factor of healing or at least advising which is more applicable to students of magic is within the field of 'psychic' activities. Many people, when they begin to experiment with esoteric techniques, find weird and upsetting things start to happen to them. Some go so far as to imagine that the moment they perform the first ritual, some vigilant black magician is waiting and watching and will immediately lay a horrid curse upon them. Certainly, when you awaken the sleeping faculties used in magical work for the first time, some extremely strange things do appear to happen to you! You aren't under attack by some evil spirit, nor are you about to lose your eternal soul to the dark forces you have inadvertently stirred up. You have opened those first doors to the inner world which has always been with you, but which you have been unable to sense before because of your own lack of sensitivity. Once you start to meditate, or perform the simplest spell, no matter how bad, feeble, or inefficient your meditation seems to be, something on the inner will happen. You begin to sense the feelings of others around you, you become aware, without realizing it perhaps, of some of the effects which the interaction of individuals always make. Clearly, some of these links will be pleasant, others not so good, and these can make you feel vulnerable or under threat from some unseen presence. It is unseen, but it is really only part of yourself. No matter what occult fiction tells you, the 'Dweller on the Threshold' is just as much a part of you as your feet!

When you sense this guardian angel or advisor or inner self you may be overawed and so feel that something is 'out to get you.' Don't worry, you will get used to the feeling and not sense a threatening presence if you keep your head and meditate upon it. The inner self is a wise and helpful companion, so value its nearness, and learn the stillness when you can turn the threat into safety and protection. Black magicians are too busy trying to destroy the world and aren't likely to waste time or effort on attacking small fry like experimenting magical students, so get on with coming to terms with your inner self, and don't try running. After all, you will never escape your own shadow!

Certainly there are situations when you can come face to face with unpleasant 'vibes,' or be in the presence of sick people whose aims are destructive and harmful. You may need to help sort out 'haunted' buildings or alleviate the sad, lonely atmosphere which can linger after an old person dies after a long illness, or at the scene of a horrific road accident. These acts are not for the novice, and it is wise to seek expert help before trying to shift a stubborn ghost, or nasty atmosphere. You may certainly try to improve the vibes of a new home though, or wipe the attachments from a second-hand item you wish to use, without too much previous experience.

People who fear they are under 'psychic attack' very seldom are, but if something has really scared them, it will take a lot of effort on your part to advise them to relax and allow their common sense to take over. What they feel may be very real, and their fears will build this up to a great unpleasant ghoul which seems about to get them. You will need to be very calm yourself, with your own psychic whiskers feeling for any actual nasties around. Definitely get your companion to help you calm down the 'victim' and try to discover what they have been up to. Many psychic upsets are the result of playing with inner matters, like using a ouija-board, or trying to get messages from the dead, or attempting to set up a seance without knowing how. Again these things will often open a crack between the ordinary self and the inner one, and if people have fears or phobias, or a lot of repressed and ignored memories of unpleasant events, these will be the first through the gap.

In the hands of trained and competent magicians some of these methods of contacting the inner are valid and quite safe but, like matches in the possession of small children, they can be extremely dangerous. Don't dabble, and try to prevent others from playing at psychic games, because they always produce surprises, some of which are hard to ignore because they are not pleasant. Messages like 'You are going to die,' true though they may be, are extremely upsetting to the average person, and can even lead them to make mistakes whilst driving, or may distract them when in a potentially dangerous situation, so that the ouija message becomes a self-fulfilling prophecy. You may find a basic consecration ceremony will help.

Blessed salt (for earth), water, a lighted candle, and some incense are carried clockwise round the person, his room, or house three times to banish fears, and actual presences. Imagine you are sweeping out bad vibes, old fears, and lurking memories as you walk round with your companion. Then fling open the doors or windows so that daylight and the healing power of the sun can shine within. If the sun isn't shining that day, imagine it strongly flooding in with pure golden-white rays, lighting up dark corners and bringing a breath of fresh, pure air inside. Cats and dogs won't go into really evil places so watch the family pet. If it still won't enter the room, refer to Dion Fortune's *Psychic Self-Defence* or the more recent book by Murry Hope *Practical Techniques of Psychic Self-Defence,* which give detailed instructions on how to cope with any similar circumstances. Don't rush in to show off your new-found psychic skills because you can get out of your depth. Do experiment by consecrating items or rooms for meditations or ritual work. Do learn to recognize problems and apply common sense to healing or psychic matters.

Your Reactions

You will need to discover how you react to ordinary things like coffee, to common analgesics like aspirin, and even foods or drinks. As your experiments in magic increase, so should your awareness of these matters. You can get to the point that a single cup of instant coffee can keep you awake all night but on the other hand a large meal may not deaden your psychic sensitivities in the slightest. You can learn to control your awareness of your state of health. When feeling weary you can increase your energy through deep breathing exercises, or when feeling tense, by switching into an altered state of consciousness, in order to become relaxed in the dentist's chair, or before the important job interview.

If you suffer allergies to foods, or substances in chemical products or nature, dowse along a row of samples to locate the precise root of the sensitivity, and then see if you can locate an appropriate antidote or way of avoiding the effects these things can have on your life. You may find, when trying the pendulum over your evening meal, that some things you have always eaten are not good for you, lowering your energy level, or causing sleeplessness or irritation. This can be quite an interesting experiment because you may end up with a list of things to avoid, but equally you may discover foods or drinks which enhance your powers of concentration or energy. You might even locate a personal 'Elixir Vitae' or a soothing substance far safer than sleeping pills or tranquillizers.

Observe Nature and see how she affects you. Watch the weather and the phases of the moon and sun cycles to see when you feel alive, and when dull, when your dreams are bright, and your inner senses alert. If you are going to celebrate magical festivals to mark the passing seasons, you will need to learn the dates and what is happening within you. Accrue information on new advances in alternative therapies and methods of healing. See how many 'old wives' tales' are proving to have grains of wisdom in them which, after being long ignored, are being rediscovered. Dig your garden and grow different plants and apply them to benefit your friends, brighten up your menus, or provide healing teas, baths, and massage oils. Read the books on trees, and listen to the wisdom in the voices of birds, the wind in the grass, and the trickle of water. Study the weather and your inner feelings so that you can become whole, with all of Nature.

15

CREATING A MAGICAL TEMPLE

If you seriously want to work magic and perform some of its most effective forms of working, you will need somewhere to do it. This place may take one of a wide variety of physical forms and obviously will depend on your purpose, resources, and intentions. It might be a whole attic in a vast country house, a secret grove in a wild wood, the cellar of a city terrace, or the corner of your bed-sit. It may be a laboratory where modern arts of alchemy may produce from the unity of two opposites, within the heart and soul, the Elixir of Life. It might be a beautiful classic temple, carved in marble and decked with the Gods and Goddesses of the ancient world. Perhaps you seek a natural secluded grove, for the word 'temple' is probably derived from the trunks of holy trees whose stems have now been transmuted into corinthian columns of stone, or the groyned vaults of early chapels. You may work through meditation and vision so that your working place is an island of dreams in the tossing ocean of the mundane world. Your practical skills may become paramount so that you have a workshop and your altar is a bench or drawing board whereon you redesign the universe. It could be as small as a cupboard into which you retreat, hermit-like, to explore through the inner perceptions the entire cosmos, or a section of an ordinary dwelling wherein the angels venture, and spread their knowledge all about you.

No matter what its physical form or size, it will have several other counterparts, for the temple is 'not built with hands,' it is built with love through the skill of the trained imagination. Once it has been set up, and consecrated in your own way, you may find some spirit will be indwelling there, ready to guide and instruct you. You cannot make this contact with the unseen by will power, nor by astral bribery, nor by any sort of threat or compulsion. If you make ready the place and send out a message through your inner self, perhaps your Holy Guardian Angel will turn up to assist you. Maybe the Gods and Goddesses you invoke will be seen in your circle, or the powers of healing, knowledge, and success will come to your special place and fill it with energy and life.

The Pillars of the Temple

You and your companion will be the pillars of the Aquarian Temple, no matter what other form it will take. Each of you represents in the world the dark and light posts which support the roof of your endeavour. In the past the pillars were inert, symbolic, and static, but in the New Age they will need to move and flow and mingle their forces, expressed through human action within the arts of magic. There are plenty of books on the symbolism of the pillars of Solomon's Temple, of Hercules, and so on, but you are the support posts of the Temple of Aquarius, each bringing your own energy and ability. The men will have the strength in the outer world, the power of the Sun, fire, and air, and all the things that such basic elements imply. The women will have the force on the inner levels where magic is real. They have the dark and changing Moon tides, the psychic skills, and the attributes of the earth and the waters. Each of you will either be a God or Goddess, a power for good, and an aspect of the total balance which is the harmony of modern magic. You will have to find ways, when working together, of harmonizing and balancing aspects of each other's natures. You will need honesty, trust, and consideration so that the two streams of power flow side by side. Imagine you are a pair of plough horses, working in double harness to plough a straight furrow, that your field may be well tended and the earth made fertile by your efforts.

To become balanced will take a lot of work because neither is the leader, for each of you will find a time to instruct and a time to learn. Each will develop skills which the other cannot match, and each will have successes and disappointments as the work proceeds. In the old alchemical texts the purpose of the very complicated process is to marry the opposites. These are usually thought to be silver and gold, or the great king and queen, or the lily and the rose. Each is a symbol of both a greater and lesser thing. In his explorations of alchemy, the great psychoanalyst Dr. Carl Jung began to discover parallels between states of consciousness and alchemical processes. He found that not only could you work at turning dull lead into shining alchemical gold, but you could turn the dim, confused consciousness of an ordinary person into the bright and shining awareness of the trained mind. He also felt that by uniting the outer male or female self with its inner and opposite female/male (anima/animus) a totally complete individual would be formed.

Many men are afraid of women and find it very hard, when set free from the chains of conventional religion, to be able to relate to a Goddess figure, or the female side of God, she who is Sophia (Wisdom), who can share her gift of knowledge and understanding with all who ask it. Once they can come to terms with this aspect of the power of creation many new doors will open up for them. The same may apply to women, who, after rejecting the pattern of 'God the Father' in all its possible forms, cling desperately to the Great Goddess to the exclusion of all else, including the fertilizing seed by which means she is a child of the mother. There is no simple way for any individual to understand the dual nature of the Creator, except to say that such understanding is very important to the work of the Aquarian Mage. Only by approaching the Goddess and the God through meditation or in the magical setting of a path-working, by getting to know these forces both as outside influences upon your life and world, and also as components of your own inner being, can you fully grasp the work of the Mysteries.

Don't imagine that after a couple of attempts to visualize a certain aspect of a God or Goddess you will be completely ready to welcome them into your humble abode, or personality. That way lies the path of the ego, the dark road to disillusion and despair. You may be able to become a channel through which some aspect of the Great Ones may work, but it is not for beginners, nor is it necessarily a pleasant or controllable experience. You will need to experiment with symbols, with basic exercises and traditional myths so that you can truly understand these powers behind the visible universe, and when you are ready, offer your dedication as their servant. You will certainly be accepted, but if you expect to be able to rule every aspect of your own destiny thereafter, you will probably be in for some surprises. Being the vehicle through which any great power manifests is not a game for novices, for as it says in many traditional lodge rituals, 'My office is greater than I am and I strive to be worthy there-of.' The forces of the universe are a good deal greater than we are, and only by knowing who we are, as the adage 'Know Thyself' over the door to the School of the Mysteries in ancient times suggests, can any of us hope not only to serve but to survive the experience!

This is another reason why a respected and harmonious partner is so vital to the work of the Aquarian magician. In the last era of magic there were learned schools, well set-up lodges, and wealthy scholars who could spend their time studying ancient texts and trying out antique rituals. Today we are living in a new world and a new age. The old knowledge cannot help us in the computer age and the books we need to study may not have even been written yet! The new magic is very different from the old, and rather than relying on lost languages and ancient symbols, it uses the instrument of the trained human mind, which, potentially, has access to far greater stores of information through the Collective Unconscious of Jung, called the Akashic Records in past ages. Either way there is far more information available to those who can learn to enter the state of mind in which it can be approached, and retain in memory whatever has been discovered there. That is the main task of the Aquarian magicians. Each must find ways to journey into this store of information and draw from it such understanding as each may safely carry, and then apply it in the world, so that through the alchemy of experience, mere information is changed into the pure gold of applied wisdom.

To continue this work, you and your companion will need to set up a suitable Temple, Laboratory, Workshop, or Grove, depending in which sphere you most wish to delve. Within that consecrated space, which may be enlarged on the inner to include the entire cosmos, or condensed to become within the whirling electrons of a single atom where the matter of creation dances eternally, you may discover the key to the universe. Which particular aspects of magic are most important to you and your companion will depend on your previous knowledge, and on your personal preferences because this is a large field of enterprise. You may fancy ritual or the arts of making talismans. You might wish to study healing or draw nearer the God and Goddesses of the pagan faith; you may prefer simple meditation and the gentle ways of pathworking; or study of lost knowledge and its application in technological times. Your individual purposes will to a certain extent influence the way your magical place is designed in the real world although, as you will have discovered through some of the earlier exercises, you can change its inner appearance and structure at will.

Furnishing Your Temple

Because this work is concerned with experiments in Aquarian magic, the final place may be the result of experiments which you have not yet tried and so the pattern may need to remain flexible and open at present. This might even be how it stays. In any case, you will need enough space for you and your partner to be able to sit comfortably, and if possible, move around a central table, altar, or work-bench. In the Golden Dawn days, temples were furnished with Victorian gothic armchairs on daises for the principal officers, and the altar often had a chunk of marble on top. In the age of melamine and Formica, you can still have your black basalt-looking altar, but you are also able to lift it! The things that are most important are the chairs in which you each sit, as many meditations, pathworking trips, and certain experiments in time and astral travel will require you to remain still and passive for some considerable lengths of time, so comfort and convenience are important. Looking at what is readily available, I have discovered that some of the high backed 'garden' chairs make ideal magical thrones. The angle of the back may be adjusted, and if you want the thing to fit in a particular colour scheme you can throw a cloth or blanket over it. These chairs are light to move about, and will fold up when not in use. By testing those available, you will find one which suits your height and is supportive in the right places. Later on, if you wish to adopt a reclining position for some experiments, it is easy to change the angle of the chair back and foot rest.

You can use these chairs if you intend to work out of doors. They won't look out of place in the garden as that is where they were designed to be used. You may need to sit on a tree stump if your sacred grove is a long way from home but you may well discover that brief visits to an actual holy forest can be replicated in the laboratory by using the creative imagination, and you won't be bothered by gnats or the weather! Magical ceremonies held out of doors are extremely powerful but they tend to be the dynamic dancing celebrations of the ancient festivals rather than the static mental journeys of exploration which many prefer. Try it for yourself and see which gives you the greatest pleasure, power, and results. After all you are an experimenting magician so you cannot settle for the first situation or test you attempt.

Symbols for the Temple

You will need some symbols, but again because of the new current of magical training, it isn't possible to simply say 'Embroider the Qabalistic Tree of Life in the Queen scale on a silk banner and hang it on the eastern wall of your temple, set up as in Dr. Ignatius Golightly's book of 1809.' You will be testing new symbols and experimenting with forms, designs, and images which are even now being formed in your consciousness. Certainly there are some symbols which appear to be important indications of balance but how you make these, and where and when you use them, will be something for you to discover for yourself. Maybe you have other ideas.

As the table/altar in your new age temple is a work-bench, it would be best not to clutter it up with instruments, candles, and statues except when these are needed for a particular working. If possible you could use the top of a bookcase, a shelf, or low cupboard as the focus of your imagery, and maybe use the wall behind it to hang a poster, mirror, or banner which is important to your present experiment. By using a length of cheap roller blind, or by making one with the discarded cardboard tubes (often found outside fabric shops), round which you attach a length of suitable material, you could create a scene, image, or symbol for the work in hand. You could paint or embroider a representation of your God or Goddess, if you have the skill, or make a montage of images from magazines. You could have an enlarged photograph of some sacred place printed onto the blind, or make a design with cut-out cloth, stuck on with rubber solution, so that it depicts the entry to a holy place, or a vista of an ancient temple. Use your imagination and your mutual skills as artists or creators of a suitable image on which you can focus. It could even be a picture of your real home so that it acts as a safety valve during workings and will bring you quickly back to the here and now. On your altar you should have a rock or slate or piece of wood which can be an earthing point too; just as electric circuits have their earth wire, so should magicians.

Sometimes you will need to sit side by side, facing this symbolic image, at other times perhaps you will prefer to be across the table, at right angles to it. Obviously the amount of space available will dictate this to some extent, as will the presence of other people, for two is the minimum, and seven probably the maximum for a group of novices. (If some of you are already senior initiates this rule won't apply!)

The other important matters to consider include the four elements of Earth, Water, Fire, and Air, for it is the balance between these forces both as symbols, and within each individual that the strength to handle the vast powers of magic can be developed. There are usually several sets of items associated with the four elements: the rock, log, pentacle, or shield which stands for Earth; the cup, chalice, or grail which contains Water; the lantern, candle, or bonfire which is the element Fire; and josssticks, scented flowers or, best of all, proper grains of incense, burned in a thurible or chafing dish for Air. Previous authors have varied this arrangement and given different attributes, but this is a safe and effective set-up if you are a novice. Once you get used to the symbols, you can change them if you want to. Many ceremonies involve a magical feast or Mass, and for these you will need consumable versions of the four elements, most often bread and wine (or for non-alcohol drinkers, apple or grape juice). Salt is frequently sprinkled on the bread, or it is dipped into the salt before being eaten. In order that Fire or Air may be shared, you have a choice of warming your hands over the candle or lamp, or sniffing the incense. In some workings a scented flower, a rose or lily, etc., is placed on the altar so that its perfume may be attributed to Air.

What you eventually choose to do will obviously depend on the state of your knowledge, the tradition in which you are working, and thus the symbols which it employs. If you have the creative skills between you, and a place which may be totally dedicated to magical experiments, you can decorate the room to represent the kind of Temple you really wish to work in. If you would prefer to work out of doors but circumstances prevent this, then by using tree branches, cut in the winter and decked with artificial leaves (the real ones dry and drop off!), you can form a tree canopy by stringing them from the ceiling. You will need to locate the load bearing joists first, though. You can carve trunks from pieces of waste polystyrene with a hot wire or sharp knife. You could also cut out mock trilithons and when painted with several coats of stone paint in various natural shades these can make a very realistic miniature 'Stonehenge.' You might find some shop display pillars in one of the classic forms to encircle your room (for the Aquarian Temple, like most of the oldest ones, is circular). If you have a green or brown carpet or even marble-type lino and can manage to paint the walls to represent a landscape at the bottom and a blue sky above (day or night as preferred), you can replicate any sort of sacred place you desire. Using white LEDs you can even have stars that light up! Visualize the ideal and then apply your creative skills to make it real. Books on theatre design will give you hints on what you can do with papier mache, chicken wire, and paint, discarded packing materials, plastics, and superglue.

Costumes

Unless you are both totally happy to work naked in your temple, some sort of costume will be useful. A simple T-shaped robe is easy to make from a strip of wide material cut to fit your shape loosely. You could simply fold a strip in half, cut a hole for your head, gather up the spare material on each shoulder with a double running thread or elastic, and tie it together round the waist with a cord, to make a serviceable tunic which suits both men and women. Of course you can be much more elaborate, but it is a matter of personal choice. You might like to have different coloured belts to match the colours of the planets, or some sort of head-dress, and a pair of sandals or slippers. Each garment has an esoteric meaning, which you will find in any prayer book which describes the items of ecclesiastical attire. Whatever you choose should not flutter over lit candles or bonfires and endanger you, and hats, etc., should not blow off in a wind or tip on to the altar if you bow your head.

When you have collected all your bits and pieces do look after them; they aren't for wearing to fancy dress parties, and your Temple ought to be a special place, set apart for ritual work, not to be displayed to all and sundry. Once everything is consecrated it is 'set apart' for ever!

Setting up a Temple takes a long time so be prepared to take it slowly. If you start with something comfortable to sit on, and perhaps a poster, picture, or symbol which appears to act as a doorway to you both, then you can call for help and guidance from your inner self, or from whatever Goddess, Deities or Powers you feel most helpful. Meditate and work through paths which lead you towards your ideal setting so that you build up information on the inner as well as collecting equipment on the outer. You might need tools and materials for talismans, or books, as well as a selection of coloured candles and safe candlesticks to burn these in. You might seek out a pleasant goblet to drink your wine from, and a food platter, carved of wood or hand-made pottery, or maybe you have the skills to make these yourself. The greater your involvement with every item used in magic, the stronger your links with it in its symbolic application and so your greater control.

Elemental Weapons

In the last generation of magical temples, the four elemental weapons played an important role in their consecration, rituals, and symbolism but perhaps now is the time for a change in this respect too. Most magicians collected a Cup and a Sword, created or painted a Pentacle, and dedicated a Wand, in accordance with the Key of Solomon or the instructions published in the texts derived from the Hermetic Order of the Golden Dawn. Each of these instruments has a large body of attached correspondences and you may wish to follow the well-trodden path of earlier magical practice. An alternative, which might align closer to the purposes of Aquarian magic, is to certainly find a cup which you will need for the wine or water, and to make a personal pentacle, showing your magical aims and mirroring your current state of advancement. Swords have always been difficult to find, expensive to buy, complicated to make and rather embarrassing to carry about if you are not performing rituals at home. Although it is possible to get a fake sword to hang on the wall or wave about during ceremonial consecrations, etc., it might not feel right for everyone. Think about what you feel is most helpful for the sorts of ceremonies you intend to perform.

If you want something which might fulfil the task of the ritual sword yet is within your capabilities to make (one for each of you) design a long wand or staff. You will need a pole about one inch (2.5 cm) thick and about six feet (two metres) long. If you are going to be indoors you will also need a support for it, made out of a large tin. Wrap several layers of card round the bottom of the pole to form a tube longer than the tin is deep and anchor this tube in the centre. Fill the tin with clean stones, sand, or gravel and then top it with some runny crack-filling plaster. Leave this to set at least overnight. It should be heavy enough to hold the pole upright as long as no great weight is attached to the top of it.

This staff is your personal Staff of Life, and so it ought to be decorated with paint, ribbons, carving, or appliqued felt shapes to demonstrate your purpose. Should one of you be working alone, the Staff can stand in for your partner, or you can compose around it during a pathworking the image of your ideal God/Goddess. Perhaps from light card you can cut out symbols which can be slid over the top of the pole to represent various forces, for example a Sun and Moon, or the sigils of the planets. One staff could be basically silver and the other gold, or they could both reflect the colour between green and blue which seems to be associated with work concerned with the Aquarian Age. You should be able to take it out of its supporting pot (which should also be painted and decorated to fit in with your purpose).

You will probably need a cupboard to keep your material in, and an electric point so that you can run a cassette recorder for music during rituals or perhaps with the words of pathworking narratives prerecorded. It is often useful to record details of any ritual, and any messages or inspiration received during meditations, as speaking requires less effort than writing, if you are very relaxed or in an altered state of awareness during your workings. It is useful to be able to dim the lights, because although candles may be magically acceptable, if you have to read a script in their flickering light, the only thing you may get from all your efforts is a headache. If you can learn to make use of all the space in your room so that the consecrated circle is actually larger that the physical space there is no reason why one of you can't lower lights, turn on tapes or music, or anything else still within the special place, by remote control.

Maybe your holy place is the Grail Castle, or one of the Temples of the Nile, or the Sanctuary of Poseidon at Sounion in all its sparkling glory, above the sun-bright sea. Perhaps you have recreated a grotto, with rocks and trees, or the Chapel in the Green, a circle of standing stones, or the entrance to the Underworld as created by the many builders of ancient earthworks, called tumuli, barrows, or burial mounds. Maybe you have designed a star-studded astral Temple, or the control room of a rocket ship to explore inner space, or a quiet, womb-like sphere where the influences of the Great Mother can be encountered. Whatever symbolism and material you have chosen, you will soon find that every ounce of effort was worthwhile, and that the time involved will quickly be repaid once you begin to make use of this 'other place' which you have created. Gradually you will find its atmosphere changes, and that simply to enter the place, adopt the robes, regalia, or even the frame of mind in which magic is a reality, will cause you to shift into that altered gear where your power and understanding may be awesome.

Treat all your equipment with respect, keep it clean and ready for use, ensure that the atmosphere of the Temple is not disturbed by entering it in a bad temper. Cool down first, and allow your magical personality to fill you. Look after your health, and by standing upright, with your shoulders back and down and relaxing the tension in your neck and back, you will find you feel a very different person—this simple exercise alone can be quite magical!

16

THE PATTERNS OF RITUAL

One of the subjects which attracts some students to the arts of magic is the idea of ritual. The elaborate robes, the equipment, and the theatrical performance of chanting words in strange languages and calling strange powers to do their bidding appeals to them a great deal. The truth of the matter is that, in today's terms, a magical ritual is more like the program in a computer. By entering certain information exactly, and in the correct order, using the language in which the machine is programmed, and interfacing with it properly, you will obtain the results you are expecting. Magic is the same. Instead of using Fortran or Basic, the magicians of past times would make their requests in Hebrew, in Latin, or Enochian, the language of the Angels (according to Dr. John Dee in Elizabethan times). Now it is much better to make all prayers, invocations, and requests in your own familiar tongue. This will ensure that if an answer is received, it will be in the same language, and you will be able to understand it!

A ritual is a way of combining the different states of awareness (which you should master through the arts of meditation, pathworking, and creative visualization first) with the equipment, symbols of the Elements, and the imagery of the 'other place' which you will have made with your Temple layout. In all systems, from those of the old, outdoor witches, to the most sophisticated lodge rooms of the Golden Dawn at the turn of the century, every group is aiming to enter a 'place that is between the worlds.' This is where the reality of the realm of magic can be approached most safely by those who live in the mundane state. Here you can confer with powers, discuss your life with your Holy Guardian Angel, receive information and healing, and accept the inner initiations which give you your own abilities.

Each ritual will have a pattern and a purpose. The pattern is generally much the same, although it may be elaborated for more important workings, and simplified if you are alone or just practising with your companion. The main sorts of rituals will fall into the following categories: active, where you are making something, consecrating a talisman, healing, or celebrating a festival; or passive, where you are seeking information, perhaps through divination, pathworking, or by direct inspiration. As you gain more skill and confidence, and as you and your partner make more of the equipment and see more clearly the path you wish to tread together, gradually your work will attract the attention of an inner link or contact with the unseen and this will add power to everything you do.

'The Dweller on the Threshold'

Because ritual can have a profound effect upon anyone who hasn't tried it before, it is a good reason not to rush into it the moment you have read the first book on the subject. As you adjust to the 'place between the worlds,' you will become very aware of your own weaknesses and fears. This is often described in older books as 'The Dweller on the Threshold,' and an encounter with it can be very frightening indeed. It is much the safest course to be well aware of any doubts, failings, or actual fears derived from your previous experiences (in this current life, let alone earlier ones!). The Dweller or Shadow, to use Jung's term, is the hidden depths of your own nature, and contains the reverse, inwardly expressed aspects of your character. When you are seemingly kind and thoughtful towards others, your inner self may harbour feelings of cruelty or selfishness. You will have learned to come to terms with some of these darker feelings and so they will not bother you, but some may have been repressed, buried in the subconscious mind, and the first, basic acts of ritual fling open the door of their prison. This can give you a nasty shock if you are not prepared.

Another thing to bear in mind is that you will be dealing with forces which can shift the stars in their courses and direct the patterns of whole universes—not to be dabbled with by amateurs for an afternoon's entertainment! You will also, within the setting of even the simplest rite, be entering a paradoxical world where everything is true and nothing is proven. On the one hand, you will be attempting to make changes, albeit small ones, in your own future, and on the other, aiming not to affect the lives of anyone else because that is unethical. It is a very narrow path, sometimes referred to as the 'sword bridge' in myth. Taking care with what you are doing before you begin can save you a lot of anguish at a later stage, and in magic, ignorance is never a suitable defence!

The Group Soul

In the inner world of the magical Temple, whether it is a properly constructed lodge room set up by trained initiates to comply with a particular tradition derived from antiquity, or the eastern corner of your Balham bed-sit, it can be a very strange experience, entering this special place and becoming one with its symbolism. You will also be sharing with your companion not only the work of constructing this Temple, but the offering of your own energies, and theirs, so that the combined work may be accomplished. In return you will both receive knowledge, strength, and insights about your work from then onwards. This sharing with another person can feel rather strange too, because each of you has a natural flow of energy, a personal level of perception and commitment, and an individual perception of what is going on. Each of you will gradually have to learn the patterns of the other or others and blend in to one harmonious and comfortable pattern. Even two people can develop a Group Soul. It will eventually be through this shared yet deeper and wider level of consciousness that you will be able to enter, through regular ritual practice, the inner world of the reality of magic. You may seek knowledge from the Akashic Record, in which all human history is recorded, on such diverse subjects as for example the method and reasons for the construction of ancient stone circles, the ceremonies conducted in the Temples of Atlantis, and minor activities in your previous life before last as a horse trainer among the Mongol hoards! It is a source of great wisdom and any attempts to enter the Halls of Learning should be seen as serious journeys of exploration and inner awakening, not a casual stroll to fill in a rainy afternoon.

Of course, it is unlikely that your first assays in ritual work will have such profound consequences, especially if you tread carefully and step onto a well-worn path, but anyone who picks up some old book, and has a go, for fun, to raise spirits or call upon the dead can scare themselves silly because they do not realize what forces they are dealing with. People who play with magic for a joke, or pretend to be wiser or better trained than they are can end up in a very unpleasant state of mindlessness, because without taking reasonable precautions, they allow other entities to infest them, like mental lice, and these are not easy to shift. Certainly the average doctor in the mental health service is hardly likely to recognize a genuine possession or know how to deal with it. There may be many people who have played with this sort of fire who are now imprisoned by some aspect of another consciousness parasitically attached to what is left of their own mind. It won't happen if you are acting sensibly because the Gods protect those who seek proper knowledge and enlightenment.

Preparation for Ritual

The patterns of rituals can be changed to suit your immediate aims and needs, but generally there are the following points which ought to be considered:

1. What is the purpose of the ritual? You can't just DO ritual!

2. What is needed to make it work—people, robes, equipment, etc.?

3. When is the best time to do it? Consider ordinary matters as well as the astrological moment, days of the planets concerned, and the correct time for the best results.

4. What sorts of results are you expecting? For example, a genuine physical healing, the arrival of a piece of information, or the specific answer to a prayer for a new job, etc.

5. How do you intend that the ritual be performed? Do you know the symbols which are most relevant, or the Goddess/God/Power whose help is required? How will you contact them?

If your purpose is very simple and you have already collected or made your robes and the symbolic elements, you will already be able to go into the planning phase. Again, although an experienced ritualist can simply get on with the action, beginners are seriously advised to plan, understand, and rehearse every aspect of a ceremony. This will make the eventual performance ten times more effective and a good deal safer than plunging in headlong. A ritual is not merely the actual rite, but the build-up of equipment, ideas, and choice of symbols, God names, and objectives too. Every factor is important because, like the computer program, each bit has a specific function which is much greater than the thing itself. Time can be important too. If you are celebrating a solstice, when the sun stands still at the junction of Sagittarius and Capricorn in winter, and Gemini and Cancer in the summer; or the equinoxes, when day and night are equal between the signs of Pisces/Aries in March, and Virgo/Libra in September, you are aiming for a precise time when the sun changes sign. This is shown in an ephemeris which is a list of tables from which astrologers derive their data. You will find an ephemeris very useful if you wish to discover days or nights when certain favourable alignments of planets are to occur. This is important in the case of initiation, which is, after all, a mystical rebirth, so you may be acquiring a magical 'rebirthday' complete with a new horoscope for your magic personality, together with an occult name or motto. It is also a good idea to consult the ephemeris if you are beginning any project, for much the same reasons. If you wish to perform a certain ceremony, a quick look at the arrangements of the planets at the time can give some hints as to your likely success, and perhaps the manner in which this might be accomplished.

Pagan Feasts

You should be able to recognize the phase of the moon from a glance at the night sky, and also know the proper dates for the old pagan feasts if you intend incorporating these into your system of ritual or worship. In pre-literate times, festivals were set by what was happening in nature and not by some pre-ordained calendar date, as they might be now. Church festivals, except Easter which is still fixed by the moon (which is why it moves about so much), have been allocated to fixed dates, celebrating the life of Jesus or of the saints and so on. Many of these festivals are much older, beginning in pagan times as high points of the story of the Goddess of the Earth and her Lord, God of the Sky. Of course this pattern, reflected in the growth of crops and the activities of animals, differs from place to place and country to country. If you don't grow corn you can't celebrate the death of the Corn King, and where vines aren't grown you can't have a vintage feast. You must look at your homeland and actually witness when the first blossoms of the hawthorn (May) are to be seen so that you can celebrate May Day!

The oldest feasts are linked with the Goddess and the God as parts of a story in which their lives reflect those of Nature, but because of climate, location, and local soil these vary quite a bit from what the books say. Going quickly through the year, you begin with Celtic New Year which is about the beginning of November, or the solar year at the first point of Aries, or the calendar year, lst January! You will need to decide which makes most sense to you and your friends. Anyway, the festivals which SHOULD BE BASED ON WHAT NATURE IS DOING NO MATTER WHAT THE CALENDAR SAYS, give you the following: Candlemas or the Feast of St. Brigit, when the Goddess is welcomed back after the birth of her Son/Sun at Yuletide. It is the time for looking for a few of the first wild flowers in southern Britain, usually snowdrops whose white and green petals show they are linked with the White Goddess. Next, after the Spring Equinox, is May Eve or Beltane, a fire festival when cattle were brought from their winter quarters and turned out on the high mountain pastures. It is celebrated when hawthorn blossoms, again white, are to be seen. After midsummer and the longest day, you have the start of the harvest, Lammas (Loaf-mass from the Saxon, when the first new grain was baked into bread). Here the God as spirit of the Corn becomes Lord of the Under/Otherworld, a place of magic and eternal youth, and corn dollies are made to keep his spirit of fertility until the spring sowing. When the harvest is in and the Autumn Equinox and the Feast of St. Michael (a very pagan saint) has gone by, comes the fire feast of Hallowe'en, Samhain, the end of summer when all flocks and herds and family are gathered in for the cold dark. Games with apples, the fruits of the Celtic Tree of Immortality, are played. People duck for them in buckets of water, eat them from strings, or cast the carefully pared skin over their shoulders to form an omen of the first letter of a special person's name. Hazelnuts from the tree of wisdom are eaten, and some are used to foretell events when cast into the fire, hissing or bursting as nature demands. If you think about it, dressing up, 'Trick or Treat' and many other games, including Bonfire Night with its fireworks, can be traced right back to much older feasts and gatherings.

If you celebrate these, together with Yuletide and Twelfth Night (when the Mabon, the young Sun King sets out on his journey as champion of the Goddess) and either new or full moon, you will have plenty of occasions for rituals incorporating part of the legend, or the symbols of each, as well as its aspects of magic. Each ancient festival has certain magical activities or powers associated with it, and if you devote a little time getting to know the cycles of Nature, she will teach you her secrets.

Planning the Ritual

Whether your ritual is to be a religious celebration of a season, or just a working for a particular purpose, you will find that developing it around a pattern will help you and your partner to achieve the steady build-up of force, and a greater awareness of your entry into that 'other world' of magical reality. You will find appropriate things to say or do (in fact you can mime an entire ritual to music, or dance it, or act out what you wish without saying a word, so you won't disturb the family or neighbours). The best for YOU will be those you have created for yourselves, rather than picking out someone else's invocations, taken out of the context they were part of, and mixing systems of symbols. This is particularly dangerous as some systems are not compatible, just as a computer programmed in Basic will not respond to commands in Algol or Fortran, and the incorrect instruction can wipe a program or blow up a chip! By all means, on different occasions, work with Egyptian God forms, or Qabalistic angels, or Celtic heroes, but don't try them all together—it's an explosive mixture. If you are a novice, work in your own language, inventing or allowing yourself to be gently inspired by the Goddess of Wisdom in the art of ritual invocations and actions. Ask and you will be taught!

Here is a list of points to go through for most rituals. You will find them in older systems, but you can design totally new workings on a similar ground plan. First you must mutually decide your purpose and collect all the items you require, both as personal attire and symbols of the Elements, bread/wine/salt for the ritual meal (or whatever set or similar items you prefer to use), then follow these steps:

1. Bless yourself—something like the invocation on page 146 will do.

2. Bless the room, making it a holy place, by first asking that the symbols of Earth, Water, Fire, and Air may purify and clear the atmosphere, and then carrying these symbols around, sharing the words/work with your companion.

3. Allow your magical personality to flow over you, perhaps during a short meditation, pathworking, or similar exercise.

4. State the purpose of the working, and call upon the Goddess of the season, or the angel of the work, or the power of healing, etc. This ensures that you and your companion(s) all know what you are doing, and can agree and focus on this aim.

5. Now is this time to actually tell the story of the festival, set out and consecrate the talisman, concentrate on directing a

healing power, or allow yourselves to sink deeper into the inner atmosphere of your Temple so that you can receive instruction, guidance, or inspiration. This may be helped with music, or by another pathworking, or by each person in turn adding to the narrative. You may seek a Guide or the Goddess now.

6. Next comes the ceremonial sharing of the Bread and Salt and Wine. The Bread is the fruit of the Earth, and the Salt represents the Mysteries which are hidden in all things, yet the magician can sense them and work with them. The Wine is both Water and Spirit, for it is the culmination of the essence of the God. You may bless each item in the name of which ever Goddess/God/Angel seems most appropriate. Always offer the Cup with both hands, and accept it in the same way. Take a piece of bread or biscuit and dip it into the salt. Acknowledge in words or gestures that in sharing the sacred feast you are one with all nature. You may pour a few drops of wine and scatter some crumbs on the earth, or onto a dish of earth placed there for libations, as a thanks offering. Again wait to see if you can feel the presence of any holy forces at this time.

7. It is traditional to face each point of the compass and offer a prayer for such things as Peace in the World; for healing of those known and unknown; for harmony with the Earth and the force of Nature; and for a greater understanding of the Mysteries. Add any other ideas you may have, slowly and with sincerity.

8. Unwind the circle and allow the ring of protection to ebb away gradually. Feel a sensation of peace, awareness, and harmony between you and with the whole world. Pinch out any candles, although a central flame may be left lit, so long as it is safe.

9. Disrobe and gently awaken to a new and clearer awareness, relaxed and fully conscious of anything which may have occurred during the ceremony. You may even KNOW by now what the result of your talisman, healing, or other work will be, and when its results will be obvious.

10. Clear up and put things away. Cast out the libation bowl onto real earth, unless you have been working outdoors, where this pattern may be followed, but with less parapher-

nalia. In a glade you can use a stone or tree stump for an altar, wands from trees as your ritual staffs, a rock for Earth, a little Water, a small, safe lantern for Fire, and a smoulder- ing incense pot for Air. Even in your Temple a sea-smoothed stone or river-rolled rock will be a useful item on which any power may safely be earthed. If it is too big to go on the altar, place it on the floor on the north side, where you can touch it with your foot or hand if necessary. (This can help you come back to reality after a simple meditation.) Climb a mountain and bring back a sacred rock or slab and with it the memories of its home.

Writing down rituals and sharing these can lessen their power, and you will discover that any prayers or ceremonial invocations taken from books will not feel as effective as those you have created for yourself. The same applies to equipment. You can order every- thing from an occult supplier but none of it will be as effective as the things you make yourself. Even if you are not very skilled at any handicrafts there is nothing to stop you learning by practical experience, and it is surprising what you manage if you try. One set of objects you and your partner might like to have a go at making are the containers for the elements. A pack of quick-drying model- ling clay will make a set to hold incense sticks or cones, a candle, water, and a flat dish or platter which is the symbol of earth. With a little ingenuity you can wind a small strip of clay around a pen- cil or wooden spoon handle and by carving the top of it with a pin, make the centre of a flower which holds the incense. Next, make a flatter dish with a thick bottom into which you can press a short, fat candle. The lower level will be a wider dish with petal edges and enough of a dip in the centre to take the water. The last piece of clay is made into a circle, about half an inch (1 cm) thick onto which you can mark or later paint leaves and symbols. Each item should fit into the one below so that the whole form a flower, either the English rose, long associated with the Mysteries of the Rosy Cross, or the Eastern Lotus, with pointed petals and the flat, almost round leaves of water lilies.

17

MAGICAL EXPERIMENTS
WITH TIME

'Eye-witness account of the Battle of Hastings,' 'Temple of the Sun finally completed—architect explains 200 year delay . . . ,' 'Housewife remembers being Rameses II.' These are often the sorts of headlines found in recent books about past-life recall, or in scoffing accounts in the newspapers, and they can detract from an important aspect of magical work.

Magic has always been associated with Time—recent research is confirming that the most ancient sacred sites have markers which indicate special rising or setting points of the Sun, Moon, or some of the stars; especially many of the great outdoor sanctuaries in the British Isles and Europe. Time was magic, especially when the priests were able to predict the coming of eclipses, storms, and important times in the farming calendar and so help their people achieve successful harvests and fruitful cattle. Magic is also associated with time in that astrology is one of the oldest arts within the scope of seekers of knowledge, and depends on the exact positions of the Sun, Moon, and planets in relation to the Earth at the time of birth of a child, from which trends in his life may be worked out. Magicians have often used astrological data to discover the most potent moment when the beneficial planets are in line to perform some complex magical operation or ritual. They also look at the horoscope of a person who may have come for help to see if his 'bad luck' or illness could be in any way affected by the planets.

Most traditional schools of magic hark back to ancient times. They are based on the wisdom of Ancient Egypt, Chaldea, China, India, or even Atlantis or earlier cultures.

People from the remote past were always considered to be more knowledgeable, philosophical, or informed and this 'lost knowledge' is sought by many students of occultism. Witches try to prove their coven has its roots in the Stone Age, or that all legends of the Gods go back to a 'common hero tale' of some lost Titan or mythological king who ruled in Lemuria. Some students forget that knowledge is expanding all the time. We now know far more about the world, its people, customs, and ancient skills than our grandparents could ever have known, and certainly generations before that had access to even less information!

However, the past does have a great attraction for seekers, especially now when the rational, standardized ideas of Pisces are giving way to the wider, free-thinking ways of the Aquarian Age. In the quest for personal identity, which is one of the first and hardest lessons of the true occult student, any application of successful techniques which leads to deeper personal understanding is worthwhile. It is for this reason that many people are now attempting experiments in 'past-life recall' by a variety of methods.

Past-Life Recall

Some venturers into times past make this mental journey because they have fears and phobias and no amount of probing into events in this current life has been able to cast any light upon the origins of these anxiety states. Some people are convinced they were kings or pharaohs, priestesses or queens in previous lives and wish to find further evidence of their historical fame. There is a wellworn joke about the guests at a 'Come as you were' party all turning up as Cleopatra, Napoleon, Julius Caesar, or Mary Queen of Scots. Sadly, many very ordinary people, in their current lives, do have these notions about their power and position in the past, but seldom do they exhibit now the wisdom or strength of character their previous 'self' would have needed to stay in power.

Magicians often make this voyage into the unknown past because they are certain many of the occult skills they seem to show now, like clairvoyance, the knowledge of symbolism, or the ability to handle the power of magic comes from advanced training in some temple school in the remote past. Many accept the fact that much of the lost wisdom of the past may be recovered if those who were living when it was first taught could remember what was shown to them. This applies in the fields of healing, especially as there is increasing interest in alternative forms of therapy, many of which (like acupuncture, for example) are extremely ancient. It is clear that a great deal of herb lore has been forgotten and that other techniques of massage, manipulation, or simple plant medicine have been lost because they were not written down.

Some people are merely curious about who they might have been in the past, or if they in fact had any kind of previous existence at all. They are encouraged in their interest by the considerable number of published accounts, books, and assorted media information on the exploits of other explorers of the inner world. Joan Grant set the scene a good few years ago with her 'novels,' which she wrote as autobiographical accounts of her previous existences among the Temples of Egypt and the forests of the Red Indians, and so on. Others have followed a similar path, sometimes interweaving their memories with those of close friends, doctors, or family, to build a complex web of relationships left over from hundreds of years before. The evidence is certainly mounting, but it would be unwise to accept every part of it without allowing your critical faculties to come into play. It is too simple to say that everyone who relaxes after a Sunday lunch and suddenly discovers he is in High Street, Jerusalem, one spring morning is actually about to witness the crucifixion of Jesus the Nazarene; or that the ladies who imagine themselves the reborn Nell Gwyn or Lady Hamilton do so because of recurring dreams or images awoken by a good novel or film.

The reason for seeking information about past events in your own life track can probably be identified as one of the following:

1. Plain curiosity.

2. A genuine desire to uncover historical facts (which may not imply personal memory or reincarnation).

3. A wish to discover all that can be known about yourself as an eternal individual, including faults, fears, and failings.

4. To see if you can uncover information or 'lost knowledge' in any field of past expertise, especially healing, science, and magic.

It doesn't really matter under which heading your own aims may lie as the techniques readily available could be useful in any case, but if you don't feel personally involved in past ages, then you will be able to view any scenes or other information which you may encounter without necessarily being 'part of' it. Certainly people's experiences vary quite a lot, depending on what method is used to invoke the past to the awareness, and it may take a number of attempts before even the slightest indication that you are able to travel back in time is apparent. Also, it is worthwhile trying out different approaches even if the first one seems to get results.

Reincarnation

If you are going to start delving about into your previous incarnations, or assist your magical partner or a friend in this work, there are a number of things you should bear firmly in mind before you begin. DELVING INTO THE PAST CAN BE VERY FRIGHTENING. Reincarnation implies previous DEATH and this is still a subject which scares people silly! Death in the past was far from pleasant—dying of disease, injury, or battle wounds without the aid of modern painkillers and drugs—and if it is your last death you are re-experiencing then you may perceive a lot more sensation than you care to feel. When you actually enter a previous life, you reawaken all your old senses too, so be prepared. (You can practise by remembering any frightening events in this life, like car crashes, accidents, or serious illnesses, to find out how well you can remember and tolerate that memory before you tackle any greater adventure.) The same applies if you are helping someone else, because they can become very scared indeed if they enter a phase from the past when they were in danger or dying and so on.

There are a number of other basic bits of information to consider fully before you set out to open old doors of memory. The first is the time factor—I mean present time. You cannot fit in a quick session before a TV programme starts, before dinner, or after putting the children to bed, etc. Time travel and exploration is a long-term and slow business. To reach even a state of mind where it is possible to go through time at all may take at least an hour, and once you do encounter a method which works you can spend hours trying to find out who you are and when you are living. And that is only the beginning! Logically, you must realize that to live through many of the episodes of a previous existence can take almost as long as the life in question. In practice, it doesn't take THAT long, but to analyse any significant amount of relived experience can take much longer than you might think. It isn't as if you can simply switch between then and now sequentially, either. The bits you recall will be fragmentary, scattered, and incohesive, just as your memories of childhood are. Some events stick out clearly in your mind, even after many years; others are totally forgotten. For example, when did you first ride a bicycle or swim one length of the pool? What did it feel like to learn to write and what books did you actually read unassisted? Who was your first friend and under what ruler was your country then? In the past all these details could help you to pinpoint the era and place, the position and authenticity of your last life. It is the minor details of costume and climate, food and scenery which tell you that you are in eighteenth century London, or fifth century Italy, or tenth century China—you don't often find a newspaper to hand!

There are a variety of methods which you can use to try to awaken past-life information, or simply rediscover historical events (from an 'eyewitness' viewpoint, if you don't accept reincarnation, genetic memory, or any other continuation of the individual, immortal human spirit). Some of these are straightforward and can be begun alone; others rely very definitely on the assistance of one or two really trustworthy companions, who must be prepared to take notes or make recordings patiently and conscientiously for however long it takes to get useful material. They must remain calm and comforting if the time traveler is going through a difficult event, and help him or her to get back into present time safely and fully at the end of each session. This is no light undertaking, and ought not to be tried unless you are sure you can commit the necessary time and effort—either as the past adventurer or companion. Even if you begin your travels using one of the most basic methods, later on you may well require assistance to document and research any material you have uncovered, or to try different ways of dipping into the past which require the guidance of a companion.

Another thing to consider before you begin is whether you already have an inkling of when you were last on earth. Quite often images from childhood, or repeated dream-scapes can give you a clue. You may also have had experiences of *déjà vu,* that is a distinct feeling of having 'seen before' some place that you are certain you haven't actually visited. Often you can remember having a dream of the place before you arrive, sometimes a long while before, or you can describe what is round corners or inside buildings before you get there. It is possible that room settings in museums or antique furniture or old objects can spark off a memory as well. In fact, these can be used to encourage or confirm material as one of the experimental techniques which are recommended for you to try.

As well as a reliable companion or two (with whom you can exchange roles, allowing them also to explore the past if they so wish), you will need a good tape or cassette recorder and notebook. Although tape recorders are useful and generally reliable, sometimes the time traveler is talking too quietly for the microphone to pick up the words clearly. This may often be the case with machines with a built-in, rather than separate microphone. Also it is possible that some sessions may run on for longer than it takes to record on one side of a cassette tape. A brief note of information, a name, place, time, or detail of costume or food written down may be the vital key not transferred to the tape recorder. It is also much quicker to flick through written notes than to search back and forth along an hour or so of taped information. In some cases, the traveler's face, expression, voice and accent will change considerably and if you wish to record this evidence you might want to resort to a video recorder if one is available. Occasionally the time adventurer might want to draw or write, so spare paper and pens should always be to hand. As the relaxed state which is best for receiving information can leave the experimenter feeling cold or hungry, a hot drink and a snack should be available so that he doesn't forget what he has discovered whilst boiling the kettle or rummaging for the biscuit tin!

There are a number of other things which, depending on your previous experience and skill in magical techniques, should be considered. It is generally thought that a witch's magical circle or the magician's temple is a place 'outside time,' or where time is stopped or changed. Certainly, if you have been meditating successfully, or even merely day-dreaming, you will have discovered how time can slip by unnoticed. Sleeping too, switches off your sense of time actually passed, and dreams can appear to have lasted for several days, or during a sleepless night, the hours of darkness may appear to stretch for ages! This applies to your journeys out of time. If you are traveling you may be totally unaware of how long you have been away from present time, and it will be your companion who grows weary and gently calls you back at the conclusion of a lengthy session.

Techniques for Recalling Past Lives

In order to escape into the past in a way in which you are totally in control, you will need to practise the different techniques to find which suits you best. The main ones are meditation and dreaming, when you are probably working alone and doing your best to record material as you remember it. Although these are suitable approaches for people with little spare time they do have snags. When meditating you cannot easily direct the line of your meditation without interfering with the flow of consciousness, and perhaps influencing the material which you later remember. In dreams you have even less ability to direct or control what you are apparently experiencing, and as mentioned before, some of the past-life material can be very frightening. It is no consolation to your sleeping partner if you wake up from one of your experiments at four in the morning convinced you have been shot with arrows, poisoned, or are dying of plague!

Methods in which the traveler retains control over his state of consciousness include magical hypnosis, the Christos technique, guided meditation, or pathworking. Other methods can include psychometry, where old objects (for example, the standing stones in an ancient sacred circle, or tapestries from a medieval castle walls) may be felt whilst in a calm and relaxed state, and so pictures may arise. These don't necessarily turn out to be actual personal past-life material, but it is an approach worth experimenting with. Again, by visiting those museums or stately homes where room settings give a clear feeling of past ages, and allowing yourself to sink into a quiet, meditative mood, you may discover clues as to whether that period seems familiar or not. Of course, your earlier lives may have been lived in different countries, cultures, and levels of society, so visiting local collections or old houses may not help. None the less, it is worth exploring a variety of ancient places or getting the feel of old tools, jewellery, or fabrics in case they do spark off that first bit of far memory from which a complete picture may eventually be built up.

Hypnotism

Although most textbooks on hypnotism suggest that the hypnotist is in control, in actual practice, within the magical (as opposed to the clinical/medical or psychiatric) application of the technique, the subject can determine the depth to which he will sink, and at what point he wishes to awaken. Although during the experiment he is willing to accept the suggestions of the hypnotist, whom he must like and trust and have already decided to cooperate with, he can terminate the altered state at will. Another misconception about hypnotism is that the subject is totally unconscious, that is 'asleep,' when in fact, he may well be even more alert and aware than he is when not in that particular altered state. That is where the crux lies—it is an altered state of CONSCIOUSNESS! Obviously, it is not a technique to be applied without training and plenty of experience, because it can be alarming to both the subject and the hypnotist if some unthinking suggestion is given which cannot be countermanded, and the very relaxed subject may not feel able to return to a normal waking state unaided. Any serious book on the subject will give clear warnings as to this point. Also, any suggestions which imply the subject is losing control of his senses, his feelings, or his body should never be given as they can cause fear and resentment, and prevent any real results being achieved. In the hands of a skilled and sympathetic hypnotist this can be one of the most useful techniques which assist the time traveler to make his first journeys of exploration. It also has the advantage that if he is given a key word or phrase, he will be able to return to the state for further explorations without needing to undergo a lengthy induction process. Unless you are very sure that you know what you are doing, though, you should not use hypnosis nor subject yourself to the suggestions of an untrained individual.

The Christos Technique

The Christos technique was first described by Glaskin, in his book *Windows of the Mind*. Here there are three operators: one is the traveler; another massages the area of the third eye on the traveler's forehead; and the other person massages his or her ankles. It is then suggested that the traveler, who usually lies flat on a couch or the floor, is able to expand and then contract his or her length. After various other instructions are given, the traveler is asked to project his or her awareness out of the body to examine the outside of the front door, and then the roof of the house. Other suggestions of flying are given, over a fairly long period of time, obviously depending on the response to the previous instructions. Gradually the traveler is encouraged to fly away and eventually land at some distant place, both in space and time, and describe to the operators what he or she is able to see or sense. There have been many hundreds of successful trips of this sort made by meditators and students of magic in groups all over the world and a large percentage of them seemed to be able to transcend time and distance and explore other ages and places.

Pathworking

Another method, which for novices is probably the safest, is the use of pathworking. It has the advantage that it may be done with a group of experimenters who all want to see if they are able to travel outside time, to give them the chance to make an exploratory journey under controlled conditions. For this, many of the original criteria apply; that is, plenty of time, a relaxed atmosphere, recording equipment including pens and paper, and a reliable and calm individual who is prepared to lead the group on their mental journey, and help any who stray off the path, or become alarmed at their experiences. Although an initial journey may be shared by a small group (not exceeding four travelers), later sessions using this technique ought to be on an individual basis. As with all pathworkings, plenty of time should be allowed for the experimenters to explore and experience whatever they come across during their mental archaeological digs.

Once all distracting noises such as the telephone and other occupants of the house have been silenced, it is as well to have a few moments of quiet reflection and calming and relaxing exercises. Everyone tries to become mentally still yet alert and ready for the adventure to begin. Each should be seated comfortably, with his head and neck well supported so that he can breathe easily, and his feet should rest on the floor or some supporting books so that he is balanced. A little quiet music may be played to set the mood, and then the leader begins her narrative, which might go something like the following:

> You are all coming with me on a journey back through time. You
> will always be able to talk and to breathe easily. Whatever you see

or experience will not harm you, and you may return here at any moment. Firstly I want you to fix your attention on the door to this room. Look at it now and remember it, and then close your eyes and allow yourself to sink down in relaxation. The reason to recall the door is that it is your 'way back.' If you become frightened, feel as if you are in danger, or you have had enough, simply see that door, as you did a moment ago, and then you will find yourself safely back here, alert and calm.

Speak very slowly, pausing between sentences both during the instructions and later on during the journey, so that everyone has plenty of time to try to see or experience (some people feel, sense, or glimpse) the scenes you may describe. Keep your eyes on the experimenters so that you notice any signs of distress. If anyone does look as if they are having a tough time, gently call their name and remind them of the door to return by. Don't panic or shake anyone who is relaxed or meditating, etc., just continue to speak firmly and quietly until they open their eyes and look alert—then continue the narrative in this sort of manner:

You are now going on a journey back through time to try and locate an age or place where you lived in a previous life. If I speak to you by name, please answer, as you will be able to do, otherwise just observe or sense whatever you can. If you get scared, look at the door and return here in your own time. You are quite safe and this is an experiment which many have safely tried before.

We are now traveling along a road which you know well. As you go along, you discover it is beginning to change from the tarmac and modern buildings which you are familiar with. There are trees and hedges and the pavement is giving way to a rough earth surface, rutted and marked by horses' hooves and the waggons they pull. As you walk slowly down this road to the past, time is flying by you, and lost ages are coming into focus. Gradually you will be able to see scenes which were familiar to you in your last life.

Elaborate this text as much as you wish, but try not to give direct suggestions, like 'There is a lady in seventeenth century dress coming towards you,' or 'Some Vikings are carrying their battle axes and shields up from their long ship moored in the river.' Set a scene which might suit any past age, or even place, so that everyone can create or remember details as he sinks deeper into this time journey. Watch each individual and then ask them in turn, by name, 'John, what can you see?', 'Mary, is there a house nearby?', 'Bill, are there any people where you are and what are they doing?', and so on, round the group. Allow then time to speak, as they may feel very remote and relaxed. Record what each says. Some will experience nothing, merely a feeling of peace and relaxation. Others may see clearly and distinctly and be able to describe intricate details of costume, scenery, activities, and buildings.

I want you now to look at any person you can see. Is it a lady or a man? Are they working at something or standing about?

Are there any houses or other buildings? Can you see any animals, trees, or other aspects of the landscape which shows you are not at home, in the time of your present body?

Turn to your right and see what lies on that side. Look at every possible thing because you will be able to remember it. Feel the air; is it summer or winter? What is the state of the vegetation, or are you inside a building? Is there any form of transport nearby? You will clearly remember every part of what you are seeing and sensing, so now try to discover as much as you can about your environment.

Allow a pause of five to ten minutes, and unless anyone is looking restless or showing any other sign of stress, leave them to it. Even those who claimed not to have seen anything, unless they are obviously already bored by the whole experiment, should be allowed time to try and find out something new. You can ask each individual after a suitable silence, if they wish to continue, or to return to the present day, or you might prefer to encourage them to remember a particular detail of the scene in their mind's eye so that they can return to it on a later occasion. Tell them to be very aware of how they actually feel: relaxed or tense, interested or weary, if they are enjoying the experiment or finding it hard to concentrate and so on. (This 'state report' can often help in later experiments because by recalling feelings and sensations, it is possible to mentally replicate these, and then return to that time or place on another occasion.)

Now it is time to return back to the old road and you will see there is a clear way for you to follow. You may walk slowly so that you perceive all the details of everything about you. Every part of the journey will remain clear in your mind as you return along the road through time. You will see that your steps are now on a smooth pavement, and the buildings are familiar. Gradually and gently you are returning to the door which you recognize as the one to this room. Slowly you will open your eyes and stretch, and before you discuss anything you will jot down some personal notes of your experiences and vision. Slowly, feeling quite safe and relaxed, you will return to be among us all here, in your own time.

There are many variations on this theme of a road or journey through time and it seems to work better than simply 'jumping back.' After a few attempts most people will begin to perceive, on one level or another, fragments of the 'other where or when.' Work slowly in this experiment, taking your own turn as a traveler, and allowing different people to narrate their version of the path through time. Learn from your group's experiences and make use of any helpful ideas which may come during any of the trips. Try to keep accurate and full records, even if you don't get clear pictures or details. These will come with practice. After all, it may well be a culture shock to discover your 'self' in another body, possibly of the opposite sex, in a distant time and place, playing a quite different role in a strange society.

How can you prove you are actually reliving a previous life and not just making it up, remembering the scenes from a vivid book or film, or simply deluding yourself on an ego trip? Well, you know yourself. If you remember a frightening moment in this life, what happens to you? How do you feel about the near or actual car accident, the serious illness, the death of a beloved? You ought to sense something in those situations which are physiologically detectable. The same applies to past life experiences. You 'feel' them just as you 'feel' fears or remembered pains in the present life. Try it and compare your reactions.

Clearly it will take many sessions before you begin to build up any great amount of information, but once you have discovered a way which opens the door to the past easily and effectively, gaining an entire collection of past-life material is only a matter of perseverance. You will probably find that your memories are not neat and sequential and that you can't leave off at one point and then return during your next attempt to the experience which follows chronologically. Often you seem to hop between several different and sometimes widely separated lifetimes, seeing scenes from different phases of each, but following no obvious plan. The same could be said about memories in this life. What you remember about your childhood may well be scattered fragments covering ten or twelve years! When you are surveying the material gathered over any number of previous lives, the problem is decidedly greater. Patience is the only answer. Gather all the material you can, and try to reject anything which you know can be traced to a book or film, etc. The human memory has enormous capacity, and though it may not always be easy to gain access to its storage system, a lot of experiences are stashed away in there somewhere, not only from this life, but from many others, in most cases.

If you find yourself living before the 1500s, traceable history becomes much harder to locate, being far more fragmentary and vague. This doesn't invalidate your recalled information, unless you are determined to convince a sceptic of the reality of reincarnation. This sort of experimental work is really for the magical student who wants to know himself in order to realize his entire potential, to develop new sources of ancient wisdom or to uncover the answers to those esoteric problems which are part of the Mysteries. Where and when was Atlantis? How did they build Stonehenge? For what purpose were the many 'burial' mounds and barrows actually constructed? Who was King Arthur and what did happen to Merlin? Do they still both sleep under some hill?

Maybe you will unravel some of these age-old mysteries, or produce the answer to the ultimate question. Perhaps you will write a series of fascinating books based on your earlier biographies, or provide information which conventional historians or archaeologists can confirm in due course. Maybe you were Napoleon or one of the Cleopatras, how does this knowledge benefit you in the twentieth century? More important, how does it benefit the rest of humanity? Karmic debts may still need to be repaid or old relationships worked through to a happy conclusion.

18

THE MAGIC OF SPACE TRAVEL

Today the idea of spacecraft visiting distant planets and space shots to explore the mantle of the sun are almost commonplace, and films and TV shows have made the universe seem quite small and close at hand. In the past such journeys, or even the notion that mankind would one day step upon the surface of the moon or planets was unthinkable, yet even in most ancient times magicians and wise folk have been able to project some aspect of their consciousness through space, and being invisible, witness events at considerable distances, or bring news of straying travelers to their families at the speed of thought.

There are really two aspects of this mental journeying and it is well worth the effort to make experiments in both types of 'space travel.' One is Divination, where by using symbols (such as the Tarot cards, the *I Ching* hexagrams, or even a crystal ball) you are helping to focus your inner sight, clairvoyance, or psychic vision on matters which may be occurring at a distance, or back or forward in time as well. Most often, this form of magical skill is applied to help or advise another person and so it carries a heavy responsibility. No one wants advice from a clairvoyant who is wrong! Also, if you give advice to other people, their lives may be shaped by your words, and you take on the responsibility for giving good and accurate assistance to them. If you should misjudge a situation you can bring unhappiness, distress, or trouble to those you are aiming to help. It is a heavy burden, too often taken up without forethought or consideration of the implications of psychic counselling. If you tell folk what to do, you get involved in their karma, and webs of commitment and attachment are woven between you.

The other form of travel is often called 'Mindreach' or Astral travel, and in this case, although it may be used as a form of clairvoyance, it is more often carried out as experiments in which your awareness is projected out of the place where your body is resting so that you can perceive events at any distance, either nearby, or at any other point on planet Earth, or even out into space. It is a skill which may be developed from basic methods you should have learned already, like meditation and creative visualization. You may also be able to master the art by developing a pathworking which begins in your own home and ends in outer space.

Of course, there are many points which are common to both approaches and both require a lot of experimental work and practice. To learn the meaning of the symbols on each of the Tarot cards can be a lengthy enough business on its own, without adding to it the ability to change into that relaxed state of consciousness where pictures arise unbidden to expand the basic knowledge of each card's meaning within the spread. This is made harder by the presence of the person who has asked you to consult the cards on his behalf. It is much easier, within the still, clear atmosphere of the magical temple or special place, to allow the extra dimensions of information to flow through your awareness, than when you have someone sitting near you, concerned about the matter for which they have sought an answer. It is like the difference between trying to read a clearly printed book in your own language, and needing to decipher a note scribbled by a friend on a piece of newsprint which has accidentally gone through the laundry! When you are 'astral traveling' you may encounter similar problems.

Divination

Taking the matter of divination first, because it is something most students of occultism add to the repertoire of healing, ritual, and meditation, there are lots of systems to choose from. Some use symbolic pictures or patterns from which information may be deduced: This covers not only the Tarot and the *I Ching* but also astrology, tea-leaf reading, the shape of an individual's handwriting, and the lines on his palm. In each case interpretations of each card, hexagram, planet's position, or line is combined with all the others in the divination, and from this much wider and more complex pattern, the future events, possibilities for the person's future, or aspects of his character which he may have overlooked can be developed and explained to him. It requires a lot of actual factual knowledge to recognize the significance of each of the seventy-eight Tarot cards, the sixty-four *I Ching* symbols, the ten planets/twelve signs/twelve houses, and all the relevant aspects of a person's horoscope, or the possible variations of line, slope, or pattern in someone's handwriting or palm. This body of information may be learned from a book, parrot-fashion, so that a beginner can chant 'Ten of Swords means complete disaster', or 'Sun in Aries shows you're a bold, assertive, bad-tempered individual . . .' and so on, which will give little comfort to the person they are, in theory, trying to help!

There are plenty of recently written and genuinely helpful books on every possible sort of divination but words are not sufficient to convey what is actually encapsulated in every symbol of any system. This wisdom has to be achieved by study, thought, and meditation. It cannot simply be read and remembered but has to come from within, and it is experimentation which brings the deeper understanding. You will need to be able to expand the bare details learned from a writer whose words make sense to you, and whose approach to the divination system you have chosen agrees with your own general theory. Some of these may be scholarly, others light-hearted; some may be psychologically orientated, some personal or historical. In each case, the way that you interpret the symbols as they have turned up in answer to some probably unexpressed question from your querent will vary with your own knowledge and the degree to which you are able to trust your own intuition in the matter. That, of course, is the key to an accurate and worthwhile reading. If your words only reflect some half-digested material gleaned from another's work, it will not show you the clear pictures, words, or other information which will help you pass on a good description of what may happen to your friend. You see, each divination symbol is really a reminder to you of some past event in your life/lives from which you can build a picture to convey to the person who needs your help. What actually happens to them won't be exactly the same as what you are remembering because that was a part of your own past, and the answer lies in their future.

The Tarot and the *I Ching*

In order to expand the amount of information you can extract from any card, you will need to work with it. (There are card packs for divination with the Tarot and its many variants, the *I Ching*, recently the Phoenix Runes as well as the Celtic Tree alphabet, and you may well encounter others.) The most effective way is to have a small, handy notebook and a new pack of your chosen cards. Shuffle the pack and place one card where you will see it. This need not be on an altar (although that is the best place), but a mantleshelf, on the kitchen wall, or even as a bookmark for when you are reading. Just allow any ideas, recollections, or thoughts which are in any way evoked by that image to filter into your awareness, and then jot these down in your notebook. Take a new card each day until you have done them all, and you will then find that simply to see any of the previous ones will immediately spark off a whole lot of information in your mind's eye. Later on you can add information gained from reading your chosen author upon that symbol. When you find the card in a future reading you will be able to draw a good word picture of it.

What will you be able to divine from such images, both on the cards and in your mind? Well, most querents will expect you to predict the future accurately. They will hope you can see the outcome of the situation they are in at present, and divine what factors will come into play in the days to come. You ought to be able to get a few details about the past of the individual or the events which have led up to the current difficulty, and even if you don't know what the exact problem is, this ought to be indicated by the first set of cards in the spread you are using, or in the initial hexagram of the *I Ching*. If the querent agrees that what you have said makes sense and relates to the problem he has in his head, or written on a slip of paper, or whatever method you use, then carry on. If the initial interpretation is way off mark, or doesn't make any sense, even to you, try again.

How does the above tie in with the concept of space travel, and how can your methods of reading be made more clear and accurate? Well, when you are performing a divination for someone else, their problem is not yours, and therefore it is at a distance from you. Whatever you discover will also happen at a distance or in the future of the other person, so in fact, this is a sort of mental space travel. In order to make it easier you should actually 'clear a space' in which you do the reading. You may well feel that you cannot put on full regalia and consecrate a circle as you would for any other ritual performance, unless (as is actually the best idea) you begin working with your magical companion on this art. If he or she is willing for you to learn to read the cards in answer to his or her future, or will perform a divination with the *I Ching* on your behalf, you can learn a great deal. You can also practise your consecrating skills, too, for any divination carried out within the mentally sterilized atmosphere of a magical temple or circle is much easier than one done in a crowded hall, surrounded by strangers. (Do bear this in mind if you have a reading done for you at an exhibition or garden fete!)

You will need to aim for a quiet atmosphere in which you can slip easily and gently into that altered state of awareness which comes from meditation and similar arts. You will be relaxed and unconcerned about ordinary events, but your mind will be clear, and whatever way information is given to you, it appears without effort as pictures, thoughts, symbols, flows of ideas, or memories, so that it is easy to grasp and understand. With the Tarot it is necessary to have your eyes open to examine the cards, but you can then close them and allow images to appear. Relate these to your companion, who should write down what you say.

Crystal Gazing

Another sort of divination you will need to experiment with is scrying. This is the art of crystal gazing or seeking pictures in a black mirror, a bowl of water, or a pool of black ink. In each case it is best tried within a consecrated circle which will banish those irritating psychic distractions which are present in everyday life. Allow yourself to sink into a relaxed state, perhaps at the suggestions of your companion, and then open your eyes to regard the crystal or other 'speculum' (scrying glass). Look within the glass, not at its surface, and ignore any reflections of your face or points of light that may be seen on its surface. Sink within it, forming a question in your mind to which you are seeking an answer. In a while, if you have reached the right level of distraction, you will find the glass seems to mist over, or become dim, and through the swirls of mist a dark patch may appear. You might find yourself sinking into this and then pictures, signs, numbers, words, or anything may appear before you. This probably will not happen in the first experiments you perform, but if you continue for a number of regular sessions, allowing your companion to try in between times, you will gradually master this ancient and very valuable skill.

Palmistry and Astrology

Other forms of divination, which may involve predicting the future, include palmistry and astrology. In the first case, as in psychometry (when you try to discover the history of an object, and thus details of its owner's life), you will be actually holding the hand of the person whose lines you are examining. Again learn this art with a friend, as holding hands with a stranger when you are in a receptive/perceptive mood can give a shock to the system—both yours and theirs! All kinds of impressions may flash through your mind's eye, almost too fast to grasp, and feelings, sensations, and even strong emotions may flood over you from this extremely powerful symbol of their past. Speak aloud whatever you discover, trying to focus your companion's attention on one particular question, for example, as this will cut down the background 'noise.' Take each of the lines in turn and try to see what has happened in that field. Health and intellect may be quite easy but the heart or 'love' line may give you some vivid impressions to interpret. Looking for the future will involve holding and comparing both hands, seeing what physical changes show between the left (potential patterns in right-handed people) and the right hand which shows what your companion has made of his or her initial advantages in life, in all fields. The shape and feel of a hand will tell you a lot about the person, as will the colour, strength, and depth of the marking indicate health and vigour. This works on an ordinary level, in that bitten nails and damaged quicks show a nervous disposition and lack of relaxation. As Sherlock Holmes knew, callouses and scars can indicate the sort of job a person does, for example. Don't ignore common sense when it comes to understanding the patterns in the lives of other people.

Modern works on psychology can provide a vast source of material about other people, and of course, yourself. Don't overlook anything which will make it easier to understand the workings of the human mind or the desires which motivate people to act. Simple introductory works on the theories of Carl Jung and other modern psychologists can provide valuable insight which can help you interpret a horoscope, read a palm, or divulge a character's secrets from a scribbled note. No one exactly fits the theoretical picture because people grow and change throughout their entire lives, and small-seeming experiences can change their attitude radically. Every divination is dealing with potential, both in the past and in the future. Not every potential musician takes up playing an instrument, any more than every healer is able to study medicine, yet now there are alternative applications of such talents, if they are discovered later in life.

To learn to travel through time for other people will require you to make some effort to understand what makes people tick, and learn the symbolism of whatever cards or other system you are using thoroughly, applying your own methods to expand and enhance that basic knowledge, probably gained from a book. You will need to practise being able to slip into a state of inner awareness where you can focus your attention on the past and future of the querent, and speak clearly of what you perceive. You will learn these arts within the quiet atmosphere of your magical circle with your regular occult companion, who can correct your visions, as you can assist him or her on experimental journeys through your past and future. Later on you may well be able to read the Tarot cards honestly and accurately, ignoring the crowds at a public show, or pick up clear and precise information about the future of a complete stranger when you take his hand at a party. This all comes with the application of concentration, study, and regular practice. Any art will get easier the more you work at it, especially if you are able to control the circumstances in which you make your initial experiments, as within a magic circle or temple environment. This also applies to your first trips 'out of the body' or astral traveling.

Astral Travel

To some students, the ability to project consciousness beyond the place where you are physically situated is looked upon as the pinnacle of esoteric achievement, to others it is as common an activity as dreaming. In all probability, dreaming in some cases is astral projection. It is an art which most people, when they have mastered it, seem to find rather unexciting. Like other forms of altered states of awareness, the concentration is on the CONSCIOUS-NESS, whether it be the ability to predict what will happen in the life of a friend, or to travel to the limits of the solar system just to see what it is like.

The methods to employ include some of those suggested in chapter 17, Magical Experiments with Time. The traveler will need to be in a comfortable position, in a place where they can be quiet and undisturbed for a considerable length of time, have a companion who can take notes and control a tape recorder or provide paper and pencils for diagrams or sketches, and the odd snack at the conclusion of an experiment. Ideally you will need to achieve a state of physical relaxation in which you are willing to accept that some part of your consciousness can extract itself from your body and venture off through space, unseen. There is quite a mystique about the idea of projecting consciousness, and some of the methods suggested by previous authors seem extremely complicated or unnecessarily elaborate for something most people do when they are asleep!

You should always have a companion on your initial journeys as you will be deeply relaxed and the prospect of disturbances such as the telephone ringing or a visitor turning up at a critical moment can ruin your explorations, and can prevent you arriving at the precise sort of balance between your 'body awareness' and your ability to be aware somewhere else, on other occasions. One very simple experiment to try is to ask your companion to go into another room in your home and place some object in an otherwise clear space, where it won't be disturbed. Your experiment is to relax and sink into an altered state of consciousness wherein your ability to see or sense things can slip away from your body. Ask your friend to be quiet for, say five minutes, and then gently say your name and ask if you can 'see' the object in the other room. It takes a certain knack to be able to do this first time, but by meditating first and getting really 'switched off,' you can often do it. Another experiment detailed in Targ and Puthoff's *Mind-Reach* involved the traveler relaxing in a silent and controlled room whilst a laboratory technician drove for half an hour to another location. Then the astral traveler 'saw,' as it were through the eyes of the other person, the location and its details which he then described in words on to tape, and in drawings or written description, after he had returned his awareness to his body. (It is possible to have dual consciousness, both of your body, and of the 'other location,' as you will probably discover during your own experiments, but it is much easier to 'return' before trying to write, speak, or otherwise communicate.) The laboratory technician in Targ's experiment also wrote, drew, and described his location, or took instant photographs, etc., and then the reports from both were compared by a separate team of judges who had to decide if the place described seemed to be the same.

These experiments were first carried out with the best 'psychics' available but later tried with all sorts of people, including the lab cleaning ladies and some FBI agents who happened to want to know what was going on. (The spying potential of perfecting this method is fairly obvious as it is difficult to prevent astral visitors exploring secret sites as they are usually invisible and won't set off detecting equipment!) You can replicate the 'traveling through space' type of experiment by asking a friend to leave something on a table in his home, or by getting your regular magical companion to set up something for you to go and examine in another place. Later on, when you have both mastered the art, you can both go to a special place and explore it, together.

One of the older magical methods of producing astral projection is by sitting in your temple and imagining yourself standing upright, preferably with your back to you, a couple of feet in front of you. Build up a strong picture of your own back, a pace away, exactly as you are dressed at the time (presumably in your magical robe), and try to see it, at least with your eyes closed. Remain as relaxed as you can and then transfer your awareness into your standing form. There is a certain art to this, which cannot be explained, but by experimenting you may well be able to get your awareness into the standing copy of yourself. This kind of astral 'cloning' has been known for a very long time, and seems to be illustrated on some old Egyptian papyri. When your awareness actually transfers from your seated, relaxed body into the image you have created, you will suddenly find that you are looking at the room from that point of view. It can be a weird experience, and the surprise will almost certainly land you back into your body with a jolt, similar to that experienced when your body seems to 'fall' when you are going to sleep.

Auras

If your companion is able to see auras, they might even see a faint figure building up in front of you, and your own auric field fading slightly, leaving the dense, inner 'etheric' or energy body around your seated form. On the subject of auras, there are basically three layers. The inner etheric is easily visible to ordinary eyesight in a dimly lit room as a smoky band about an inch wide outlining the figure, and is seen best against naked flesh. Beyond that is a wider band of the astral health region, seen as faint coloured filaments, such as you would see if you squint through your eyelashes at a candle flame. Outside that again is an even fainter layer, stretching away, of finer threads of the emotional aura, which connects to all the people, places, and objects with which you have any link. Although there are numerous books on interpreting the colours of other people's auras, as to their state of health, moods, and so on, you are never told that as you are looking through your own aura, the colours are a blend of yours and theirs! If the apparent colour is muddy and unpleasant it may not mean they are weighed down with ghastly karma, but that a combination of their colour and yours is not very pleasant. You can learn to see your own aura by standing naked in front of a large mirror in a dimly lit room, and squinting with your eyes unfocused, a few inches away from your reflection. The colours of the outer aura will be changing all the time, varying with emotion, hunger, and temper, as well as general state of health, alertness, and concentration on other people, which will brighten the filaments of auric material by which you are linked to them. It may well be that it is along these delicate threads the shared thoughts of telepathy may flow, and when you are psychometrizing an object, the impressions you receive are obtained from the same source. It is an enormous field of experimentation as yet unexplored for it will have valuable information to give about diagnoses of impending illnesses, mental depression, or unstable relationships.

Archetypal Magical Temples

The most important magical aspect of being able to project your consciousness (with or without the astral body), is to be able to enter the archetypal magical temples. Each tradition of High Magic and of ancient Natural Magic has its sacred place. Some of these have a sort of history, like Atlantis or Avalon, or a genuine earthly base, like the ancient temples of the Nile in Egypt, each dedicated to its particular family of Gods and Goddesses, or our 'home grown' stone circles and sacred earthworks. Although these have some links with earth, they are really only replicas of great sacred buildings or constructions which never existed as physical places. It is from these astral temples that power may flow into the small ritual rooms we construct to work in, and it is priests or powers which originate from these which convey most of the force we are able to raise in our workings. Magical tools, properly consecrated, become linked with their astral counterparts, as do robes and regalia, talismans, and even people. It is through this contact with the 'Great Temple' that the most important and well established lodges draw not only magical forces for healing and esoteric workings, but great sources of knowledge and wisdom. Inspired teachings have their reality in an astral world, perhaps parallel to this one, yet invisible, like radio waves or television pictures, which constantly flow through us, undetected unless we have a receiver and aerial connected up. Here the great communicators or masters have their existence, and the 'Cosmic Civil Service' which seems to plan and direct the general pattern of certain individuals' lives on earth, have their offices. They are the ones who arrange those odd 'coincidences' which in retrospect prove to have been the most important meetings or events in our lives.

Your Reactions during Astral Travels

On astral journeys, as opposed to ordinary pathworkings, meditations, or visualizations, you may find it hard to speak or indicate your impressions because you are not in your body, as you would be for these other experimental techniques. However, you should be able to recall the details later on and so give your companion any information regarding the object you went to visit, or the other location you explored. Your companion should also watch how you are reacting to your astral travels and may discover you look very relaxed and still. It is certainly worthwhile to have your companion suggest you can breathe normally, and speak, at the beginning of your adventure, and that if you make a movement of your right hand, for example, he or she should then gently call your name. You will be able to remember such keys to returning to your body.

If you use the 'building an astral form' method to get out, you may be aware of a slender, silvery or rainbow hued strand which seems to link your astral and your ordinary self, although it is not apparent to everyone. There are reports of it being joined at the navel, or the top of the head or heart area, so see if it is visible in your own case. The Bible says, 'If the silver cord is loosed or the golden bowl broken . . .' when talking about death, and it is thought that the silver cord is that which connects the astral or spiritual form to the physical, and the golden bowl is the aura, shown as a halo around the heads of Christian saints and martyrs, though the size, density, and colours will vary a lot, as explained before. If you find yourself in your astral form, floating through walls presents no trouble and you can fly (as do many children in dreams, regretting that they can't do so during the day) and so visit distant places or scenes. You will learn to speed up your rate of progress by concentrating on the place you wish to visit. You can explore inside volcanoes and try skydiving without a parachute, but make sure you are on the astral plane first, and not actually about to leap out of a tenth floor window! When you want to return, see the place from where you set off and then re-enter the room. It can be extremely disconcerting to see yourself sitting quite still in your temple and this alone may well jolt you back into your physical aspect, but otherwise you will need to stand in front of yourself, and sink backwards into the seated position. Allow yourself a few moments to truly merge and become centred before leaping up and telling your companion all about your adventures. You will have been very relaxed for some considerable time and may feel a bit stiff or wobbly at first.

If you have succeeded in doing these exercises in the company of a friend, you may try them alone, or in bed, projecting yourself up and out of your body, or as R. A. Monroe did, by rolling out of his body, sideways through a wall, as he explains in *Journeys Out of the Body*. It is possible to get into all sorts of weird situations, so do exercise common sense. It might seem to be fun to spy on people or 'overlook' someone you don't like, but they might actually see you! The astral police force, servants of the Great Temple, can also catch you at it, and if nothing else, limit your ability to do it at all, or any other work which involves the application of hidden knowledge.

Like time traveling, the more experience you have, especially when working with a trusted companion, the greater will be your self-confidence, which in turn will help you gain skills in all the other magical arts which are allied to travel, such as divination, scrying and clairvoyance. Gradually you will build up a link with one of the great teachers who will find ways of instructing you, often through those coincidental meetings or the sudden discovery of a book or other source of knowledge. You will be surprised what doors these experiments can open for you, if you persevere with them.

19

MINDS OVER MAGIC

Most magical arts are very serious and require hard work and dedication. However, there is a diverse range of other 'supernatural' skills which you might never have considered. These can be valuable training techniques, or can even provide a variety of esoteric party games which your friends can play, and demonstrate their possible psychic talents. It is true that some people who have taken part in seances, played at 'raising ghosts', or light-heartedly dabbled with ouija-boards and the like, have scared themselves, and opened doors to psychic perceptions which they did not know how to close, or attracted the attention of entities which they could not control, but if you are aspiring to master the skills of magic, you ought to know what you are doing.

The occult arts have always recognized the reality of the 'unseen' forces which may help and heal, instruct and guide. Magicians do not usually call up the spirits of dead people, accepting, on the whole, that the immortal human spirit needs to rest and assess its past life before being brought back into incarnation—it doesn't want goading by friends or relatives still alive into giving an account of its activities after it has cast off its mortal body. Nor will it necessarily have instantly gained profound wisdom, thus being able to answer all the questions which still beset those remaining in the 'vale of tears.' Certainly there are discarnate sources of knowledge which may be contacted through magical applications of some of the spiritualists' methods, but magicians generally prefer to use their own ways to receive information from hidden masters.

It is worth trying some experiments in Extra Sensory Perception (ESP), psychokinesis (PK, affecting material objects by 'mind power'), and expanding psychic awareness. If you and your magical companion, or perhaps a slightly wider group of your friends and family, for example, can get together to try out skills like telepathy (conveying information from one mind to another), precognition or clairvoyance (guessing what card, for example, will be turned up next), or post- or retrocognition (listing the order of an already shuffled pack of cards). Scientists working in laboratories, with carefully selected subjects, using well-tested methods under strictly controlled conditions, have made some progress in pinning down these elusive skills. In less formal tests it has been found that new subjects often score higher than those who had tried, and become bored, with card guessing, or attempts at bending metal. It was also found that a relaxed frame of mind, often difficult to achieve in a laboratory, was a help to 'traveling clairvoyance' (astral travel to the magician), and in tests in telepathy when one subject tried to 'see' the picture being looked at by a 'sender' in another room.

You may already have found that your magical interests have led to you getting 'hunches' about doing, or not doing, certain things, or that hints and clues are found in dreams, or that you actually perceive bits of the future clearly in meditations or during divination sessions. So long as you have control over your ability to use psychic faculties you won't get into trouble, but if you allow yourself to relax your guard and become frightened by your sudden clairvoyance, or power to seemingly affect and change the future, you will need to watch out. Don't play about with trances or try to contact 'spirits of the dead,' as these can lead you into deep water, and if expert help is not to hand, can cause mental disturbance or depression. There are lots of safe and interesting experiments you can try and when you have fully mastered many of the psychic skills, then, if you are still interested, you may attempt more advanced journeys into the unknown regions.

Testing Your 'Supernatural' Skills

If you have a pack of Tarot cards or ordinary playing cards, you can begin some simple tests with your friends. Get someone to sort out the playing cards and then shuffle them very thoroughly. You then take this pack, face down, and picking the cards up one at a time, try to guess, imagine, or 'see' what colour (or suit if you are using Tarot cards) each falls in. Place each card in turn on one of two or four heaps. If you get stuck with some cards make another heap, and go back to them at the end. You might be surprised how many you get right first go! Let your companion have a go and see if she does better or worse. You can even buy decks of special Zener cards which have five symbols on them. These are star, circle, square, wavy lines and cross, and they were invented to make scoring easier. If you make some of these cards you ought to score five out of the twenty-five cards right in any run through them by sheer chance. If you get six or more correct that is called a 'psi-hit' and is significant to investigators, especially if you can always score like this. If you always score less than five that is called 'psi-missing' and is just as significant. That proves that some aspect of your consciousness does see or guess what the cards are but deliberately makes you say or write down the wrong answer. To produce results which actually prove you are psychic may well take far more time and trouble than you are willing to devote to this experiment, but consistent significant scores do show you are waking up new areas of awareness.

An interesting method (though it is sometimes harder to work out statistical scores) is to repeat the tests using a selection of picture postcards with clear images or designs. One person looks at the picture chosen at random from a selection and tries to convey the illustration to the receiver in another room. The receiver gets into a relaxed and meditative state, allowing his or her mind to be empty, and tries to sense what is being seen. Although it is not easy to be able to draw exactly the same picture, receptive people (as all magicians ought to be) should get some aspect of the design, or indicate the feeling of the sender's mind. For example, if the card showed yachts sailing on a calm sea, with birds flying above, the receiver might draw triangles and say it felt windy, or sunny, or that he or she had a feeling of swaying, etc. Sometimes the emotion of a picture of lovers, or the scent of a flower, or the speed of racing cars can be sent more easily than the actual shapes, colours, or minor details of the design. If possible, get a third party to match up the sender's and receiver's material, or allow the receiver to try and recognize the 'target' in a selection of cards. Again psi-missing can apply, shapes and colours being avoided!

You can use Tarot cards instead, and by sensing something of the meaning, even if it isn't an obvious tie-in with the scene shown on certain of the more elaborate decks, it may well link in with the symbolism of the card, either your own, or a more traditional interpretation. This 'game' has the added advantage of helping you form telepathic links with your partner, as well as possibly discovering deeper levels of meaning to the Tarot or any other system. Later on you may be able to send messages to each other at a distance, at first by trying to get your friend to recognize a colour which you send at one o'clock, for example, and by identifying a simple shape received from him or her at two o'clock. With practice, you might be able to send a number and a suit of playing or Tarot cards which would include a message, derived from the interpretation of that card or cards. Find out what sorts of information you can pass from mind to mind, starting with colours, plane shapes, numbers (either as the written figure, or a number of lines, dots, or symbols, as that may be easier), feelings like energy, calm, and so on. Use your own imagination to invent some suitable experiments to try. Each will help awaken, strengthen, and control your psychic faculties.

Metal Bending

One subject which had a lot of coverage in the press and media a while ago was 'metal bending' and though some of the most famous demonstrators of this ability may have faded from public life, there are a number of eminent physicists in university laboratories still carrying out tests with both admitted experts and young people, to train them in this rather destructive and not very useful art. If you want to try for yourself, you can resort to bits of cutlery, which were the things which made the headlines a few years ago, or strips of iron, steel, or thick aluminium, if you come across any. You should simply relax into that useful mood of distraction, with the attitude, 'This is a game, it doesn't much matter if I succeed or not, but it would be fun to show that metal bending is possible.' Allow that sort of idea to flow through your head for a while, and then very lightly stroke part of the metal with one fingertip, whilst holding the bar gently with the other hand. Imagine it is a piece of plastic which can be sufficiently warmed by the heat in your finger to become soft and bendy. Even if you are just playing, don't exert any kind of bending force as this will invalidate your experiment, and prevent the 'psi-force' from working. Relax and imagine the metal doing the same. You may well be surprised after a few minutes to discover a slight bend in the bar—or possibly not! Certainly metal can be bent by forces as yet not fully understood by physicists, and far more people can develop the ability if they really want to, but it doesn't have many peaceful applications. Try it for fun, and if you succeed and want to demonstrate your skill to the experts, find one of the serious books on the subject, and write to the author, care of the publisher. You might find an outlet for your new found skill on television!

Psychokinesis

Although the above application of PK is not very useful and you may not have that many spare spoons and forks, you might like to try some other tests which show the same forces in a more entertaining and less destructive manner. One way to find out if you can move things by will power, apart from sitting staring at a ping-pong ball on a tray, out of draughts, and willing it to move, is to obtain a Crooke's Radiometer. You may have seen these at shows or in shop windows. They are glass spheres, about four inches across, and inside is a pair of fine wires, balanced on a pointed pivot. At the end of each arm is a small diamond shape, coloured white on one side, and black on the other. The whole thing is sealed in a vacuum. The Radiometer will remain quite still in darkness or dim light, but if the sun, or even a candle, shines upon it, the white sides will reflect the heat and the black sides absorb it, and so untouched by human hands, it will slowly begin to turn clockwise. Your task is to make it go the opposite way by will power. You may not thump the table, and blowing will not help as the unit is sealed, but some people can actually make it go round the wrong way by psi.

A simpler set-up you can make yourself consists of a slender straw or grass stem attached to the finest hair or strand of a terylene thread and hung from the lid of a screw-top jar. At each end of the straw a vertically mounted circle of coloured paper is attached forming 'paddles.' This should be able to turn easily within the container, which should be sealed so that the air within may become totally still and any natural twisting movement left in the supporting strand can unwind. The whole set-up should be placed on a totally firm and stable bench and you will see that any slight movement of the table, floor, or even house might be enough to cause the bar with its paddles to turn. Once you have allowed the apparatus to become absolutely still after a day or so, without touching the jar or table, begin to 'will' the bar to turn on its spider thin thread.

Poltergeist Activity

You may already have noticed a psi force at work in your home which makes objects move without any obvious touch or jarring. Of course, if you live near a main road, railway, underground line, or airport your whole house is likely to shake a bit. Even factories which use heavy machinery can have a subtle effect on places at a considerable distance, depending on the soil type in the area. If things do seem to move about, or vanish, or even strange items suddenly appear, it means there is a psi force operating in your home. This may emanate from you, as a result of your magical practices, or it could be the energy field of a young person. Many teenagers do develop this strange flood of energy, usually between the ages of about ten and fifteen. Quite dramatic poltergeist activities have been recorded with furniture flying about, noises in the night, the telephone going mad, and electrical equipment turning on and off without being touched. This energy never does any harm to anyone, but it can be terrifying for those involved. However, once you pay attention to the youngsters and allow them to let off steam with games or outings, by sharing their emotions and guiding them during this critical stage of growing up, these phenomena soon vanish. They don't require exorcism nor the intervention of priests, merely loving care, time, and the release of tension and zest through normal activities like sport, dancing, or drama.

Ouija-Boards

Many people, who do feel they are under psychic attack, have done something to open a door to some of the playful energy which lurks about in the unseen world which flows through us. Often they have tried raising spirits, played with a ouija-board, or held seances, without having any real idea how to go about it safely.

Like any experiment with unseen forces, whether magical or psychic, you will be working with altered states of awareness. In magic you, as the magician, are trained to be in control—in playing with ouija-boards and the like, this is usually not the case. When a few people sit in the light of a guttering candle around a table, circled with the letters of the alphabet, with quivering fingers placed on the stem of an upturned wineglass, it is no wonder that everyone is keyed up for a visitation. Very soon, if the tension and expectancy is sufficient, the glass will begin to move. Will it spell out 'death' or 'I am the spirit of the devil' or any other such common comment? Possibly, and everyone will get very excited or scared, depending on their nature. Perhaps the glass will zoom across the table, or jerkily start to spell out messages from the departed. Tension among the participants increases, and doubts and queries arise in their minds. 'Is there some spirit moving the pointer?' 'Yes' the glass will answer, or 'No' if it is in that sort of mood. Sometimes clear messages are laboriously spelled out, or else there seems to be a great force causing the glass to jerk violently from letter to letter, trailing garbled words or plain nonsense. Whatever happens, everyone taking part will have had a weird experience which they will find curiously hard to forget. It can prey on the minds of unhappy people and cause them to have strange dreams and become unsettled so that any out of the ordinary happening takes on a great importance, and they become very frightened. Often, because their awareness has been sharpened by this slight brush with the unseen, they convince themselves they are under psychic attack when they break a favourite ornament, and that the itches of gnat bites are some imps sent to torment them. It really does happen!

If you get invited to join in such a game do make it clear to the others that it is not the best sort of activity to dabble with and that the consequences can be far reaching. When the glass does spell messages, these are almost always derived from the subconscious of one or other of the participants, or from the collective unconscious mind if it is a well established group. Because people expect to get messages from dead relatives, that is the form the words may well take. If they expect to feel cold or clammy, sense touches, or hear knocks and thumps, the chances are that they will. The same applies to table-turning or tilting, when a circle of people sit with their hands lightly on the surface with little fingers and thumbs just touching. After a while, in the dim red light, after the singing of some eerie hymns or prayers, the table will seem to move, sway, and even tap out letters. The slightest nudge will set it off on its erratic course through the alphabet, or even careering about the room with the disturbed sitters in hot pursuit. This is an extremely slow and clumsy way of getting divine instructions or communicating with the discarnate masters, and magicians will soon find that safer, quieter methods of meditation and contemplation provide far more reliable sources of information than cracking glasses or breaking the legs off tables!

Unidentified Flying Objects

Although magicians may have individual views on the subjects of unidentified flying objects (UFOs), and may not personally have seen that many ghosts, they accept as a part of their mystical heritage, the reality of elemental spirits of nature, and the fairies of past times, as well as the giants and heroes of myth and legend. It may not be immediately obvious that there are definite links between all these different sorts of visitors. Recent surveys have indicated that many UFO sightings appear over ancient sacred sites; fairies or elves are often seen at crossroads; ghosts haunt churchyards (or staircases); and elementals can be found in wild places. Most of these are 'places between worlds' or 'set apart.' Churches are often built on much older pagan sacred places; crossroads were frequently locations of meetings of witches; and fairy folk will turn up anywhere where nature has enough energy to support their existence. Most of these beings exist primarily on another plane and come into our set of dimensions where the veil is thin and the separated worlds meet. In many cases these places have always been sacred, weird, or set apart. Usually they have rocks beneath them which are crystalline, radioactive, or have some other property which our ancestors recognized as a power source, and made use of when constructing circles, standing stones, or earthworks.

The art of shape-shifting has been attributed in turn to witches, angels, fairies, and the occupants of flying saucers. It wouldn't be too great a leap of the imagination to say that all these creatures have certain things in common, if, in fact, they are not indeed the same. They turn up at the same sort of places, seem to be able to draw on energy supplies which well up from the earth, and even those who might have originated in spacecraft from the other side of the galaxy tend to appear close to the ground, hovering, glowing, and leaving little or no trace of their visit. It seems extremely strange that extra-terrestrials come all the way to earth and then vanish without saying 'Hallo'! If they are wiser, more advanced and so on, which they must be to have got this far successfully, it is a shame that they don't leave a calling card. Even the people who are invited aboard their craft do not receive a souvenir of that momentous visit to show their earthly friends.

In biblical time spacecraft didn't exist, so it was 'Chariots of Fire' and flaming wheels; today we have intergalactic spaceships and science fiction films showing ETs and Vogons. In the Middle Ages only angels flew through the air and, apart from the odd saint, human beings stayed safely on the ground. Today flying faster than the speed of sound is commonplace, and trips to the moon frequent, at least by man-made research craft. However, we still have our share of fairies, elementals, and ghosts appearing where they always have done, as recorded in local tales and legends, but now they may appear as space travelers, and their balls of light as UFOs. One curious fact about these visitors is that if something is seen by a psychic person, he can draw the attention of his non-psychic friend to that object or creature, who can then see it too. Now, that is a piece of magic!

There are undoubtedly forces around ancient sites, be they what scientists can measure and record as ultrasonic pulses, high frequency radio waves, or energy surges which appear as shape-shifting balls of light in the sky, and are seen as UFOs, angels, etc., depending on the psychology of the viewer, rather than the actual object. Magicians may not need to give these forces technical names, but they ought to learn to detect them, by dowsing with rods or a pendulum, or actually by feeling the power in a standing stone when sitting relaxed against it, or by discovering the bands of energy with their hands. It is this force, which can be detected in the ley lines, that seems to link ancient sacred sites, standing stones, mounds, moats, marker cairns, notches in ridges, and groves in a vast web of energy. Whether this was created by the wise ones of old, or whether they detected its force and wove the strands between certain places is not yet known, but gradually its secrets are being uncovered and the Gordian knot of this antique power source is being unravelled by those with the width of understanding to delve into it. Maybe, in the future, the power for peace on earth can be fed into the network, to flow through all the places where war and hatred rage, calming and stilling the anger and restoring peace and prosperity. Let healing, love, justice, and plenty flow through the decayed veins of Mother Earth, and all her children may benefit from this power, once they learn to recognize it.

Psychic Healing Power

You can apply psychic forces to healing in a variety of ways, healing not only people, but animals, trees, and perhaps the very Earth herself. One of the simplest things to do is to get some fresh spring water, preferably from a healing spring, and then bless it in the name of the God or Goddess of Healing. This can be a Christian saint or simply 'Lady of Health' as you wish. Place your hands around the container for a few moments and then experiment with the 'holy' water on things like potted plants or even seeds. Compare a pot of seedlings sprinkled with the consecrated water with a similar pot given only tap water—you could be very surprised at the difference. This water may also be added to a bath, for relaxation and healing, or given to ailing animals or children, as well as to any friends who wish to share your experiments. Aches and bruises may be bathed with this healing water, and sickly trees or shrubs, even in public parks, may well benefit from a dose of blessed spring water. You might find your healing power is such that each time it rains you can stand in a doorway or under a tree and bless the rain as it falls, to bring healing and fertility to the land, and all that grows there.

You might also apply your psychic healing power through consecrated oil. Take a little almond or 'baby' oil and bless it, and use this as a healing balm for sunburn, itches, and to enrich your hands and feet before a ritual. Offer your magical companion samples of blessed and untouched oil and see if she is able to detect the difference. If you have done the consecration correctly and brought down the power of healing into it, you will be able to detect a difference in temperature, or a feeling of glowing, or some other sensation. The same is true when you bless a humble candle before a ritual, or consecrate a talisman. To the psychic senses it will feel very different. Experiment with something as ordinary as a pair of postcards of the same picture. Bless one and not the other and see what the difference is.

If you can't sense it with your left hand, or by looking with your inner eye, maybe a pendulum will help. Ask 'Is this the consecrated item?' over each in turn and see which it indicates as positive. Learn to get it right. Dowsing is a very simple art, and anyone can soon get a pendulum, made of any small, symmetrical object, like a bead or plumb-bob on a thin thread, to give a definite positive swing and a clear negative swing, which will be easy to tell apart, even if they don't comply with the patterns of swing given in a book. It is your inner awareness which is helping the pendulum to swing, and it will react as it chooses. Check each time that it is being consistent, then you can add another game to your psychic repertoire.

Playing 'Hunt the Thimble' may sound a bit childish, but if you go about it as a training exercise, or as yet another in a series of experiments, you and your companion can try to expand your awareness of your unexploited talents in the psychic field. With a pendulum in one hand, use the other as a pointer after your friend has hidden a 'thimble', which is best if it is something like a significant lump of rock, or a consecrated object, as it is easier to find. Point around the room and watch for the pendulum to change from swinging idly to a positive movement, and then gradually move nearer to the place it seems to indicate by cross referencing until you locate it. Again it takes both practice and confidence in your inner sight to be able to see through walls or under cushions to locate a hidden, or later on, lost item.

Until you gain expertise it is worth playing a few games with a pendulum—this is one of the subtler skills you can teach children too. Hide a coin under a loose carpet and let them take turns in dowsing for its location. Help them trace water pipes or cables under the lawn in the garden, or, indoors, blindfolded, follow the courses of rivers or the sea coast on large maps. Get samples of as many metals as you can and hide each under an upturned cup and award a small prize for the person who gets the most right. Ask 'Is this silver?' over each cup in turn, or brass, stone, copper, glass, or plastic and see how expert you and your companion are getting.

When you do have confidence you may use the pendulum in healing, not only as a way of diagnosing the seat of an illness, but also as a radionics tool for creating a healing potion. Again, using spring water, or the basic milk-sugar tablets used by homoeopaths to make their medicines (available from natural chemists), you can create a useful therapy. With a clipping of hair, a signature, or some other 'witness' of a sick person placed under the container of water/pills, hold your pendulum over it and say 'Make this a medicine to cure so-and-so's illness.' You will find it will begin to swing in large circles over the medicine and continue for some time, gradually slowing down and finally stopping. This has then made radionically (the art of using dowsing for diagnosis and healing, or other methods which use the same underlying principles) a potion which the sick person should take each day, for a whole moon, starting as soon as possible. Note whether the moon is full, new, waxing, or waning, and see how the patient progresses during the next four weeks. You can even hold the pendulum over the person, if they are willing to try this unusual form of healing!

Experiment with Psychic Forces

If you are certain you have psychic powers (which most people possess though they haven't all bothered to learn about or train them), you can make a 'poltergeists' playpen' which is, in fact, a miniature laboratory, combining a number of experiments for these loose psychic forces to interact with, inside a sealed container. If you can get an old aquarium, or even a large sweet jar with a lid from a shop you can develop a number of things which the forces may use. You will need some kind of striped or squared paper to make a background so that even tiny movements of objects will be apparent. Some stationers sell large squared sheets, or even fancy wrapping paper with a chequer-board pattern might be available. Stick this firmly to the longest side of the tank/jar. On the floor you will need to spread a light powder which will show when objects have been moved. This could be talcum powder or flour, or even instant coffee powder. You will need to make little swings as suggested on page 240, suspended from the thinnest thread, and provide a ping-pong ball or other light object which might be moved or rolled about. It is worth putting in a heavy stone or lump of wood in case there are very strong forces wishing to demonstrate their power. Get a couple of interlinked metal rings which are soldered so they won't simply unlock, and a dice to discover if it will roll on its own. All these things will need to be placed inside the 'lab' and then it will have to be sealed, perhaps even getting the lid glued or fastened with a small padlock so that no tiny human fingers can get in among the playthings.

The 'lab' will need to be placed on an immovable support, for example on top of a wardrobe, and well away from anyone or anything which can physically jar, shake, or affect it, if the experiment is to have any validity at all. Set it up, and allow each item to take up its natural position. In a few days, as long as nothing has obviously interfered with its resting state, you can begin to call upon any psychic forces which happen to be around to enter this esoteric funfair and try the equipment provided. It may take ages before anything noticeable happens, but you may find that there are tracks of movement in the dust, or that the trapeze has turned round, or even that closely sealed interlinked rings have unlocked—or that unlinked solid rings somehow defied logic by interlocking. Springs might be found straightened out and unbent pieces of wire curled into patterns. No one knows what these forces are, but they do seem willing to play in such equipment, and if you get results, please let me know. In many universities and laboratories all over the world, technicians are striving to evolve suitable tests which will demonstrate the sorts of powers magicians take for granted.

20

THE ARTS OF TALISMANIC MAGIC

Amulets, charms, spells, and talismans are all used in various books dealing with magical arts and often it is not made clear precisely what is being inferred, so it is important to start off with some sort of definition of these various artefacts.

Amulets

Amulets are an extremely ancient form of PROTECTION, especially against the 'evil eye,' and are often made to represent an eye, or are natural stones, pieces of wood, or pottery in that shape. In ancient Egypt the symbol was called 'The Eye of Horus' and was drawn like the natural black lines of feathers around the eye of an Egyptian falcon, whose head was often used for that of the young sun god. The shape, which some modern magicians believe represents the inner parts of a human brain, the seat of esoteric power, is still found on modern medical prescriptions as ℞, which is taken from the Latin word 'recipe' meaning 'take thou . . .' Amulets ward off harm by drawing the glance of the ill wisher to the carved imitation eye rather than to the real eyes of the victim so that the evil intent may not land and enter his soul through the gateway of his eyes.

Charms

Charms may be natural objects which are intended to bring luck or ward off other sorts of evil intent. They may also be chants or simple rhymes which are intended to dispel a problem, like warts, or protect the charm bearer or singer from a specific sort of harm. Many of the oldest charms are derived from nature, often being fossils or naturally occurring crystals. As our ancestors had no clear understanding of what caused fossils to be formed, these were looked upon as strange works of the Gods. Some were lucky and would attract health, and others were the harbingers of misfortune or sickness. The good stones included ones with holes in, for these were hung over the doors of byres and stables to prevent the animals being attacked by spirits in the night, when they would be ridden to exhaustion or milked dry. It was believed that evil sprites would try to get through the holes in the stones and become trapped, so that every seven years the stones had to be thrown into running water and new ones found. Usually these stones were tied with red ribbons as the colour of life. These 'holey', holy, or Hag stones turn up all over the country and in Europe. Other almost perfectly spherical holey stones are actually fossil sponges which vary in size from that of a pea to that of a walnut, and they were sought by witches who made them into necklaces. They also make excellent magical dowsing pendulums.

Fossil ammonites curled like snakes were believed to ward off the poison of snake bite, and those found in Ireland were thought to be the snakes which St. Patrick had turned to stone when he rid that green island of its venomous serpents. Belemnites, bullet-shaped fossils derived from some kind of squid or sea creature, often turned up by the ploughshare, were called 'elf bolts' and were supposed to have been shot to inflict harm on children or cattle. Similarly, ancient flint arrowheads made by Stone Age people were looked upon as harbingers of evil, and unless ceremonially cast into running water or buried deep, they too might bring sickness or ill luck.

Spoken or sung charms were usually used to drive away sickness and were often doggerel rhymes, made up to suit the person for whom they were intended. A simple, but still effective wart charm may be said as follows:

Wart, wart, black of heart, I command thee to depart.
As our Lady Moon do wane, be he free of spot and blain.

Usually there were fairly elaborate instructions to be followed in that each wart had to be counted and a leaf picked from a sacred tree for every one. These leaves were buried, thrown into water, or even impaled upon the thorns of a May Tree, or perhaps the sap from a dandelion was smeared on each wart to show it up black, or a piece of meat or a snail was rubbed on every blemish, and in turn impaled, buried, or drowned, depending on the local theories. Many of these ancient charms do literally 'work like a charm,' but be careful if you start experimenting with spells using creatures, even those as lowly as snails and slugs.

Some of the well-known children's nursery rhymes were originally charms against the plague. For example, 'Ring a ring o' roses, pocket full of posies, atishoo, atishoo, all fall down' was hoped to keep away the miasmas which caused pneumonic plague, as were the scented posies of herbs mentioned in the rhyme. There is a vast mine of information scattered among these old rhymes and folk songs which have preserved for hundreds of years both magical charms and valuable pieces of myth and legend, upon which the work of modern occult groups is ultimately rooted. The common country folk were wise far beyond the educated, book learning of the town folk and religious orders. They preserved in folk song, ditty, spell, and symbol, a great deal of very old knowledge, which, because it retained its virtue even in the face of science, has in some part come down to us today. Much is still to be rediscovered from these sources of knowledge and practical crafts.

Spells

Spells are again the application of the spoken word. In the days of the Druids, their Bards could win battles by singing satires against the leader of the opposing army, revealing the secret names of their Gods and the weaknesses of character of the leader. The voice or the musical note, used correctly in magic, is a very powerful instrument. Spells may be woven to enchant and entrance by hypnotically repeated phrase, both the singer, if he is a shaman, or the hearer, who may be lulled into a peaceful sleep in sickness, or incited to riot and fight by the battle hymn of the blood chant. The stamp of the foot, beat of a drum, or jangle of the sistrum in the hands of true priests can invoke in the hearers all kinds of powerful emotions and actions. Pop music can do the same by inflaming the fans in wild adoration, and the shouts of the military junta can lead the mob into slaughter and pillage. Trained occultists are aware of the forces which sounds can call up, and use their voices with care when calling upon the sacred names of their God and Goddess.

Experimenting with Sound

The old books of magic hint at the 'unspeakable names of God.' These aren't so much unspeakable but unpronounceable. Most of the old alphabets did not have vowel sounds as we know them, so a combination of consonants might be spoken in a variety of ways, as the letters 'tn' could become 'tan,' 'ten,' 'tin,' 'ton,' and 'tun,' each with a different meaning. Expand the word to more than three letters and it becomes vastly more complex. In some systems it is the vowel sounds themselves, which pronounced alone, invoke power. One way to experiment with this is to find a place where a bit of noise will be tolerated, under a railway arch, or in an empty bathroom where there is some echo, and by dropping your voice to a lower note than that used for ordinary speech, vibrate the letters A, E, I, O, and U. The results will certainly surprise you if no one has shown you the trick before. With practice, you can get your whole body apparently vibrating in harmony, once you have hit the correct pitch. When you then invoke the words of power during a ritual, it will have a great deal more effect. Vibrating sounds need not be very loud; you aren't aiming to shout at God, but to send out a powerful call which will resonate on the other levels of existence. You will need to do some breathing exercises, so experiment with whistling and deep breathing to increase the power of your lungs and the length of time you can vibrate any note. Work with your companion too, for he or she will resonate to a different note and you ought to be able to harmonize so that when invoking together you have an even more devastating effect.

Another technique which is worth learning is the use of chanting or humming as a way of releasing tension. You can teach this to children too, because they often like to shriek and scream, unknowingly for this very reason. Start off by groaning low and loud, putting into it all the held in feelings of disappointment, despair, and unhappiness you can actually manage. A whole roomful of people doing this is an amazing sound! Groan and moan out all the mental pain and repression you can, and as you feel the burden of it slipping from your mind, let the sound rise in pitch, gently and gradually, so that after a few minutes you are beginning to sing, on any note which pleases you. Try small runs of notes or scales, in any mode or key, until you find a simple tune forming, which you may hum or sing. Perhaps a single note seems totally satisfying to you, or you wish to change pitch and add rhythm until you have made a tune. If you are with other people you may well end up singing in harmony, and you will feel much better for the exercise.

As you develop a pattern of ritual with prayers, invocations, and chants, you will see how music or vibration of certain words will add a new dimension to your working. You can chant a simple spell each day for health, based on Coue's theme, 'Every day, in every way, I am getting better and better!'—a much safer tranquillizer than some of the chemicals on the market! You may like to learn a musical instrument or find recordings of either classical or modern tunes which fit the theme of your rituals, meditations, or pathworkings. You may well be able to fill in gaps of silence with background 'musak' as there is a good deal of meditation music available now. Experiment with all kinds of sounds; drums, bells, gongs, and flutes have all been used to add to the atmosphere of religious and magical ritual through the centuries, and even the addition of single dings on a pleasant-sounding bell can add effect to the simplest ritual.

Talismans

When you come to the making of talismans, the most complex art of this kind, you will need not only the words to say for the consecration, but the elements with which to bless the completed work, as well as the skill, equipment, and materials to design an effective talisman in the first place. Each one is a specific magical charm designed for one person, to work on one occasion, so you can't make a batch of 'good luck talismans' despite the claims made about such items that you can buy through the post! Every talisman has to be made for a particular person and situation and you can't practise or have test runs, any more than you can have complete rehearsals of magical rites!

Talismans require several sorts of information and skill and should not be undertaken until you are competent at the basic arts of visualization and human psychology. Anyone who makes a magical charm, with the application of intent and will, is responsible for the outcome, for it forms very strong karmic links, so do think first before showing off this aspect of your magical know-how. You will need to know the correspondences of planet, colour, number, God/Goddess names, gems, plane figures, and astrological information relating to each talisman and all the people involved. It is always best that you and your partner start off by working on your own behalf so that you can observe what happens during the making, consecrating, and finally the working of the talisman. You will need a genuine reason to launch this difficult branch of magic, not just a trumped up excuse to play with clay and coloured pens.

As well as knowing on what day and at what hour the work should be done, you will need to assemble material for the talisman, either the correct planetary metal (gold is a bit pricey, so gold foil or paper will probably have to do, for example), and inks to write on it. You will need a connecting link to the person it is intended for: hair, a signature, or photograph, etc., and some silk or fine cloth of the right colour to make a cover for it. You might need clay or wood, jewels and sewing thread, felt-tip pens and parchment, metal foil, or particular gums for the incense sacred to the powers whose influence is to be woven into the talisman. These items may well not be to hand, unless you are already a competent magical jackdaw, hoarding all the necessary bits and pieces. You may well also need to learn certain practical arts, like calligraphy, astrology, metal engraving, poker-work, embroidery, or herbalism, in order that you have the necessary skill to make, consecrate, and empower the talisman in a way that will ensure its success.

Magical Correspondences

The most obvious set of magical correspondences which will cover most of the situations you will meet to begin with are those associated with the days of the week. You should know the planets from the names of the days: Monday—Moon; Tuesday—Mars (Tiw, Saxon, or Mardi in French); Wednesday—Mercury (Wotan, Saxon); Thursday—Jupiter (Thor, Saxon); Friday—Venus (Freya, Saxon); Saturday—Saturn; and Sunday—Sun. Each of these planets, astrologically speaking, has certain associations with influences, colours, incenses, flowers, and so on. You will need to research the underlying symbolism and arrive at a set of correspondences, which even if they don't agree with anyone else's, satisfy you and your magical partner. Don't rush this research; it is a part of making a talisman, which is a much longer process than scribbling a brief spell on a bit of paper and wrapping it in green paper! From the moment you decide to make a working, you are already involved in the process, and it will not be completed until the aim for which you are working has been accomplished.

Often there are several forces whose help is needed to complete the work and these must be understood and balanced so that each is given its due. For example, a talisman to get a specific job would involve Jupiter (business), the Sun (for yourself), and Saturn (because you want a particular job concerning the Law or old people). If you are trying to interfere in the lives of other people—DON'T! Do not make 'love spells' or potions, because whether or not they work you will have created unnatural and lasting links between people and have interfered with their destiny. You cannot see the outcome of any relationship, nor what is planned for each individual to achieve, so don't meddle. If someone asks for this kind of help you can assist them to attract a suitable partner or lover but only by AFFECTING THEMSELVES, not some other person, no matter how good the argument seems to be. You will only win love, affection, and respect if you are WORTHY of these feelings, not because you have bespelled and lured the affections of someone who you may heartily dislike once you have got together! Earn love by being lovable and by giving out warmth and compassion to all those around you; it is the strongest and safest love potion in the world

Making the Talisman

You will need to establish the colour, materials, day, and God forms related to the subject of your talisman and gradually gather such equipment as you need in order to make it. You can simply manufacture the charm and then consecrate it, but as you are experimenting with different techniques, actually making it magically can teach you a lot. After checking the correct items are assembled on the right day, you and your partner can enter a kind of shared litany of question and answer which adds enormously to the power of the completed talisman. When you begin, for example, with your piece of new parchment, cut accurately to a square (for a Jupiter talisman), and take up a blue pen to write upon it as she asks 'Who is this talisman to be made for?' and you answer. She then asks 'Is it with his/her will?' and go on, after your replies each time, to enquire 'Why that shape?' 'Why that colour?' 'What words/symbols/jewels/metals are you using?' 'What is the purpose of the talisman?' and 'By what right do you set this plan in motion?'

If you are genuinely sharing the work, she should also be allowed to have a part in making the talisman, and then you can ask her how it is to be consecrated, why a particular incense is being used, how the cover which has also been made will help to retain its power, and so on. By doing this you will both learn a great deal, especially if the questions are prepared by each of you and not asked before the work begins. Ensure that the work is complete, that the talisman states its purpose and is linked both with the person for whom it is made and with the god/power which will bring its intent to fruition. If it is for yourself, you can link it by writing your magical name or motto on it, signing it, or by adding a drop of your blood or saliva. Even so, it should be completed by both of you and finally sealed in a bag or wrapping of new cloth (silk is far the best) of an appropriate colour, and bound with a different coloured thread, perhaps plaited from the number of strands to correspond with one of the factors involved. The final parcel should be carried around with you close to your heart, if its purpose is knowledge, health, or some on-going matter. If you want a bit of specific luck, a new job or home, then it is best to place the completed talisman, when it has been consecrated, under your bed, out of the way, until one moon, or three signs of the zodiac have passed.

Consecrating the Talisman

When the practical part of making the talisman is complete, you still need to consecrate it. This need not be on the same day, for example something with both the Sun and Venus involved, such as a talisman to bring success to a growing partnership, could be made on a Sunday and consecrated on the following Friday, or vice versa. This will also need preparation, as you will need the elements of earth, water, fire, and air in the form used in your ordinary rituals, and if the talisman has been made of wood, metal, or clay (which may need to be fired and glazed, possibly, before consecration), you will need some holy oil. This is usually made from almond or olive oil to which herbs, gums, resins, or chips of wood from the tree dedicated to the planets concerned is added. This is left in the sun for a while so that the essential oils and perfumes may suffuse the oil. You can buy it ready made and appropriate to any planet or power, but it is much better to make your own for magical purposes. It can also be used to dedicate people at initiation or degree ceremonies, if these should fall within the compass of your activities, in due course.

You will need to set up the temple, with the altar in the centre, and next to the altar lamp the newly made talisman and its cover. When you have blessed each other and sealed the circle, you should sit opposite each other across the altar. If that isn't possible due to lack of space, try to make an equal-sided triangle with the altar and your seats as this gives power to the working, as does the first position suggested. Don't rush through the words or the actions as it takes time for the powers to build and the help you are asking to come and enter the talisman. Using words like:

Lord (or Lady) of Air (*Fire, Water, and Earth, in turn*), bless this thy symbol, and let power be indwelling.

Go round all the symbols, and if possible carry them to each point of the compass, or elevate them in the right direction. Share this work between you because this is both consecrating the area and the items themselves, which in turn, you will use for empowering the talisman. Each holding one hand over the oil say your own version of:

Great Lady/Lord (*name of planet or other force you wish to infuse into the talisman*), enter into this oil, that it may bless and dedicate this symbol and give it the power to work effectively in this plane of Earth.

If you each normally work with two of the elements, it is a very effective way of first cleansing the new talisman of your own influences by, in turn saying:

Spirit that moveth on the face of the waters, wash from this symbol all past associations that it may be pure and dedicated to its new purpose.

One of you should say the words whilst the other sprinkles a few drops of water on the talisman, using a twig of the appropriate plant if you know which one is dedicated to the planetary force you are using. Then the other one sprinkles a little salt upon it and you say:

Lady of Earth, foundation of our lives and work, take away the links of the past, and instil into this talisman the strength and stability that it may perform its true destiny.

Try not to actually touch the talisman after it has been cleansed unless it was made specifically for you. Lift it on a cloth or piece of cardboard or slide it into its cover, at the end of the ritual, using a wand or dagger.

You still need to circle it with fire, which as the energizing element will begin to make it come alive. If you can't pass it through the lamp flame, that is if the talisman is made of paper or cloth, circle the lamp about it. The same applies to the incense smoke, which as a representation of the 'Breath of God' will blow life into the talisman, so that it is fully effective. Work out an invocation which mentions this, so that you can put into the talisman all your feelings about it. You can even have another set of questions and answers which explain to the powers you are calling upon what the talisman is intended to accomplish, who it is for, and so on.

You may like to sit in silent meditation or even listen to some appropriate music for a few moments to allow any energies to spiral into the new talisman before you complete the work by 'switching it on' with the holy oil. When you are ready, both dip your forefinger into a little of the oil, placed on a small dish on the altar. Imagine there being a pool of light which you can transfer on to the talisman. You will need to find some powerful words to exactly express your intention for the charm. Together say firmly, as you touch the oil onto it,

'In the Name of . . . I consecrate this talisman of . . .'

Wait for a moment, as it may be that a surge of energy is actually felt or the incense smoke will swirl or you will perceive light flowing around the new talisman. Carefully slide it into the cover which should be fastened securely. Then share a cup of wine and bread if that is a usual part of your ceremony. Do not hurry, just because it seems you have completed the work. Gently unwind the circle, put the equipment away, disrobe, and slowly come back to earth. Leave the talisman on the altar before the centre lamp for as long as you can.

This may not seem a very powerful ritual, but if you carefully choose words and actions and research the correspondences of the planets and so on, you will be surprised what forces you are able to see or feel when you complete the work. The entire ritual is roughed out for you as writing all the words and actions of any ceremony can take away a great deal of its power. If you work through the chapters of this book you will find all that you need to master most of the arts of a really competent magician, in your own style. The experiments here are meant as a guide so that you can find your own individual path through the Mysteries, which you would not get if the whole of a ritual system, used and developed by other people, was simply set out before you. By making up your own ceremonies on a conventional framework you will discover a far more potent system, exactly suited to your own needs and abilities, than merely copying, parrot-fashion, someone else's work. Be patient and you will grow in knowledge and understanding.

Other Magical Charms

You will find lots of information on traditional charms and amulets in books of folklore. Some lucky stones are large, like the Men-an-Tol, the 'stone with a hole' on the Cornish moors which has a legend about people who crawl through it. Many similar stones or nooks and crannies in cromlechs and dolmens were set up to represent the womb of the Earth Mother, and by ritually crawling through the hole, a candidate became a 'Child of the Earth Goddess' and one of the twice born, or initiates. Horseshoes, so long associated not only with the mysterious, magical crafts of the smith, were symbols of the Horse Goddess, called Epona by the Romans. She is the great ancient image carved on White Horse Hill, near Uffington. Nearby is the long barrow called Wayland's Smithy, a site of ritual and initiation, still filled with power. Both these, and their associated sites, lie close to the ancient Ridgeway path, which is almost literally, as old as the hills. Along it there are many places where luck or magic might be sought, and where gatherings of folk were held, to work the magic which makes the corn spring green each year, and the ewes bring forth twin lambs.

Many ancient earth works and settings of stones map out great talismans on the very face of the earth; certain stones act as 'acupuncture needles' bringing healing and certain energies, either from the sky to the earth, or from the inner earth to those who walk on her surface. There are numerous healing springs or wells which are famous for their magical associations, and lots of places where traditional ceremonies are held, even now, to bring fertility, luck, or success to the surrounding lands. Fire festivals in Sussex echo the bonfires of Hallowe'en, and burning 'guys' and setting off fireworks were common activities before the Gunpowder plot in 1605. Burning ships in Shetland at January's 'Up Helly Aa' is reflected in the flames of the Rye bonfire in November. These are all genuine spells to ensure harvests of fish or field or to burn out ill luck or sickness. So when you are trying to decide how to tackle a small personal problem, remember that such arts were used on a far greater scale in times past, and that your experiments are only repeats of things wise folk have been doing for thousands of years, all over the world. Museums are full of ancient curses scratched on lead (the metal of Saturn, Lord of the Underworld) or of cuneiform inscriptions which are medical or magical spells. Corn dollies are charms in which the spirit of the Corn King lives out the winter. Seashells, fossils, and strange shaped stones ward off harm, or attract success. You are certain to find some magical charms in your local museum, during traditional festivals celebrated in your own area, or where you may go on holiday, not only in Britain, of course!

21

GODS FOR THE FUTURE

Most of the previous experiments have fairly obviously been concerned with some aspect or other of magic, but how can you experiment with religion or your relationship with God, or even with a
total disbelief in any supernatural agency? You will probably have
been brought up with the tenets of some orthodox faith, accepting
perhaps 'God the Father,' 'Thou shalt have no Gods before me . . . ,'
'There is no God beside Allah, and Mohammed is his prophet . . .'
and 'God, the Father, Son, and Holy Ghost.' You may have been
taught about the Virgin Mary, or having taken to pagan ways have
learned of the Earth Goddess or Mother Nature. As a magician you
will have to examine the concept of the male and female sides of
deity, the God within, and the idea put forward by Dion Fortune,
in several of her books, 'All Gods are One God, and All Goddesses
are One Goddess, and there is One Initiator.'

A magician does not have faith; he is not taught to believe,
but just as he gradually becomes aware of his powers to change
events by the logical application of his magical intent, he will
have EXPERIENCE of God and the Gods during his work. Most
conventional religions make the point that God is unknowable,
being too great and complex for mere humans to grasp in total-
ity. This has led to the introduction of hierarchies of priests,
bishops, and the like, and even modern witch covens have High
Priests and High Priestesses. In each case these priests may set
up a barrier between the seeker of God and some aspect, at least,
of Deity. It is possible to come to terms with the idea, as Dion
Fortune has done, that there may be many gods and goddesses,
just as there are many planets and stars whose influence is apparent in any horoscope, but that there is a Creator/Initiator/Primal
Stream from which comes the energy of change. Qabalists may
talk of the 'Logos,' biblical scholars of 'the Word,' Skywalkers of
the 'Force,' and you may discover some other term which seems

absolutely right and totally descriptive for your own experience of Deity.

In working magic it is necessary to understand that the power you use to alter events, effect healings, and bring about the accomplishment of your magical intention, need not only be directly contacted and that there may be other ways in which you can communicate, but that by interacting with this power, a strong link may be formed. This is a link of personal, direct experience. You KNOW your prayers can be answered from firsthand experience. You may read that within you there is a spark of the Divinity. You will gradually discover that this is both male and female and is much greater than simply being of a neutral spiritual nature.

Many people, in the last few decades, have expressed their dissatisfaction with the Christian church and have sought other paths to spiritual fulfilment. Some have taken the seemingly easy path of agnosticism, denying deity, and then wonder why their spells have no power or effect. Many have been led along the oriental ways of Zen and Buddhism, meditating on the goal of samadhi and total detachment. In the Middle Ages there were a large number of sects which separated creation into two sections, matter and spirit. Matter was ruled by Rex Mundi, the King of the World whose image still appears on the Tarot trump of the Devil. The Cathars, the Albigensians, and many other similar groups maintained that God was a spirit and could not live in the flesh, and so Jesus the Nazarene was a prophet and preacher but because he lived and died on earth, could not be God. They were the keepers of great secrets, one of which might have been the Holy Grail. This is usually thought of as a cup or cauldron, according to the Christian or pagan sources, but it was described as a stone or as a secret, perhaps not material at all, which could be perceived in some special manner by the chosen few.

The Shroud of Turin

Research is unravelling bits of the story of Jesus, and even after 2,000 years new material is coming to light about his life, work, and death and either survival or resurrection. The Shroud of Turin may hold some vital clues as to the state of the body around which it was wrapped, in antiquity. If carbon dating tests are finally permitted to demonstrate its age, it will provide a very interesting piece of evidence for religious detectives. Maybe the body was still alive when placed in the shroud, although in a state of deep trance, similar to that often recorded by fakirs and holy men in India, who were buried alive, in lead coffins, sometimes for months, and yet came forth alive and well at the end. If Jesus had studied with the Essenes, or any other ancient mystery school, he may well have learned the arts of suspended animation. Being nailed to a cross for only a few hours would hardly kill a man in his prime, and in good health. Felons were hung until eaten by birds yet Jesus was taken down and reverently laid in a cave tomb, where, in some of the New Testament accounts, two white robed 'angelic' figures attended him. Were these healer priests from his own order who stood by after this extreme sort of initiation test to ensure the candidate survived, as did the Sioux warriors when candidates suffered the ordeals of the flesh hooks?

No one really knows if Jesus existed, how closely his life fitted any of the stories, which themselves are extremely varied, in the New Testament. None of this information was written down at the time, and it has been much edited, changed, and influenced by the views of the different people whose hands it passed through. Much has been omitted too. Perhaps he did survive the crucifixion, and married Mary Magdalene, as has been suggested. Maybe he continued his travels with Joseph of Arimathea, who legend reports, brought him as a child to Cornwall or Glastonbury, or both. He may have lived many years after recovering from his ordeal of 'birth/death/rebirth' on the cross, and the blood of his children may well live today among the powerful families all over Europe. When they find his body and match it with the Turin Shroud and openly reveal all the ancient texts which deal with his life, ministry, and message, it may be one far closer to the hearts of many people than some watered-down religions seem to be.

Paganism

People turned to paganism as a way to escape the formal dogma of the orthodox religions, but in some cases cast off one set of beliefs for another equally alien one. It is pointless, spiritually, to deny the value of the Church and then bow down to some self-appointed priest who still acts as a go-between, separating the Gods and the people. Religion is a matter of personal experience and should not need to be mediated by anyone. You will have to decide how you can think of the Creative force which set the path of evolution going, and which seemingly, still has some effect upon living things. You must decide if you are happy worshipping a Goddess who may be, in fact, the very earth beneath your feet, or Mother Nature, invisible yet living in every plant, animal, tree, and stone. You might like to work with the image of Isis, so beautifully described at the end of *The Golden Ass,* a book of initiation and mystery written in the second century of the Christian era by Apuleius. The pagan Goddess is symbolized by the shifting pattern of the moon's face and she usually has three names, Maiden, Mother, and Crone, and different attributes for each phase. In the calendar of the pagan year, each of the nine main festivals celebrates some aspect of the life story of the Goddess of Nature/the Earth/the Moon and her Son/Consort/Lord whose symbol is the Sun, whose growing and fading strength is echoed in the part he plays in the rites. Many of the ancient festivals have modern counterparts and the old sacred dances, for example, are still performed by Morris men.

Many of the ancient sites have religious as well as calendar associations. The vast hill figures are both depictions of aspects of the Gods of Old and clearly seen gathering places where folk came to share their feast days and work their magic. Cerne Abbas has its vast virile giant as does Wilmington in Sussex, although he is only seen in outline these days. The great white mare who is also a dragon, showing the association of the powers of inner earth with the serpent or dragon force of the whole planet, is still the focus of magical workings. Remember, if you wish to celebrate your rituals at some ancient sacred site you do not have to be there physically. No one can stop visitors photographing, not only onto film, but into the library of the inner vision, all the details of such important places as Avebury, Stonehenge, the White Horse, Arbor Low, the Rings of Callenish, and the Avenues of Carnac. Look at these places, absorb their atmosphere and you will learn that you can recall it in great detail at home, in the quietness of your own temple.

You must come to understand that spark of God/Goddess within you so that its voice can advise, its power can direct, and its influence help you grow in all the fields which you are capable of mastering. YOU can be the greatest in the world, if you first discover in which area you wish to excel, and by cultivating skills guided by that inner contact, you alone can help yourself to succeed. You may also find ways of encountering each sort of God and Goddess you have ever heard of. The most effective way of meeting the Deities for yourself is by steeping yourself in the legends or mythology of any given era. Don't mix these up. Isis won't appreciate being called up in the company of Wotan, nor Lakshmi with Cernunnos. Start with the Gods of your own people, because their symbols, sacred places, and tales will be closest to you. This is not easy, but then nothing worth doing ever is. Suddenly you will find the flat pictures in some book or the patterns of stones in a field near you come alive, and you will become aware of great presences with whom you can communicate.

The Four Elements

Many of the books on paganism and witchcraft insist upon superhuman type figures for the God and Goddesses, but this does not appeal to everyone trying to escape from the images of the orthodox faiths. There is no reason why you cannot envisage the powers as abstract forces or energies and interact with them accordingly. The most powerful magical system, no matter what it may be called by its followers, still relies on a special relationship between the magician and the four elements, Earth, Water, Fire, and Air. Many lodges work with these forces in the form of the Archangels: Auriel, or Uriel, is generally associated with Earth and clad in robes of the colours of Malkuth, black, olive, citrine, and russet; Gabriel is the blue-robed archangel of Water, and healing; Michael, dressed in armour of flaming red and gold and bearing the great sword is an angel of fire; and Raphael in airy golden robes guards the quarter of Air. These aren't gods, but great forces traditionally personified as taller-than-life figures, stationed at the four points of the compass. In the witch's circle the elements are offered in salutation at each quarter in turn at the opening and closing of the ritual and there the Lords of the Watchtowers (derived from the works of Dr. Dee in the sixteenth century), are requested to surround the working. Traditional witches raise a castle within which time is stopped, and in many other ceremonies some sort of representations of Earth, Water, Fire, and Air are placed about the circle or on the altar. Again these are not specifically related to gods or goddesses, although they may be given the names of pagan deities in some groups.

You may feel happier working with forces that are symbolized by the four elements, by the male/white/positive pillar and the female/black/negative pillar. A few sessions of meditation on this dichotomy is very worthwhile and it may well uncover aspects of deities about which you had not previously thought. Remember, dark and light are not good and evil! You cannot have up without down, left without right. Everyone should strive to be in a state of balance and equilibrium. If you are convinced that the insistence on 'God the Father' has to be counterbalanced by 'Goddess the Mother' alone, you will swing the pendulum just as far in the other direction. The world needs stability of God/Goddess, Father/Mother, Day/Night, and Summer/Winter. Even the Bible, using the term 'Elohim', implies male and female deities.

Do not simply reject all previous religious upbringing and turn to some neo-pagan rituals just because it seems a good move. Within every sort of faith there are keys to the mysteries, and even the Christian message was for the few and not the many. 'Love thy neighbour as thyself' only makes sense if you are willing to love yourself, not in a selfish way, but by truly understanding who you are and where you are going. You are the standpoint by which you judge the rest of the world, and the closer you are able to get to perfection, the better is the whole of humanity. If you become part of a group and have to accept different Gods and Goddesses to those you have encountered before, meditate upon them, in the forms in which your group works with them. Get to know them and any stories or legends associated with them. Many of the Gods and Goddesses may have been human heroes once, or, like the Gods and Goddesses of Classical Rome and Greece, each had a specific job or association and these characteristics were linked with one of the traveling stars which we know now to be planets.

The Need to Worship

Dr. Carl Jung became convinced that as well as a need for food, shelter, love, and security, mankind needed to worship something. In modern times many people worship a pop-star, a football team, or even a possession like a car or house, rather than a God or Goddess. It is because people have reduced this innate longing to such mundane levels that they are feeling cut off and disconcerted about their lives. We are living in an age of great changes, but then the human race has almost always been in times of change, ever since the discovery of fire. Instead of living, as the farming folk did for hundreds of years, knowing their successes or failures were in the hands of God or the gods, people seem to have come to rely totally on the State for their well-being, housing, and other needs. Some have cast off the responsibility for almost every aspect of their health, occupation, and situation. Now it is time for every aspiring magician, at least, to examine his or her feelings about religion, God, the Gods and Goddesses of pagan times, and maybe even discover new deities for the new age.

If you really are drawn to the Lord of the Wild Hunt and the Great Earth Mother you will not be able to encounter them in your ordinary home, unless you live in a cottage in the middle of Dartmoor. You will have to make a modern pilgrimage to a wild place, to sit in the depths of a winter wood, or a summer moor, where cloud shadows chase across the purple green hill-sides. You will have to cast off the mode of thinking of the town or city and allow your deeper, wilder nature to come to the surface so that you can feel the presences of the Great Ones. You may see them as vast figures looming across the sky, or feel the breath of the Lady on a spring wind, filled with the scent of primroses or hawthorn. You might begin to realize that the whole globe of the earth is actually a living, sentient being, the goddess Gaia or Ge, and that you are living as a creature upon her mantle. You may begin to realize how the earth has been spoiled and how greed has begun to destroy the very foundation upon which we live. You will have to go through some strong feelings if you open up one of the doors to this sort of religious experience. It might even lead you to the way of the shaman, who abandons awareness for the ecstasy of unity with the Goddess who inspires him. This is very different from the groups of modern witches who dance around in a candle-lit basement with artificial flowers, and images of the Goddess in glo-lite plastic!

To embrace the Old Ones honestly will require a great deal of dedication and change in your life. Whether you are initiated by someone with superior knowledge, or if you choose the lonely path of the solo seeker who becomes one with the Great Goddess, to be reborn her child, you will be changed. You cannot remain the same person. Your view of life, modern motivations, and personal objectives will change because she has blessed you; or because you have genuinely encountered the Lord of the Wild Things, you can no longer feel safe among man-made walls. Material possessions and mundane security will no longer seem important, and your whole outlook will be radically changed if you dare to take this path to the wilderness.

If you cannot commit yourself to being truly pagan you may take the softer option of reawakening the contacts with the classical Gods of Rome, Egypt, and Greece. Their stories are well documented. Many of their temples or sacred places are still to be seen, and in some of the more remote ones, the power still lingers, or can still be perceived by those who know how to open their inner vision. You may be able to build something of the surroundings at home in your own temple, but you'll need to experience these ancient sacred sanctuaries firsthand for the contact which will make their gods apparent to you. Once you have absorbed as much of these places as you can, you can develop pathworkings which lead you to the innermost inner, where the classical Gods and Goddesses had their dwelling. Begin by simply setting the scene, and allowing the vision to build up, and you may well be surprised how strongly the pictures before your inner eye develop and become 'real.' If you and your partner have both visited the same places, you can take it in turn to create scenes from the relevant temple or grove and as you become more expert the pictures will unfold before you so that you can report them to each other.

The Gods and Goddesses need the worship and contact with humans just as we need their help and inspiration. By allowing their will to work on earth they are strengthened to perform greater miracles, in conjunction with their followers. Everyone who serves the classical Gods or is united and reborn into the family of the Great Ones is in some way helping them to accomplish their wills for mankind. We are all a part of the whole, be it cosmos or universe, or even thoughts in the mind of the Creator. 'God created mankind in his imagination, male and female created he them . . .' We must try not to forget this very important fact.

Working with Ritual

When you begin to build up elaborate rituals, you will probably become aware that when you consecrate the elements you are making a change, not perhaps physically visible, but just as a good priest at mass symbolically changes the bread and wine into the body and blood of Christ, so are you changing mundane objects into spiritual ones. They become 'of the Gods' by the blessing of those Gods whose aid you invoke. You may wish to make some of your rituals entirely religious, either by celebrating the traditional feasts or by making your working a method of speaking with or observing the Gods of your chosen system. Here you will either need to go to the wild places to meet the Great Ones who are reluctant to come to cities and towns, or you will need to create the images of the Temples of the Nile, the heights of Olympus, or the Standing Stones of some British sacred site. To do this is an inspiring activity and, like most magical acts, it is the performance and the resulting experiences, which are the real secrets of magic, and will prove whether or not you have actually made a contact with your deities.

As well as celebrating the many festivals, you might choose to work with the Moon Goddess in her threefold form, as Maid, Mother, and Crone, and use her power for each aspect to help with your work. She will bring magical inspiration if you dare to allow her mystic influences to seep through your inner being. This is another form of dedication which must be without reservation. You cannot command the Gods, you can only try to align yourself with the associations traditionally linked with them and allow the magic to work through you. This requires courage and commitment and cannot be simply withdrawn if you discover a new hobby. Magic and initiation are forever, no matter how feebly they are done in the first place. If your intention was to serve the Great Ones (even if the coven or lodge you joined proved to be a bunch of amateurs), it will be taken as such and you can't just back out!

Observe how the God of the Sun and the Lady of the Moon affect your waking and sleeping life. See how the tides of the year, separated by the solar solstices and equinoxes, change your feelings and magical abilities. See what each phase of the moon does to your dreams and visions, and you will soon learn how strongly the bonds with the God and Goddess have been forged. Experiment with different sorts of religious activities. Try pathworking to the sacred places, experiment with conjuring visions of the deities you choose to work with. Consecrate and bless things in their name and see how their influences change ordinary items into magically powerful instruments. Make up ceremonies of thanksgiving—not only for ordinary help received, but for all the good things in life— butterflies, beautiful flowers, strange animals, and wild places. Get into the habit of talking to your Gods and Goddesses as if they were invisible friends. Imagine they are part of your family, as you have become a part of theirs. Get to know them and all the symbols associated with them. Discover their feast days and what sort of offerings of grain, flowers, or incenses were prepared for them. You cannot sacrifice life to the Creator or any of the Great Ones because they gave it in the first place; you can only offer yourself and any work you may do on their behalf.

Prayer

At the end of each ceremony, close with prayers or poems of thanksgiving and praise. Ask for peace, for harmony in the world, love to overcome hatred and health to conquer disease. Think not only of your own land and people, but of the sufferers in other places, those without any of the things which you take for granted—clean water, shelter, help in sickness, and relief from poverty. There is enough for all and the world can be made into the paradise it is meant to be by the properly applied magic of prayer. This is the force which works unseen and causes changes at an inner level, allowing power to flow outwards, bringing benefits and changes for the good of all. Illness is cured from within, in a sick person, either by his own will helping him to regain the balance of true health, or by the medicines which he has taken assisting in the healing process. This is also true of the whole galaxy. Ask that the Great Ones bring peace and true understanding and somehow those in high places will become inspired with thoughts of peace. You would never be able to change their minds by argument or brute force, but by the subtle application of the seeds of wisdom sown by people of goodwill, and tended by the ancient Gods on the inner, all things may be brought to change.

Prayer doesn't have to be performed on a certain day each week, in a particular building. The influence of the Great Ones is all round you wherever you are, and they will listen to your words and hopes at any time. You do not need priests to guide you or intercede for you. If you have sinned, then the laws of karma will show you how reparation may be made. Muttering a grudging prayer to the Lady Mary will not necessarily relieve your feeling of guilt, nor will it help whoever you have wronged. Punishing the body will not affect the soul and confession to someone as human as you simply shares the burden, it doesn't relieve it. You will have to consider the matter of wrongdoing and forgiveness in the light of your understanding of your original religion and that of the deities you now choose to worship. Again, this is a personal matter which you should work out for yourself.

There are a couple of other points about becoming a working magician or witch. If you feel that you are able to become a mediator of the power of a particular God or Goddess, you must recognize that you must become worthy. There is nothing less pleasant than encountering some egocentric High Priestess who believes she can call down the power of Isis, yet has not the humanity to get on with her fellow coven members and treats them like dirt. If you want to become the vehicle of the Great Ones you must not only strive to become worthy in your everyday life as well as magical life, but you must recognize the responsibility that such an act entails. You can't play at being Isis, Horus, Cernunnos, or Artemis without understanding what that involves. You can only really be the servants of the Old Ones, trying to do their will and work on earth. If they choose to temporarily dwell within you it is a great honour and a heavy burden.

The same responsibility rests with people who take the names of Gods and Goddesses as their magical names. If you can live up to the onerous task of being the Goddess of Wisdom or the Lord of Travel and Thievery all the time, well and good. If you are really only a simple human being striving to master the arts of magic, then calling yourself 'Servant of Saturn' or 'Child of Isis' is infinitely safer!

The Path of Unity

Everyone is a child of earth, each of us can look up at the sky and know that without the power of the sun we would have no being. From this simple notion you can build up an important relationship between yourself, the created world, and all the other inhabitants. Many people on drug trips have experienced a feeling of oneness with all creation; others, who have studied long and hard in the Eastern yogic traditions, hold such unity as an objective. In the West it was the shamans and priests of the old ways who so involved themselves with the patterns of the earth and sky that they became absorbed into the oneness and unified with creation. This can happen to you. There is no sure way of going about this dissolution into the infinite, but it is a goal to aim for if you accept that we are in fact parts of a greater whole, but cut off by false beliefs and separated by having forgotten our roots. As with all other magical acts, you need to be in control and not under the influence of drugs or any other person. The path of Unity is a lonely one, and will cut you off from many of the human contacts with which you are familiar. That path will set you apart and change your views of modern life even more radically than true initiation might. It is not an easy way to travel, and there are no signposts and few fellow travelers on that strange way. You alone can choose to set out on that journey, for it is another experiment, but if you feel it is your way, what you learn upon it could help all creatures understand their unity and involvement with one another's plight.

Do examine the religious ways of other people, read their books, and experiment with the tenets of their faith, for though you may reject much of it, underneath many different religions lie the same ideas and aims, most of which should make sense to a modern magician. Soon we may be living away from earth, and having to discover a new set of sacred places and acts of worship to suit the space age, yet the new ideas will have been grown from the seeds of the old. Perhaps research in archaeology and science will uncover material on which the major faiths are based, and radically change them into a belief for the coming age. Maybe a new Messiah will emerge, or the old one come back for a rerun! Perhaps people will realize that all of them have the spark of the Divine within them and do not need outside Gods or priests. If they can understand the nature of the human spirit, both male and female, which lies within the core of every individual and make this a life-giving force for healing, creativity, and contentment, many of the long-held hopes for the future of mankind on earth will be achieved.

As a magician you will need to discover by experiment your own true feelings about God, the Gods and Goddesses, the Creator, and the invisible, unknowable power which exists within everything from the tiniest microbe to the greatest universe. To change one part of that creation is in some way to change the whole. If you make changes by magic, you hold the whole responsibility for what happens to the entire cosmos. It is an awesome concept, but magic is an awesome undertaking, not for those of weak will, nor feeble intention. Every ritual is an experiment, and can never be exactly repeated.

Another aspect of religious experimentation is in the keeping of a shrine. Britain is dotted with ancient sacred sites, springs, groves, hills, tumuli, stone circles, and prehistoric settlements, all of which may well have had their priests, priestesses, and oracles in times gone by. You may be drawn to explore such a place near you, clearing away rubbish, planting bulbs or flowering plants, and making it a good place to visit. Some traditional holy sanctuaries are well known and visited by thousands of people each year, others have been long forgotten, but their sacredness and the wisdom stored in their stones is still there to be reawoken by a devotee. It is in this way that the highest form of worship and magical aspiration can be drawn down to the earth, and links between the forces which govern the whole cosmos and us below may be strengthened. Even a small corner of your room can become a dwelling place of the Gods and Goddesses, or the Creator, if you wish.

It has become clear during the last few years that ancient sources of knowledge and wisdom are once again being opened to us, if we treat them with reverence and respect. From the oldest sacred places in the land to the newest location of the inspired seer, drops of the elixir from the Cauldron of Inspiration are pouring into our world of consciousness. Used correctly this information can go a long way towards rebalancing the forces for peace, for love, and for eternal justice in our world, so long as the new venturers into the paths of magic do not take it upon themselves to preach, to indoctrinate or to pressure other people to follow their personal vision. The magic of worship, calling on the Great Ones for help or guidance and healing is something between you and them, shared only by your working partner or group. If you have a clear vision of the Gods, angels, or powers, that is a special thing which should be kept private and respected. Converting the masses to yet another faith or promulgating your inner vision will not lead those who have not found the way for themselves one step nearer their own destiny. The message will come from within as a direct revelation, it cannot be enforced from outside, as history so clearly demonstrates.

Magic is not a light undertaking, especially as it works in all aspects of your life and no one can be absolutely certain of the outcome of any act of magic. It is always an adventure, a journey into the unknown regions of your inner experience, so venture with care and forethought. Adhere to the ancient adage 'To know, to will, to dare, and to keep silent' and you will find that the Gods guide your travel and the Lady will keep you safe in her care.

CONCLUSION

Magic is a vast subject. Even the study of its history can take a life-time. Every magician will be making a new path through the various traditions, selecting the symbol systems and God forms which most closely match their own aspirations. From the simplest rites of the Natural magicians to the most complex and elaborate ceremonies of advanced Qabalist adepts, each will have researched, experimented, and discovered a way which satisfies their magical will. It is a matter of personal choice which you will have to make for yourself.

Today there are plenty of new books written by competent practitioners of every possible path, both Eastern and Western, simple or complicated, religious or dedicated to the service of creation. If you have been able to use this book as it was intended, you will have experimented with a number of techniques, compared theory with practice, and explored areas which you may never have dreamed were parts of the work of the occultist. Your work will never be finished, for in magic, as in life, you never cease to learn new things and undergo new experiences.

Perhaps you had been hoping this book would reveal all the secrets of magic for the dawning age of Aquarius—in fact, it has. The secrets of magic are concerned with experience. Unless you are willing to try the various arts suggested here, or work through the methods of the ritual magician or the festivals of the modern witch, the secrets remain secrets. YOU will have to experiment, sometimes facing the hard lesson of failure, which teaches you a great deal more than the success which seems to be a 'fluke.'

You will learn how to shift your awareness to a level when meditations, pathworkings, and visualizations create the images and then the reality which you are seeking. No one can do that for you, nor can reading every book published demonstrate to you the power to heal, the curious coincidences which bring about your magical will, if you will not exchange your armchair for your temple throne.

A new magic is being created now, suitable for the people of the end of the twentieth century. Gradually, like a tree growing, the first leaves are spreading so that we can begin to recognize its nature and perhaps its ultimate form. At present we do not know how tall it may grow, nor what its flowers or fruit may be—these may take years to develop fully. But everyone who is willing to make the experiments here, in the attitude of exploration and wonder, all manner of things may be revealed to you. It will be your work which will help to unlock the secrets of the Gods for the future, the magic arts and skills which you learn and practise may assist those who follow in your footsteps. Our lives are so much changed from the simple ways of the first magicians who watched the stars and speculated on their powers and effects upon the earth. They left us no books to read, nor videos to watch, yet somehow, within such artefacts which have come down to us, is enshrined a great store of wisdom. It is up to us, using our will, consciousness, and inner perceptions to discover how this knowledge may be recovered. Already many alternatives are seeping into everyday life—in healing, alternative therapies, often based on ancient natural methods, are being made more readily available; in entertainment, all sorts of options are to be tried; in food and drink, natural and untreated produce is being sold or grown at home. We have the option to live as slaves within a system which we cannot alter, or to take destiny into our hands, through the application of our trained magical wills, and so bring knowledge, healing, and peace to all about us.

When the circle of those wise in the hidden ways of magic can join hands around the great circle of the earth, and gather in the greater circle of the skies, then surely the will of the Gods for mankind upon earth will come into being and a new and magical future will open before us. Take up your courage, your common sense, and your sense of humour, fasten these within the magical sphere of your trained attention, and set off into the unknown that you may bring back a light to guide those who walk behind you. There is a blessing on all who serve.

FURTHER READING

Ashcroft-Nowicki, Dolores, *First Steps in Ritual* (Aquarian Press, 1982).

———, *The Shining Paths* (Aquarian Press, 1983).

Glaskin, G. M., *Windows of the Mind* (Arrow paperbacks).

Hope, Murry, *Practical Techniques of Psychic Self-Defence* (Aquarian Press, 1983).

Green, Marian, *Magic for the Aquarian Age* (Aquarian Press, 1983).

Jung, C. G., *Man and His Symbols* (Pan, 1978).

———, *Memories, Dreams, Reflections* (Collins, 1983).

Knight, Gareth, *The Secret Tradition in Arthurian Legend* (Aquarian Press, 1984).

Matthews, J. and C., *The Western Way* (Arkana Paperbacks, 1985).

Stewart, R. J., *The Underworld Initiation* (Aquarian Press, 1985).

Toffler, Alvin, *The Third Wave* (Pan, 1981).

SULIS MUSIC produces cassette tapes of magical meditations by Marian Green, Dolores Ashcroft-Nowicki, and R. J. Stewart. List available from SULIS MUSIC, BCM Box 3721, London, WC1N 3XX, England.

INDEX

Akashic Record, 197
alchemy, 185
allergies, 181
alternative therapies, 164, 280
amulets, 249
Applied Kinesiology, 175
Aquarius, Age of, 164
Ashcroft-Nowicki, Dolores, 152
astral travel, 221, 228–230
astrology, 226
auras, 230–231

Bach Flower Remedies, 173–
    174
balance of forces, 135–136

Celtic Tree alphabet, 224
charms, 249–251
Christos technique, the,
    213–214
collective unconscious, 137, 186
correspondences, magical,
    255–256
costumes for ritual, 191
creative visualization, 140–142
    experiments in, 142–144
crystal gazing, 160, 225–226

death, re-experiencing, 208
Dee, Dr. John, 195, 268
déjà vu, 210
diet, natural, 166–167
divination, 155, 221, 222–224
dowsing, 174, 245–246
Dweller on the Threshold,
    the, 178, 196

Elements, the Four, 268
energy-raising methods,
    144–147
extra-sensory perception
    (ESP), 235

Fortune, Dion, 180, 263
Fountain of Light Exercise,
    175–178

Golden Ass, The, 266
Group Soul, 197–198

healing, 169–172, 244–245
healthy living, 163, 164,
    168–169
herbal remedies, 172
homoeopathy, 172–173
Hope, Murry, 180
hypnotism, 212–213

I Ching, 155, 221, 222, 223,
    224–225
invocation, 146

Jesus, 264–265
Journeys Out of the Body, 233
Jung, Carl, 137, 185, 227, 269

Lesser Banishing Ritual, 141

Magic for the Aquarian Age,
    135
magical partner, 149
    choosing a, 151–152
meditation, 137–139, 150, 151

metal bending, 238–239
Mindreach, 221
Monroe, R. A., 233
Moon, the, as healing force, 167–168

Nature, healing power of, 165–166
ouija-boards, 241–242

pagan feasts, 200–201
paganism, 266–267
palmistry, 226
past-life recall, 206–208
techniques for, 211–212
pathworking, 152–155, 214–217
Phoenix Runes, 224
Pisces, Age of, 164
poltergeist activity, 240–241, 247–248
Practical Techniques of Psychic Self-Defence, 180
prayer, 273–274
psychic activities, 178–180
Psychic Self-Defence, 180
psychokinesis, 235, 239–240
psychometry, 212, 226

reincarnation, 208–212
ritual, 195, 271
planning, 201–204
preparation for, 198–199

salt intake, 168
scrying, 160–161, 225
service, 134
Shining Paths, The, 152
Shroud of Turin, 280–281

sleeping difficulties, remedy for, 147
spells, 251–252
Staff of Life, to make, 192–193
stress, 163
sugar consumption, 168–169
Sun, the, as healing force, 166
'supernatural' skills, 236–238

talismans, 253–255, 256–260
Tarot, the, 224–225
Temple, Magical, 183
Archetypal, 231–232
Pillars of the, 184
symbols for, 188–190
to furnish, 187–188
Third Wave, The, 149
time travel, 209
Toffler, Alvin, 149
Tree of Life, 152

UFOs, 242–244

weapons, elemental, 192
Windows of the Mind, 213

TO OUR READERS

Weiser Books, an imprint of Red Wheel/Weiser, publishes books across the entire spectrum of occult, esoteric, speculative, and New Age subjects. Our mission is to publish quality books that will make a difference in people's lives without advocating any one particular path or field of study. We value the integrity, originality, and depth of knowledge of our authors.

Our readers are our most important resource, and we appreciate your input, suggestions, and ideas about what you would like to see published.

Visit our website at *www.redwheelweiser.com* to learn about our upcoming books and free downloads, and be sure to go to *www.redwheelweiser.com/newsletter/* to sign up for newsletters and exclusive offers.

You can also contact us at *info@rwwbooks.com* or at

Red Wheel/Weiser, LLC
665 Third Street, Suite 400
San Francisco, CA 94107